LIVING IN PRISON

LIVING IN PRISON
A History of the Correctional System with an Insider's View

STEPHEN STANKO, WAYNE GILLESPIE,
AND GORDON A. CREWS

FOREWORD BY MICHAEL BRASWELL

GREENWOOD PRESS
Westport, Connecticut • London

Library of Congress Cataloging-in-Publication Data

Stanko, Stephen.
  Living in prison : a history of the correctional system with an insider's view / Stephen Stanko, Gordon A. Crews, and Wayne Gillespie ; forword by Michael Braswell.
    p. cm.
  Includes bibliographical references and index.
  ISBN 0–313–31856–5 (alk. paper)
    1. Imprisonment. 2. Prisons. 3. Prisons—United States. 4. Prisoners—United States. 5. Criminal justice, Administration of—United States. I. Crews, Gordon A. II. Gillespie, Wayne. III. Title.
  HV8705.S73 2004
  365—dc22   2003056801

British Library Cataloguing in Publication Data is available.

Library of Congress Catalog Card Number: 2003056801
ISBN: 0–313–31856–5

First published in 2004

Greenwood Publishers, 88 Post Road West, Westport, CT 06881
An imprint of Greenwood Publishing Group, Inc.
www.greenwood.com

Printed in the United States of America

The paper used in this book complies with the Permanent Paper Standard issued by the National Information Standards Organization (Z39.48–1984).

10 9 8 7 6 5 4 3 2 1

CONTENTS

Foreword by Michael Braswell — *vii*

Part I   Justice: Introduction, History, and Philosophy   1

Chapter 1   Crime and Justice in the United States   3
Wayne Gillespie

Chapter 2   Justice and the Origin of Corrections   25
Gordon Crews

Chapter 3   A Brief History of Corrections in America   43
Gordon Crews and Wayne Gillespie

Part II   Contemporary Correctional Issues   61

Chapter 4   The Context of Imprisonment   63
Wayne Gillespie

Chapter 5   Women and Prison   89
Wayne Gillespie

Chapter 6   Prisoners' Rights and States' Responsibilities   111
Wayne Gillespie

Part III   Living in Prison: One Man's Journey   129

Chapter 7   A Prisoner's Narrative   131
Stephen Stanko

Chapter 8   The Prison Environment   149
Stephen Stanko

Chapter 9   Surviving in Prison   171
             Stephen Stanko

Index   *187*

FOREWORD

A number of books have been written over the years about life in prison, including the autobiography of Bill Sands, who initiated a twelve-step program for prisoners, to the powerful descriptions of inmate violence and despair by Jack Abbott to the practical and enlightened essays of prisoner-turned-Buddhist Jarvis Masters. *Living in Prison: A History of the Correctional System with an Insider's View* by Stephen Stanko, Wayne Gillespie, and Gordon A. Crews adds another worthy volume to this topical area in criminal justice and criminology studies.

An interesting characteristic of this text lies in its organization. Professors Gillespie and Crews provide the reader with a useful overview of prisons in both a historical and systemic context. Their discussion includes criminal classification, prison organization, the rights of prisoners, women in prison, and prison violence and corruption. They provide a framework against which Steve Stanko, a prisoner, describes life in prison. The result is a stimulating interaction between the personal story of a prisoner and the academic observations of two criminologists.

Inmate Stanko offers an intimate narrative of his experiences, from pretrial detention through the appeal process to all aspects of incarcerated life. Descriptions of food services, health care, violence, prisoner relationships, dealing with corrections officials, and attempting to maintain communication with family and friends remind the reader of the stark contrast between the "free world" and the world of prisons.

It is not enough that we observe, analyze, and describe life in prison from an outside vantage point. We also need to let prison life describe itself through the voices of those who have lived and worked in such environments. Each perspective provides a balancing point for the other. Personal recollections can be judged against what theories and research suggest as well as put flesh on the bones of academic literature on imprisonment. This book achieves such a balance.

Stanko, Gillespie, and Crews have created a text that offers us a synthesis of experience and expertise—what prison life feels like inside an inmate's mind and heart, and what it looks like through the external eye of the criminologist and corrections professional.

Michael Braswell
East Tennessee State University

Part I

JUSTICE: INTRODUCTION, HISTORY, AND PHILOSOPHY

1

CRIME AND JUSTICE IN THE UNITED STATES

Wayne Gillespie

INTRODUCTION

The gavel is a symbol of power. It represents the authority of the justice system. Of course, the gavel also brings to mind the vision of a judge cloaked in a black robe sitting atop a raised bench presiding over cases in a courtroom. Judges perform a variety of tasks in the courtroom. They are considered experts on law and facts. They oversee bailiffs and court reporters. They may order search warrants, confer sentences, and revoke probation in criminal cases. The gavel is simply a tool used by the judge to command attention or to confirm legal action (Grana, Ollenburger, & Nicholas, 2002).

Upon closer inspection, the true power behind the gavel, and behind the judge, is located within the law. The two major forms of law in the United States are criminal law and civil law. Civil law deals with torts or wrongs against certain persons, whereas criminal law is concerned with crimes or wrongs against the state. Another common definition of crime is any judicially determined violation of criminal law (Tappan, 1947). Grana et al. expanded the definition of crime to include the following characteristics:

1. There must be certain external consequences or harm to society.
2. The act must be legally forbidden or proscribed by law.
3. Some form of conduct must occur, either intentional reckless action or inaction.
4. Criminal intent, or mens rea, must be present.
5. Mens rea and conduct must occur together.
6. There must be a causal relationship between the social harm and the misconduct.
7. There must be a legally prescribed punishment. (p. 76)

They also maintain that all seven conditions must be present in order to consider behavior criminal.

Brown, Esbensen, and Geis (2001) also outlined several important distinctions between civil and criminal law. First, the victim or complainant in criminal law is the state, whereas in civil law it is an individual. In terms of legality, Brown et al. argued that criminal law calls for no crime without corresponding laws on the books, although civil law is broader and retroactive. Next, the standard of judgment in criminal law is proof beyond a reasonable doubt, yet in civil law all that is required is preponderance of evidence. Brown et al. also acknowledged that criminal law generally requires intent, whereas intent is not required in civil cases.

It is also possible that some behaviors are violations of both criminal and civil law. Consider the O. J. Simpson case. On June 17, 1994, the one-time professional football player was arrested and charged with the murders of Nicole Brown Simpson and Ronald Goldman (Cable News Network, 1997). The criminal trial lasted for over eight months. Finally, on October 3, 1995, a jury of nine African Americans, two whites, and one Hispanic acquitted Simpson of the crimes. The jurors did not find Simpson innocent; rather, they had some reasonable doubt of his guilt. However, the Goldman and Brown families sued Simpson in civil court for the wrongful deaths of Ronald Goldman and Nicole Brown Simpson, respectively. Those proceedings began on October 23, 1996. A jury of nine whites, one African American, one Hispanic, and one person of African and Asian descent found Simpson liable for the slayings and, on February 4, 1997, awarded $8.5 million in compensatory damages (Cable News Network, 1997). Thus, in this example, the defendant was acquitted in criminal court but found liable in civil court. As Knight (1996) suggested, "Verdicts that are actually based on reasonable doubt, as Simpson's may have been, inevitably seem irrational and wrong" (p. 263). However, this is the burden of proof that is required by the criminal law.

The O. J. Simpson case was somewhat unique because it involved a violent crime, a jury trial, a high-profile defendant, and savvy attorneys. It was also televised. However, these crimes were not representative of most cases in the justice system. Felson (2002) argued that people are swayed by certain fallacies about crime. Crimes that actually receive television coverage are unusual, passionate, or violent. By focusing on sensational offenses, the mass media keep the public watching. Television ratings increase, and the media companies make money. In fact, Felson reported that murders account for less than 1 percent of serious crime.

CLASSIFICATION OF CRIMES

Crimes are defined and classified in the United States today based on common-law practices. Common law originated in England and spread to North America during the colonial era and was made by judicial decisions in court cases. In the absence of written law from the king, judges based their rulings on the customs of the people (Wallace & Roberson, 2001).

Klotter (1990) provided an overview of common-law definitions for violent crimes. First, murder includes the "unlawful taking of a human being by another human being with malice aforethought" (Klotter, p. 56). Non-negligent manslaughter differs from murder due to the lack of malice aforethought. Thus, "Manslaughter may be committed without malice as where one kills in sudden passion aroused by lawful provocation" (Klotter, p. 68). Rape refers to the "act of having unlawful carnal knowledge by a man of a woman, forcibly and against her will" (Klotter, p. 114). According to common-law definitions, robbery includes multiple elements. Klotter acknowledged that robbery involves "the taking with intent to steal property in the possession of another, from his person, or in his presence, by violence or by putting him in fear" (p. 197). However, other conceptualizations describe robbery as aggravated larceny or the felonious taking of goods by another by violence. Finally, assault is "any unlawful offer or attempt to injure another, with apparent present ability to effectuate the attempt under circumstances creating a fear of imminent peril" (Klotter, p. 87). Murder, rape, robbery, and aggravated assault are generally considered to be serious offenses against persons; these crimes are also believed to be *mala in se* in nature.

Most crimes are traditionally classified according to either their nature or their degree. Acts that are wrong in and of themselves are referred to as *mala in se* crimes. Klotter (1990) commented, "*Mala in se* crimes are wrongs that are considered wrong in any society, and include the common law crimes such as murder, rape, arson, burglary, and larceny" (p. 14). Crimes that are prohibited by law but not naturally evil are dubbed *mala prohibita*. These acts are generally illegal because they infringe on the rights of others, whereas *mala in se* crimes involve moral turpitude. *Mala prohibita* crimes include offenses such as prostitution, illicit drug use, and vandalism. Although the distinction between *mala in se* and *mala prohibita* crimes is an interesting dichotomy, it is not readily used by state legislatures.

Today, statute or law prohibits most criminal behavior in the United States. Crimes are classified based on their severity and fall into one of three categories: violations, misdemeanors, and felonies (Brown et al., 2001). Violations are the least serious category of offense. Persons convicted of violations typically only receive fines as punishment. Misdemeanors are considered less serious than felonies, and an individual may receive up to eleven months, twenty-nine days of imprisonment in a jail if convicted of a misdemeanor offense. Felonies are the most serious offenses and are punishable by at least one year of incarceration in prison. Both felonies and misdemeanors are further broken down into different classes (e.g., Class A, B, C, D, and E), according to the seriousness of the crime. Of these different classifications, Class A felony offenses carry the lengthiest prison terms and the greatest fines. For example, in Tennessee, Class A felonies such as second-degree murder, aggravated rape, and especially aggravated robbery are punishable by up to sixty years in prison and a $50,000 fine (Anderson Publishing Company, 2001).

However, definitions of crime, classifications of degree, and associated punishments vary from state to state. According to Grana et al. (2001), the United States operates under the concept of dual federalism. In essence, there are fifty-one systems of law (i.e., the federal government and fifty state governments) in the United States. This arrangement of law restricts the power of the federal government by preserving state autonomy. Unfortunately, one unintended consequence of this bifurcated system is that the law becomes somewhat relative. Illegal behavior in one state may be legal in another. Punishments also vary across the states. For example, not all states practice capital punishment. Thirty-eight states currently have the death penalty, and twelve do not (NAACP Legal Defense and Educational Fund, 2001).

In fact, the death penalty is a contested issue in the United States. Because the Eighth Amendment to the U.S. Constitution prohibits cruel and unusual punishment, several notable Supreme Court cases challenged the constitutionality of capital punishment. In *Furman v. Georgia* (1972), the Supreme Court decided that the death penalty was being applied unfairly on the basis of race. African Americans were more likely to be executed for capital crimes. It was both arbitrary and capricious. The Court reasoned that the death penalty was indeed cruel and unusual punishment due to its inconsistent and uneven application in Georgia. In light of this verdict, many states modified their statutes regarding capital punishment to eliminate arbitrary and capricious methods and to make the imposition of this sentence consistent. After changes were made to the appropriate statutes regarding the application of capital punishment, the Supreme Court reversed its initial stance and upheld the constitutionality of the death penalty in *Gregg v. Georgia* (1976). However, the death penalty debate is far from complete. As recently as 2000, Republican governor George Ryan imposed a moratorium on capital punishment in Illinois. In 2003, he commuted the sentences of all death row inmates in Illinois and pardoned four (Cable News Network, 2003).

CRIME STATISTICS

Despite the relativity of law, it is important to standardize reports of crime in order to measure the extent of criminal behavior in the United States. Nettler (1984) suggested that crime statistics allow researchers and policy makers to accurately describe crime, assess risks, evaluate programs, and explain criminality. Describing the extent of crime in the United States allows criminal justice personnel to efficiently use resources. Risk assessment involves predicting future patterns of crime and victimization. Crime statistics can also be used to evaluate the effectiveness of criminal justice policies. Finally, knowing the amount and distribution of crime in the United States helps criminologists explain why some people break the law.

Several agencies compile reports of criminal behavior from all over the United States. Each year, the Federal Bureau of Investigation (FBI) collects police reports from local law enforcement agencies around the United States. The resulting Uniform Crime Reports (UCR) include twenty-nine different crimes broken down into two sections. Part I of the UCR, known as the Crime Index, covers four offenses against persons (homicide, forcible rape, robbery, and aggravated assault) as well as four offenses against property (burglary, larceny-theft, automobile theft, and arson). Part II includes twenty-one "other" crimes such as drug offenses, prostitution, embezzlement, and juvenile status offenses. Status offenses are essentially crimes that apply only to juveniles due to their age, and examples include truancy and running away.

Table 1 shows arrest information for Index offenses from 1997 to 2001. The five-year average for all arrests in the United States was 9,682,715. That is, almost 10 million people in the country are arrested each year. However, there is some debate over the extent to which data in the UCR are an absolute indicator of crime in America (O'Brien, 1985). It is generally believed that the UCR provide a gross underestimation of the number of actual crimes. However, O'Brien noted, "The number of homicides is well reported in official records" (p. 34). The accurate representation of homicide makes comparison between jurisdictions valid. Some researchers focus solely on this measure and use it as a proxy for all forms of violent crime (Blumstein & Rosenfeld, 1998; Fagan, Zimring, & Kim, 1998).

Table 1
Arrests in the United States, 1997–2001

	1997	1998	1999	2000	2001
Murder	12,764	12,335	9,727	8,709	9,426
Rape	22,133	21,922	18,759	17,914	18,576
Robbery	94,034	87,129	73,619	72,320	76,667
Aggravated Assault	372,422	359,892	318,051	316,630	329,722
Burglary	245,816	233,435	192,570	189,343	198,883
Larceny-Theft	1,033,901	940,243	794,201	782,082	806,093
Motor Vehicle Theft	116,052	107,003	94,335	98,697	102,607
Arson	13,831	12,144	10,811	10,675	12,763

Source: Uniform Crime Reports, 1997–2001

TRENDS IN VIOLENT CRIME RATES

The U.S. Department of Justice uses both the UCR and the National Crime Victimization Survey (NCVS) to provide as accurate an account of violent crime rates as possible. In 1992, violent crime rates for rape, robbery, and assault were 9 percent below the peak rates of 1981. The U.S. Department of Justice (1994) reported "the percentage of households with a member who had been a victim of violence (other than homicide) in 1992, 5%, was the lowest recorded since 1975, when these estimates were first available" (p. 1). More recent data indicate that robbery rates dropped by 31.8 percent from 1991 to 1997. Rape rates declined by 15.1 percent for the same period, and aggravated assault rates fell almost 12 percent (LaFree, 1999).

From the mid-1960s until the late 1970s, the homicide rate doubled in the United States (U.S. Department of Justice, 2000). The highest homicide rate since the early 1960s occurred in 1980, when it reached 10.2 per 100,000. The rate peaked again in 1991 with 9.8 per 100,000. However, the homicide rate has been declining substantially since this last surge, plummeting 30.6 percent from 1991 to 1997. In 1998, the homicide rate was 6.3 per 100,000. Thus, the drop in the homicide rate over the past few years has been quite profound.

The homicide statistics compiled by the FBI are a good estimation of violence in the United States; the other crimes indexed in Part I are less representative of the actual level of violent crime in America (Hindelang, 1974; O'Brien, 1985). Therefore, researchers look at the official homicide statistics as an indication of violence in this country. For example, Blumstein and Rosenfeld (1998) focused primarily on explaining recent trends in U.S. homicide rates. Initially, they looked at the changes in age-specific homicide rates (the increase between 1985 and 1993 and the decrease from 1993 until 1998). They described the increase in homicide rates during the late 1980s and early 1990s as reflecting increased activity among younger offenders operating in large cohorts, or groups. Between 1993 and 1997, the homicide rates for all ages declined. Yet, as of this writing, the teenage homicide rate was still 60 to 80 percent above the 1985 rate; rates of offending among older groups were down as much as 40 percent. Blumstein and Rosenfeld (1998) attributed part of the downturn in the total homicide rate to a sharp decline in offending among older groups and noted that "between 1991 and 1993, the rates for younger people were generally flat . . . thus the decline among older age groups dominated the aggregate, and so the down-turn began in 1992" (p. 1186).

Blumstein and Rosenfeld (1998) also described the effects of a changing demographic composition on homicide rates. In particular, they reviewed the unfulfilled prophecies of the "crime bomb" that was set to explode during the 1990s. Growing cohorts of teenagers and young adults were expected to increase crime over time. However, Blumstein and Rosenfeld determined that cohorts only "grow" about 1 percent per year, and that this demographic shift produces a negligible effect on the current homicide rate.

Weapons may affect homicide rates as well. Initially, Blumstein and Rosenfeld (1998) noted that "the sharply increasing prevalence of handguns in youth and juvenile homicide must be considered of fundamental importance in any explanation of the homicide increase of the late 1980s and 1990s" (p. 1196). In terms of the decline in homicide rates during the 1990s, Blumstein and Rosenfeld made the following observation:

> The flattening of the growth in the handgun homicide rate between 1993 and 1994 is consistent with the decline in youth homicide rates [therefore] suggesting that the decline in homicide is also associated with the decline in the use of handguns by young people. (p. 1199)

However, these speculations remain untested.

Finally, Blumstein and Rosenfeld (1998) explored the influence of big cities on changes in homicide rates. In particular, they looked at the effect offending in New York City had on the national homicide rate. In 1991, New York City accounted for 9 percent of the national homicide rate, but in the late 1990s it contributes only 5 percent to the national rate. In order to explain this difference, Blumstein and Rosenfeld tied the fluctuations in urban homicide rates to the instability of the crack-cocaine market. They believed that the illicit drug trade was impermanent during the mid-1980s and the early 1990s. When it first hit the street, selling crack cocaine was especially dangerous and risky; the distribution and sale of crack resulted in lethal situations. However, the violence associated with it steadied once the market was established, and the murder rate declined in the major cities.

Of the metropolitan areas in the United States, New York City has received national media attention and accolades for decreasing violent crime. Fagan et al. (1998) focused specifically on declining homicide in New York City. They summarized the New York experience as follows:

> The drop in homicides was both large and abrupt—the homicide rate in the nation's largest city fell 52% in five years. In its relative and absolute magnitude, the homicide drops after 1992 were by far the largest in the postwar history of New York City. The number of lives involved is even more impressive, with more than 1,100 fewer homicide victims in New York City in 1996 than in 1992. This reduction in homicide far exceeded the total number of homicides the city experienced each year in the 1950s and early 1960s. (1277–1280)

The authors considered several factors that might account for this decline. First, the idea of regression to the mean could explain declining homicide rates. That is, increases in homicide rates are typically followed by decreases; mean rates represent the average, central tendency of the fluctuations over time. Fagan et al. commented that "sharp downward momentums in the homicide rate might be expected after sharp upward movements" (p. 1283). However, the declining homicide rates in New York City are probably not entirely due to cyclical variations.

Like Blumstein and Rosenfeld (1998), Fagan et al. (1998) believed that changes in homicide rates might be dependent upon the use of firearms. They offered convincing evidence that there are actually two separate homicide trends in New York City. The first trend, or the nongun homicide rate, has been decreasing steadily since the mid-1980s and is now half of the 1985 rate. However, homicides linked to firearms increased substantially from 1985 until 1992 and then fell sharply from 1993 until 1996. Fagan et al. suggested that these trends are independent of each other and should be treated as such. Additionally, they noted similar dichotomous pathways for robbery. In essence, the presence of a firearm *categorically* changes the nature of the criminal event.

THE CRIMINAL JUSTICE SYSTEM

Most crimes that occur in the United States never result in arrest, let alone trial or imprisonment. The dark figure of crime refers to the portion of crime that goes unreported each year. For example, Travis (2001) noted that about 1.6 million people were arrested for drug offenses in 1997. However, it is estimated that more than 24 million people in the United States used illegal drugs during that time frame. In this case, 93 percent of drug offenses went undetected by the criminal justice system in 1997—an example of the dark figure of crime.

Many crimes that are reported to the justice system go unsolved. Of those cases in which an arrest is made, only a small percentage result in imprisonment. One reason for the attrition of cases is a result of the funnel-like nature of the criminal justice system (Silberman, 1978). The criminal justice system has been compared to a funnel because, at each processing stage, cases exit the system. Brown et al. (2001) offered an insightful comment:

> Of those crimes reported police only solve about 20 percent. Prosecutors, in turn, file charges in only about one-half of the cases referred to them. Finally, for many, charges will be dismissed or result in acquittal at the judicial phase. (p. 57)

As such, cases may exit the criminal justice process at key decision points within the system. These decision points are tied to the roles of personnel within the criminal justice system. For example, police officers initiate the process with the decision to arrest a suspect. Lawyers help suspects enter the appropriate plea. Juries and judges decide guilt and impose sentences. Correctional officials and parole board members determine the context of punishment and, occasionally, its length.

Police, courts, and corrections are generally considered the three components of the criminal justice system. Police are the first to respond to a complaint and initiate the processing of individuals through the criminal justice system. The courts are responsible for fact-finding, assessing guilt or innocence, and sentencing. Correctional institutions deliver these sentences through punitive and sometimes therapeutic sanctions.

The Police

Policing involves three primary stages: detection of crime, investigation, and arrest (Travis, 2001). The most common way that the police detect crimes is reactively through reports by citizens. However, police also detect criminal behavior proactively through patrol or undercover operations. In addition, some crimes are uncovered through investigative grand juries and legislative committees. Police are often called the gatekeepers of the criminal justice system because they are involved in uncovering criminal behavior (Brown et al., 2001; Travis, 2001).

Examples of police investigatory practices include search, interrogation, identification (e.g., lineups), surveillance, informers, crackdowns, and undercover operations (Travis, 2001). The main objective of police investigations is to gather as much evidence as possible that connects a specific person to a particular crime. However, as Inbau (1961) remarked,

> Many criminal cases, even when investigated by the best qualified police departments, are capable of solution only by means of an admission or confession from the guilty individual or upon the basis of information obtained from the questioning of other criminal suspects. (p. 1404)

Eck (1992) concurred that investigative work is often not productive in solving crimes.

Regardless, police investigatory practices such as interrogation, search, and seizure are subject to certain limitations under the U.S. Constitution. The Fifth Amendment protects suspects from self-incrimination. That is, persons cannot be forced to testify against themselves. The Miranda warning is based on the Fifth Amendment against self-incrimination. Travis (2001) summarized the typical warning police give citizens concerning their Fifth Amendment rights:

> You have the right to remain silent. Anything you say can and will be used against you in a court of law. You have the right to an attorney during questioning. If you cannot afford an attorney, one will be appointed for you by the court. Do you understand these rights? (p. 175)

The U.S. Supreme Court ruled that police must inform suspects of their rights before any interrogation may commence.

Constitutional safeguards protect citizens during other investigatory phases of policing. For example, the Fourth Amendment to the U.S. Constitution is supposed to prevent unreasonable searches by law enforcement. Likewise, the Supreme Court established the exclusionary rule to curb police misconduct during searches; evidence that is improperly or illegally acquired cannot be used in trial (Osborne, 1999). The Fourth Amendment is also applicable to seizure of the suspect during apprehension or arrest.

Law enforcement officers sometime must use physical force to control violent offenders, prevent escape, and protect themselves and the public (Kappeler & Kaune, 1997). Occasionally, deadly force must be elicited when the situation deteriorates. National statistics on the use of police deadly force are lacking, and research findings are ambiguous. For example, Walker, Spohn, and DeLone (1996) suggested that the number of arrestees who were shot and killed by police peaked in 1975 with 559 instances but declined to 300 in 1987. Moreover, Kappeler and Kaune (1997) found that the number of persons killed by urban police officers was cut in half from 1971 to 1984, with 353 and 172 occurrences, respectively. Both sources indicate that the police use of deadly force is declining.

The Supreme Court's decision in *Tennessee v. Garner* (1985) most likely initiated the drop in use of deadly force. Before this court case, police officers could shoot to kill (in order to affect arrest) any suspected fleeing felon (Walker et al., 1996). Edward Garner was a fifteen-year-old, unarmed, African-American male who had stolen about $10. An officer shot him in the back of the head as he was trying to avoid arrest by fleeing from officers. Edward's father filed a lawsuit in federal court. The resulting decision in *Tennessee v. Garner* determined that the fleeing felon rule was unconstitutional; it violated the Fourth Amendment. The Supreme Court ruled that the officer had used excessive force against Edward Garner and was liable for the death of the juvenile.

The *Garner* decision greatly restrained police discretion (i.e., decision-making power) in regard to deadly force, and in 1987 Smith published a study on arrest decisions made by police. He predicted that extralegal factors such as race and sex would influence arrest decisions as much as legal variables like offense severity and victim complaint. Smith also noted three styles of control that police apply to cases involving interpersonal violence: penal, conciliatory, and avoidance. The penal style of control promotes arrest as the remedy to violence. The conciliatory police response focuses on mediation of complainants in order to overcome a temporary dispute. Finally, the avoidance style favors separating the combative parties in order to restore immediate order. Smith's analysis suggested that officers are more likely to separate disputants if both persons are nonwhite and involved in a male-female relationship. Arrests are even more likely if both individuals are white and male. Smith concluded that extralegal characteristics are as prominent as legal factors in police decisions to arrest.

The Courts

Just as there are different stages in policing, the U.S. criminal court system entails a sequence of events. According to Travis (2001), the court process may involve an initial appearance, a preliminary hearing, formal charging, an arraignment, a trial, and sentencing. Each of these stages may vary from state to state due to the system of dual federalism in the United States. However, bail is usually set during the initial appearance. Bail is money that the defendant gives to the court to ensure appearance at a later court date. During the preliminary hearing, a judge reviews the case to decide whether there is enough evidence for a trial. At the formal charging phase, the prosecutor files formal charges. This stage may in some states involve a grand jury; in about half of the states and in the federal system, the grand jury delivers an indictment. Grand juries exist in all states, except Pennsylvania, and they have the power to investigate the case. During arraignment, the defendant is required to appear in court, at which time he or she is notified of the charges and asked to enter a plea.

The jury trial is considered the quintessential element of criminal court. However, it is rarely used. Grana et al. (2002) generalized that only about 5 percent of criminal cases go to trial; the vast majority (over 90 percent) are plea-bargained. Plea bargaining is actually an admission of guilt in exchange for a reduction in the charge. If a case reaches the trial phase, the most common form is a bench trial, one that is held before a judge with no jury present. Trials are fact-finding endeavors that ideally are concerned with uncovering the truth. However, many trials take on an adversarial nature and become counterproductive.

Sentencing is the crux of the court process. It is at this phase that the offender's punishment is decided. The sentencing decision occurs in two parts. First, the sentencing judge must determine if the offender should be imprisoned. Then, the exact conditions of the sentence are rendered. The conditions may be determined jointly by judicial and correctional officials. Examples of the conditions of a sentence include the length of imprisonment, fines, restrictions, and probation. Sentencing in criminal cases has been researched quite extensively in recent years (Caulkins, Rydell, Schwabe, & Chiesa, 1997; Dixon, 1995; Griset, 1991; Spohn, 2002; Tonry, 1996; Ulmer, 1997; Wicharaya, 1995).

Dixon (1995) examined the factors that influence judges' decisions to sentence an offender to prison and the length of the sentence meted out. She used three theoretical models to predict which variables would be influential in predicting sentencing decisions: the formal legal theory, the organizational maintenance perspective, and the substantive political model. According to formal legal theory, criteria such as offense severity and prior record will have the greatest effect on judicial sentencing decisions. However, the organizational maintenance perspective predicts that both legal and processing variables such as plea bargaining and jury trials should have the greatest impact on sentences. Finally, the substantive political viewpoint suggests that legal and social variables such as the offender's race and gender will have the greatest impact upon judicial sentencing decisions.

In addition to these three general theories of judicial decision making, Dixon (1995) offers two more perspectives: a combined substantive/political organizational model and the organizational context theory. The substantive/political organizational maintenance model holds that "politics are institutionalized in organizational practices" (Dixon, p. 1163). Minorities are likely to receive differential treatment and biased sentences as a direct result of this institutionalized political prejudice. The organizational context model maintains that judicial sentencing decisions are affected by the "political, social, and organizational contexts of the court" (Dixon, p. 1164).

In Dixon's (1995) study, legal variables had the greatest influence on both sentencing decisions and sentence length, thus supporting a formal legal model for judicial decision making. Three of the four legal variables she tested (offense severity, prior record, and use of a weapon) had a significant effect on the judges' decisions to sentence offenders to prison. For example, offenders were 103 percent more likely to be sentenced to prison for a severe crime, 588 percent more likely to be sentenced to prison if a weapon was involved in the crime, and 288 percent more likely to receive a prison sentence if they had a prior criminal record. Four legal variables (the previous three and multiple charges) affected sentence length. In addition, the processing variable of plea bargaining had a very significant effect on both the decision to sentence to prison and sentence length. If a plea agreement was reached, offenders were 75 percent less likely to be sentenced to prison. Thus, both the organizational maintenance theory and the formal legal perspective were supported by Dixon's findings. She also tested the effect of race on sentencing decisions, but it did not have any significant effect on judicial sentencing decisions in her study. The substantive/political perspective was not supported by her research.

In his analysis of sentencing decisions in Pennsylvania, Ulmer (1997) also found that legal variables such as offense type, offense severity, and prior record had the greatest effect on sentencing outcomes (i.e., the decision to sentence to a correctional institution and length of sentence). However, race, gender, and mode of conviction had significant effects on sentencing outcomes as well. Pennsylvania's sentencing guidelines require that offense severity and prior record serve as the major bases for sentencing decisions. Ranges for offense severity and prior record are combined into a sentencing matrix. Additionally, the guidelines in Pennsylvania encompass standard, aggravated, and mitigated ranges, which are applied to both misdemeanor and felony cases. The sentencing guidelines in Pennsylvania were implemented, in part, to reduce the effects of extralegal and processing variables on sentencing outcomes. Since Ulmer's analysis revealed that these factors still influence sentencing, it may be tempting to conclude that the guidelines are not serving their purpose. However, he suggested that "it is necessary to tease out the processes behind the statistics by connecting court community organizational contexts to workgroup interaction strategies, and interaction strategies to sentencing outcomes" (Ulmer, p. 164). The courtroom work group generally consists of the judge, the prosecutor, and the defense attorney.

Ulmer (1997) outlined twelve ways in which court community contexts can lead to sentencing disparities. His first proposition concerned the stability and the familiarity among members of the court; these factors can result in either interorganizational consensus or conflict and coalition. Next, Ulmer discussed how interorganizational consensus on sentencing goals (e.g., rehabilitation, retribution, etc.) affects relations among judges, attorneys, and sentencing practices. He also pointed out the political ideology associated with each sentencing goal. For example, Republicans were inclined to favor retribution, whereas Democrats were more likely to favor rehabilitation. The third proposition dealt with news media coverage. Negative media attention may disrupt relations among court members and create conflict between political parties. News coverage can become a political weapon and influence sentencing decisions. Ulmer then noted how attorneys, depending on the court docket, attempt to match themselves with a judge sharing the same political or sentencing ideology. This practice is known as judge shopping. His fifth and sixth propositions concerned the balance of power between judges and attorneys. Sentencing discretion is sometimes displaced from judges to attorneys. Ulmer found that the balance of power favored judges in more urban counties characterized by an efficient district attorney's office; the balance of power in more affluent counties favored the district attorney's office.

Ulmer (1997) described his seventh proposition as the effect of case processing on sentencing decisions. Courts with high degrees of both familiarity and sentencing consensus are likely to develop going rates to determine sentences and are not likely to abide by sentencing guidelines. Courts with high degrees of familiarity but low sentencing consensus are likely to follow sentencing guidelines to mediate between conflicting parties. The eighth proposition deals with the work group case-processing strategies that develop from stability and consensus among court members. High stability and high consensus lead to a negotiative process. Low stability and high consensus lead to a unilateral method. Finally, an antagonistic process results from high stability and low consensus. Ulmer's ninth proposition concerned sentencing guidelines directly. He suggested that sentencing guidelines may promote sentence bargaining by specifying the exact factors that mitigate and aggravate. In the tenth proposition, Ulmer acknowledged that open guilty pleas and prosecutorial tactics might influence sentence bargaining. Likewise, he claimed that sentencing guidelines occasionally lead court members to reward offenders who plead guilty and punish those who eventually go to trial.

In the twelfth proposition, Ulmer (1997) explored how sentencing outcomes may be affected by the racial and sexual stereotypes held by court members. Sentencing decisions may be influenced by stereotypical beliefs about the characteristics (e.g., danger, rehabilitative potential) of certain groups. For example, women may be seen as more amenable to rehabilitation than men. However, Ulmer claimed that an offender's prior record should temper the effects of extralegal factors on sentencing outcomes. These propositions, taken together, indicate just how extralegal and processing variables still influence sentencing outcomes in the presence of state-mandated guidelines.

The goal of sentencing guidelines in criminal court is to reduce discretion and thereby enhance due process of law. Due process rights are embodied in several key amendments to the U.S. Constitution. The Fourteenth Amendment extends due process into criminal law at the state level. As previously mentioned, the Fourth Amendment is particularly germane to policing because it protects citizens against unwarranted searches or seizures. The Eighth Amendment is relevant to the defendant's initial appearance in court because it prohibits excessive bail. The Fifth and Sixth Amendments deal directly with court processes. In particular, the Fifth Amendment offers protections against double jeopardy (i.e., accusing or trying the same person twice for the same crime) and self-incrimination. The Sixth Amendment calls for notification of charges, a speedy and public trial, the right to confront witnesses, and the right to an attorney.

Harlow (2000) recently looked at defense counsel in criminal cases for the U.S. Department of Justice. Specifically, she was interested in whether defendants who are represented by private attorneys fare better in court than do offenders who have public defenders. She discovered that, in both state and federal courts, there is no difference in the conviction rates of defendants with publicly funded attorneys versus those with private legal counsel. Interestingly, Harlow found that most offenders charged with violent, felonious crimes were represented in court by public defenders. On average, violent offenders received longer prison sentences than persons convicted of drug, property, or public-order crimes. She also noted that a greater proportion of persons with a publicly appointed counsel pleaded guilty than did those with private counsel. Additionally, Harlow's analysis revealed, "Convicted defendants represented by publicly financed counsel were more likely than those who hired a private attorney to be sentenced to incarceration" (p. 6). However, those with private counsel had, on average, a longer period of incarceration if they were sentenced to prison than did offenders with a public defender.

Corrections

The correctional subsystem of the criminal justice system may be divided into two broad categories: institutional/residential corrections and community corrections. Institutional corrections include prisons, jails, and other regional detention facilities. Community corrections encompass a wide range of alternatives to incarceration such as probation, parole, home detention, electronic monitoring, community service, weekender programs, day reporting, work or treatment programs, or other types of nonresidential supervision. The number of persons subjected to community corrections is far greater than the number of those who are incarcerated in institutional settings. For example, in 1998, over 4 million persons were under probation, parole, or some other type of community supervision, as compared with only 1.89 million in jail or prison (U.S. Department of Justice, 2000). Thus, in 1998, there were over twice as many persons under community supervision as there were under institutional control.

Jails and regional detention centers are the first correctional environments to which persons accused of crimes are typically exposed. In fact, jails serve multiple purposes. They may hold persons before, during, and even after court. Criminals convicted of misdemeanor offenses may also be sentenced to serve time in jail. Jails sometimes are used to hold inmates during times of prison overcrowding. The U.S. Department of Justice (2000) estimated that 592,462 individuals were held in jail at midyear in 1998. Likewise, another 72,385 were allowed to participate in alternatives to jail such as home detention, electronic monitoring, community service, weekender programs, day reporting, work or treatment programs, or other types of pretrial supervision.

The maximum length of incarceration for persons convicted of misdemeanor offenses is eleven months, twenty-nine days. Persons convicted of felony offenses have sentences of imprisonment in excess of one year. Criminals sentenced to serve time in prison have been convicted of at least one felony offense. Misdemeanants are incarcerated in jails, and felons are incarcerated in prisons.

Prisons may be differentiated between state and federal facilities. There were 1,375 state and 125 federal prisons throughout the United States in 1995 (Stephan, 1997). Furthermore, prisons are also distinguished by level of security. Stephan reported on three security levels: minimum, medium, and maximum. A prison's level of security is determined by a variety of factors such as the design of the facility, the amount of staffing, and operating procedures (North Carolina Department of Corrections, 2003). The security level involves the extent of control over inmates and the amount of separation of inmates from their communities. Maximum-security prisons are the most restrictive and controlled of the three, and minimum-security facilities are the least restrictive and controlled.

Like the correctional institutions in which they are housed, prisoners also have different classification or custody levels. Levels of custody vary from state to state. However, most states use at least four levels: minimum, medium, close, and maximum. An inmate is classified into one of these categories based on the perceived public safety risks he or she presents. Most states also consider institutional risk criteria when classifying an inmate. For example, the Oregon Department of Corrections (2001) uses seven criteria to compute public safety risk: crime severity, extent of violence, use of weapon, history of violence, escape history, time left to serve, and arrest warrants that have not been resolved (i.e., felony detainers). That agency also determines institutional risk by looking at six additional factors: frequency of institutional misconduct, severity of institutional misconduct, primary program compliance, gang affiliation, substance abuse, and age.

The number of people incarcerated in prison each year in the United States has been steadily increasing since the 1980s. According to Blumstein and Beck (1999), the number of inmates in state and federal prisons increased by as much as 260 percent, from 315,974 prisoners in 1980 to 1,138,984 in 1996. The U.S. Department of Justice reports that the number of inmates in state correctional facilities alone increased from 708,393 in 1990 to 1,231,475 in 1999, indicating a gain of about 74 percent. These numbers illustrate how dramatically the prison population has increased during the 1990s.

Blumstein and Beck (1999) were also concerned with the rationale behind this marked increase in incarceration. They conducted a study in which they examined a number of factors that could contribute to high prison populations. In particular, Blumstein and Beck examined offending rates, arrests per offense, commitments to prison per arrest, and time served in prison. They determined that inmates are serving longer sentences nowadays. Longer prison sentences seem to be the main reason for the dramatic increase in incarceration rates in the United States. In fact, Blumstein and Beck remarked that "the preponderance of the responsibility for prison population growth lies in the sanctioning phase, the conversion of arrests into prisoners and the time they serve in prison" (p. 55). Time served is thus the key to understanding prison population growth.

Recent changes in criminal justice policy have played a role in the current incarceration binge. Both legislation that calls for stringent sentences (e.g., "three strikes" laws, sentencing enhancements, selective incapacitation, and mandatory-minimum laws) and protracted durations until parole (e.g., "truth in sentencing" laws) contribute to more time served, which in turn has fueled the population explosion in American prisons. Selective incapacitation is a relatively new correctional practice that involves incarcerating individuals who commit a disproportionate amount of crime for longer periods of time than other offenders (Pollock, 1998). Through statistical analyses, Greenwood (1982) demonstrated that habitual offenders can be identified by a number of characteristics, including age of onset for criminal behavior, their criminal histories, and substance abuse or chemical dependency. Selective incapacitation involves incarcerating criminals for what they might do in the future as well as what they have done in the past. Of course, an unfortunate consequence of this practice is that some offenders who would not commit more crimes are not released. The practice of selective incapacitation seems ethically problematic; it does not seem right to incarcerate men and women for crimes they have not yet committed. However, it continues to be a popular correctional policy.

Proponents of selective imprisonment maintain that the benefits derived from it far outweigh the associated costs. For instance, Forst (1984) suggested that selective imprisonment is ultimately the best crime control strategy to safeguard a community against future violent criminality. He also noted that selective incapacitation would not necessarily lead to more prison crowding. Only those who are predictably the most violent, criminally active, and harmful would be imprisoned. Less serious offenders under such a correctional practice would receive alternative sanctions such as probation, community service, restitution, and so forth. A variation on this theme of selective incapacitation involves segregating high-risk violent offenders in super-max facilities.

Super-max is a term used to describe a prison with a super-maximum security level that houses the most dangerous and violent criminals. Inmates in super-max prisons are segregated in single small cells with solid steel doors. They are isolated from other inmates and receive minimal time outside their cell each week. When inmates move outside their cell, they are typically handcuffed, shackled, and escorted by two or three correctional officers. Human Rights Watch (2000) recently estimated that around 20,000 prisoners are now incarcerated in super-max prisons throughout the United States. Punitive criminal justice policies, growing prison populations, and budgetary cutbacks have made it difficult for prison officials to safely, securely, and humanely operate traditional penitentiaries. According to Human Rights Watch (2000), these factors create thinly staffed and overcrowded prisons that produce tension and violence. In an effort to decrease these risks and increase control over inmates, prison officials turned to prolonged, super-max confinement. Human Rights Watch noted that assignment to super-max facilities might be for an indefinite period, continuing for years. And although super-max confinement was developed for high-risk violent offenders, the practice is being used on inmates with medium- and minimum-security classifications. Super-max confinement is just one correctional trend sweeping the United States.

Privatization is yet another popular correctional practice that policy makers have endorsed in light of overcrowding and budgetary cutbacks. Expenditures for imprisonment are becoming some states' largest spending category. In an effort to relieve part of this burden, some state governments have allowed private businesses to assume management (and ownership in some cases) of their correctional facilities. McCrie (1992) noted that the privatization of prisons generally involves a combination of a build-operate-transfer agreement and a contracting-out policy. The build-operate-transfer agreement allows private companies to build a major project, operate it for a certain length of time, and then possibly transfer it to the state if necessary or at the end of the contract term. Typically, the contracting-out policy simply allows public services to be assumed by the private sector.

Lauen (1997) reported that private prisons exist in at least thirteen states. From the correctional officer's perspective, private prisons offer lower starting salaries than those at state facilities. In fact, Lauen looked at several detrimental effects of privatization and remarked that "Some of the impacts of this public/private differential on private programs include the following: staff turnover rates in private programs are high, staff morale is low, and the general quality of services is low" (p. 23). However, the main impetus behind the privatization trend appears to be operating-cost reduction. Many public officials believe that private prisons can be operated less expensively than public facilities.

There is some empirical proof to support the claim that private prisons are cheaper to manage than those in the public sector. For example, Culp (1998) looked at thirteen different evaluations of private and public correctional facilities in the United States. He found that private prisons are about 4 to 14 percent less expensive to run than state institutions. He also claimed that the cost savings associated with private prisons are not the result of poor working conditions for correctional officers or inadequate conditions of confinement for prisoners. Although Culp endorsed privatization, he recommended new research into its long-term consequences.

Heightened state expenditures tend to accompany the new correctional policies that put lawbreakers behind bars for longer periods of time. As the U.S. prison population grows, the costs associated with imprisonment increase as well. Expenditures for state prisons grew from $6,778,000,000 in 1985 to $22,033,000,000 in 1996, representing an increase of 225 percent (Bureau of Justice Statistics, 1999). However, Maguire and Pastore (1997) estimated that the cost of corrections in the United States today is actually closer to $32 billion than $22 billion. Eckl (1998) also noted that from the 1980s to the late 1990s state corrections budgets tripled, and these costs surpassed all other state expenditures to become the fastest growing state spending category.

A future extrapolation can be made from these current trends in corrections. In short, more individuals in the United States will be incarcerated for longer periods of time, and expenditures for imprisonment will rise in tandem. Social institutions such as education and the family will suffer, and state support to related social organizations like schools, shelters, and certain businesses might decline. In fact, Walker et al. (1996) have already determined that, in 1992, more African American males were under correctional supervision (e.g., jail, prison, probation, and parole) than were enrolled in college. Likewise, Hagan and Dinovitzer (1999) noted, "Several large states now spend as much or more money to incarcerate young adults than to educate their college-age citizens" (p. 130). These are both dire financial and social consequences of the law-and-order mentality that is popular among the contemporary American polity.

CONCLUSION

A sequence of events is set into motion when behavior that violates the criminal law is detected by the criminal justice system. Police work is typically associated with uncovering crime through investigation, and the results of police investigation may lead to an arrest. After arrest, an individual will appear in court. Court involves a variety of stages, including initial appearance, arraignment, trial, and sentencing. The final phase of the criminal justice system involves the supervision of an individual if he or she is found guilty in court. This supervision may be based in the community or in an institutional or residential setting.

This chapter provided a brief introduction to the criminal justice system. The subsequent chapters deal with aspects of the correctional subsystem. The history and philosophy of corrections are explored in chapters 2 and 3. Chapter 4 examines the context of corrections and includes topics such as prisonization, institutional dependency, and misconduct in prison. Chapter 5 addresses the differences and similarities among male and female inmates. Prisoners' rights and states' responsibilities are presented in Chapter 6. The experiences of imprisonment from an inmate's point of view are described in chapters 7 through 9.

REFERENCES

Anderson Publishing Company. (2001). *2001 Tennessee criminal code: Handbook for law enforcement officers with selected traffic offenses.* Cincinnati, OH: Author.

Blumstein, A., & Beck, A. J. (1999). Population growth in U.S. prisons, 1980–1996. In M. T. Tonry & J. Petersilia (Eds.). *Prisons* (pp. 17–61). Chicago: University of Chicago Press.

Blumstein, A., & Rosenfeld, R. (1998). Explaining recent trends in U.S. homicide rates. *The Journal of Criminal Law and Criminology, 88*(4), 1175–1217.

Brown, S. E., Esbensen, F., & Geis, G. (2001). *Criminology: Explaining crime and its context* (4th ed.). Cincinnati, OH: Anderson.

Bureau of Justice Statistics. (1999). *State prison expenditures, 1996* (NCJ-172211). Washington, DC: U.S. Department of Justice, Bureau of Justice Statistics.

Cable News Network. (1997). *Key dates in the O. J. Simpson case* [On-line]. Available: http://www.cnn.com/US/9702/05/oj.timeline/index.html

Cable News Network. (2003). *'Blanket commutation' empties Illinois death row* [On-line]. Available: http://www.cnn.com/2003/Law/01/11/illinios.death.row/index.html

Caulkins, J. P., Rydell, C. P., Schwabe, W. L., & Chiesa, J. (1997). *Mandatory minimum drug sentences: Throwing away the key or the taxpayers' money?* Washington, DC: RAND Drug Policy Research Center.

Culp, R. F. (1998). *Evaluations of prison privatization* [On-line]. Available: http://www.geocities.com/CapitolHill/Lobby/6465/eval.html

Dixon, J. (1995). The organizational contexts of criminal sentencing. *American Journal of Sociology, 100*(5), 1157–1198.

Eck, J. E. (1992). Criminal investigation. In G. W. Cordner & Donna C. Hale (Eds.), *What works in policing? Operations and administration examined* (pp. 19–34). Cincinnati, OH: Anderson.

Eckl, C. (1998). The cost of corrections. *State Legislatures, 24,* 30–33.

Fagan, J., Zimring, F. E., & Kim, J. (1998). Declining homicide in New York City: A tale of two trends. *The Journal of Criminal Law and Criminology, 88*(4), 1277–1323.

Felson, M. (2002). *Crime and everyday life* (3rd ed.). Thousand Oaks, CA: Sage.

Forst, B. (1984). Selective imprisonment should be used. In D. L. Bender & B. Leone (Eds.), *America's prisons: Opposing viewpoints* (pp. 92–96). St. Paul, MN: Greenhaven Press.

Grana, S. J., Ollenburger, J. C., & Nicholas, M. (2002). *The social context of law* (2nd ed.). Upper Saddle River, NJ: Prentice-Hall.

Greenwood, P. (1982). *Selective incapacitation*. Santa Monica, CA: RAND Institute.

Griset, P. L. (1991). *Determinate sentencing: The promise and the reality of retributive justice.* Albany: State University of New York Press.

Hagan, J., & Dinovitzer, R. (1999). Collateral consequence of imprisonment for children, communities, and prisoners. In M. T. Tonry & J. Petersilia (Eds.), *Prisons* (pp. 121–162). Chicago: University of Chicago Press.

Harlow, C. W. (2000). *Defense counsel in criminal cases* (NCJ-179023). Washington, DC: U.S. Department of Justice.

Hindelang, M. J. (1974). The uniform crime reports revisited. *Journal of Criminal Justice, 2,* 1–17.

Human Rights Watch. (2000). *Out of sight: Super-maximum security confinement in the United States* [On-line]. Available: http://www.hrw.org/reports/2000/supermax

Inbau, F. E. (1961). Police interrogation: A practical necessity. *Journal of Criminal Law and Criminology, 89*(4), 1403–1412.

Kappeler, V. E., & Kaune, M. (1997). *Critical issues in police civil liability.* Prospect Heights, IL: Waveland Press.

Klotter, J. C. (1990). *Criminal law* (3rd ed.). Cincinnati, OH: Anderson.

Knight, A. H. (1996). *The life of the law: The people and cases that have shaped our society, from King Alfred to Rodney King.* New York: Oxford University Press.

LaFree, G. (1999). Declining violent crime rates in the 1990s: Predicting crime booms and busts. *Annual Review of Sociology, 25,* 145–168.

Lauen, R. J. (1997). *Positive approaches to corrections: Research, policy, and practice.* Lanham, MD: American Correctional Association.

Maguire, K., & Pastore, A. L. (1997). *Sourcebook of criminal justice statistics, 1996* [On-line]. Available: http://www.albany.edu/sourcebook.3

McCrie, R. D. (1992). *Three centuries of criminal justice privatization in the United States justice system.* Jefferson, NC: McFarland.

NAACP Legal Defense and Educational Fund. (2001). *Death row U.S.A.* [On-line]. Available: http://www.naacpldf.org/pdfdocs/deathrow_%20fall2002.pdf

Nettler, G. (1984). *Explaining crime* (3rd ed.). New York: McGraw-Hill.

North Carolina Department of Corrections. (2003). *Assigning inmates to prison* [On-line]. Available: http://www.doc.state.nc.us/DOP/custody.htm

O'Brien, R. M. (1985). *Crime and victimization data.* Beverly Hills, CA: Sage.

Oregon Department of Corrections. (2001). *Custody levels* [On-line]. Available: http://www.doc.state.or.us/programs/intake_center.shtml?custody_levels

Osborne, E. (1999). Is the exclusionary rule worthwhile? *Contemporary Economic Policy, 17*(3), 381–389.

Pollock, J. M. (1998). *Ethics in crime and justice: Dilemmas and decisions.* Belmont, CA: West/Wadsworth.

Silberman, C. (1978). *Criminal violence, criminal justice.* New York: Random House.

Smith, D. A. (1987). Police responses to interpersonal violence: Defining the parameters of legal control. *Social Forces, 65*(3), 767–782.

Spohn, C. C. (2002). *How do judges decide? The search for fairness and justice in punishment.* Thousand Oaks, CA: Sage.

Stephan, J. J. (1997). *Census of state and federal correctional facilities, 1995* (NCJ-166582). Washington, DC: U.S. Department of Justice.

Sudnow, D. (1965). Normal crimes: Sociological features of the penal code in a public defender office. *Social Problems, 12*(3), 255–276.

Tappan, P. W. (1947). Who is the criminal? *American Sociological Review, 12*, 96–102.

Tonry, M. (1996). *Malign neglect: Race, crime, and punishment in America.* New York: Oxford University Press.

Travis, L. F. (2001). *Introduction to criminal justice* (4th ed.). Cincinnati, OH: Anderson.

Ulmer, J. T. (1997). *Social worlds of sentencing: Court communities under sentencing guidelines.* Albany: State University of New York Press.

U.S. Department of Justice. (1994). *Violent Crime* (NCJ 147486). Washington, DC: U.S. Government Printing Office.

U.S. Department of Justice. (2000). *Homicide trends in the U.S.* [On-line]. Available: http://www.ojp.usdoj.gov.bjs/homicide/hmrt.html

Walker, S., Spohn, C., & DeLone, M. (1996). *The color of justice: Race, ethnicity, and crime in America.* Belmont, CA: Wadsworth.

Wallace, H., & Roberson, C. (2001). *Principles of criminal law* (2nd ed.). Boston: Allyn & Bacon.

Wicharaya, T. (1995). *Simple theory: Hard reality.* Albany: State University of New York Press.

2

Justice and the Origin of Corrections

Gordon Crews

INTRODUCTION: THE EVOLUTION OF JUSTICE— FROM BANDS AND TRIBES TO STATES

No one knows exactly when criminal law and corrections began in human society. However, it probably would have occurred at the point in social evolution when collective vengeance was first substituted for private vengeance. That is, people realized that feuding was costing the group too much in terms of injuries and lives, and some individual's behavior was first imagined to be harmful to the group as a whole. The entire group, or the leader(s) acting for the group, took action against the offender.

As small primitive bands grew into sizable tribes, there was a need for more organization. With this shift came an increase in the number of tribal rules that individuals could violate. Also, there were more feuds among individuals and families. Social order simply could not be maintained in a large group by relying mainly on private vengeance; it was too costly in injuries and lives of tribal members. Therefore, some tribes set rules for third-party intervention, which established forms of "corrections" that were less injurious than private vengeance (e.g., verbally insulting each other until the feuding parties were satisfied) (Bohannan, 1967). More often, it seems, an order was made for some sort of payment in personal goods by the designated offender to the injured party or his or her relatives, depending on the seriousness of the victim's injuries, or for the victim's death (Hoebel, 1954).

The size of tribes continued to grow, and feuds among members and families also increased. As Mays and Winfree (2002) described the transition from tribal to state justice, the chief and tribal elders or the king and his counselors had to establish consistent procedures for controlling feuds and keeping the peace.

> Chiefs and kings were supposed to act themselves, or assign a third party to act, as final adjudicators of the [settlement] of wrongs, and thus the idea of a court was born. When this happened, the tribal group or state assumed responsibility for all offenses committed within its jurisdiction. (p. 348)

Although the beginnings of courts and corrections probably occurred in wandering tribes, most historians mark the discovery of agriculture, which allowed the shift from tribes to states, as the major turning point in this and all matters of human civilization. The development of agriculture occurred when primitive people discovered how to grow food, instead of having to move around hunting for it. Agriculture changed virtually every aspect of human life, and certainly criminal law and corrections. Up to that time, the land had not belonged to anyone; or, to put it another way, it had belonged to everyone. Different tribes had well-defined areas for hunting and gathering, just like other animals; and, just like other animals, there were skirmishes when the members of one tribe invaded another's territory. Still, individuals and groups did not think of the land as something they owned personally, like they owned their clothing, utensils, weapons, and other things they made. It was simply the area of earth on which they were trying to survive, rather like guests of nature.

In order to provide for different needs and interests, and to prevent the social chaos of private attempts to "get even" for perceived wrongs, rules were invented to protect property ownership and control the exchange of goods and services (including domesticated animals and slaves from other tribes to do the hard labor). From these rules, the ancient feudal system began to emerge. The rules of ownership and exchange of goods and services made it possible for increasingly larger areas to be claimed by those who were not just the strongest, but also the best organizers and managers—those who could make or use the rules for their personal advantage. They became feudal lords, and everyone who lived on their lands worked for them in exchange for economic support and physical protection. Not only were the lords the administrators of lands, but they also became the administrators of justice for all persons who lived on their lands. The lords then increased their domains through wars with their neighbors, and the ultimate winner became king of the region or empire.

EARLY CODES OF CORRECTIONS

The Egyptians had developed hieroglyphic picture writing about 3400 B.C., but their pictures did not communicate spoken words and ideas. However, along with other high levels of cultural progress, papyrus rolls became the material for "books" throughout the ancient world around 1300 B.C. (Hayes, Baldwin, & Cole, 1962). The advent of papyrus rolls was an important step in the development of law because it allowed for the communication of ideas through an easily transportable material medium.

From all accounts, the first code of law and corrections was written in wedge-shaped cuneiform symbols representing spoken syllables. This was the Sumerian Code, which emerged in Sumer at about 3500 B.C. However, these rules and procedures "were fragmented, rather than being a true 'code,' and dealt with pleadings and land transactions" (Fox, 1985, p. 5).

The first fully developed written code that provided a systematized source of criminal law and corrections was that of Hammurabi (1947–1905 B.C.), the sixth king of Babylonia. This code was in use for about two centuries. Then, in 1750 B.C., the Hittites invaded and destroyed Babylonia, expanding their own empire and their legal code throughout the Mesopotamian region. Another code, the Hebrew Law of Moses, was evolved and refined from the Ten Commandments between 1500 B.C. and 900 B.C. There were a number of lesser codes in the ancient world, but those mentioned here are the most notable in the history of Western civilization.

Insofar as criminal law and corrections were concerned, all of these initial codes were designed to control private vengeance and preserve public order. Whatever the king's justice called for was given as "collective vengeance" on behalf of all members of the realm. The underlying principle of justice in these codes is the law of Talion (i.e., the consequences for the offender should be equivalent to the injury sustained by the victim). Initially, this meant not only an eye for an eye, a tooth for a tooth, and a bone for a bone, but also exactly the same eye, tooth, and bone, if possible. By the eighteenth century, a long history of interactions among religious belief systems, individual behavior systems, and governmental justice systems had taught the lesson that if the official punishment was much more or less than "getting even," private feuding would continue and more crime and social disorder would be promoted.

The principle that the severity of punishment should fit the severity of the crime has been recognized in virtually every criminal code in the history of Western civilization, from Hammurabi to the present time. Although legally prescribed correctional practices have changed dramatically throughout this history (e.g., society no longer legally sanctions putting out offenders' teeth and eyes, breaking their bones, and severing hands and feet), the basic idea of the Talion principle has remained fairly constant to the present time.

The problem with the Talion principle, from the very beginning, was not in figuring out how severe the punishment should be. The principle is clear: The punishment should be no more or less severe than the offense. The real difficulty comes in determining how harmful various behaviors actually are, when considered as offenses against the whole society.

Overall, the earliest written sources of law relied mainly on one of three correctional outcomes for convicted offenders: death, Talion for physical injuries not resulting in the victim's demise, and payment of restitution. Death was frequently decreed in Hammurabi's Code, whereas restitution was far more prevalent in the Hittite Code. Considering that the Hittites dealt with homicide by restitution to the victim's relatives, it would seem that the economic well-being of living survivors was viewed as a more important aspect of "justice" than exacting the vengeance of Talion against the offender. Presumably, the Hebrew Code placed a greater value on the sanctity of human life, and was therefore more vengeful than the Hittites' in calling for the execution of the murderer.

THE GREEK EXPERIMENT WITH DEMOCRACY: POLITICS AND CORRECTIONS

Ancient Greek civilization began around 1200 B.C., was at its height in about 500 B.C., and began to decline with the Macedonian conquest in 338 B.C. Through all this time, the Greeks never really developed as a politically unified nation or empire with a single legal code. They settled in city-states, each of which developed and maintained its own social, economic, and legal system.

The Greeks differed from other ancient societies in that they did not consider themselves to be totally subservient to a monarch or king. Public opinion was always a strong force in Greek government and administration of justice. In this respect, they recognized their differences from the populations of neighboring kingdoms and empires, and they took great pride in their status as "free citizens" of their respective city-states. Actually, they were free men, since women, children, and slaves did not count politically. In the developmental era before the seventh century B.C., there were kings, or "tyrants," as they were called. However, except in war, they were strongly influenced, if not controlled, by Councils of Elders.

By the eighth century B.C., the citizens of Athens had managed to rid themselves of the tyrants. However, the Council of Elders had become a council of aristocrats whose rules favored wealthy families and made slaves of the poor who could not pay their debts. The experiment with democracy and the system of law and corrections associated with it were essentially reactions against this aristocratic elitism. Despite the lack of written statutes at this time, a system of courts had developed that served the interests of all citizens, in principle if not in practice. During the eighth century B.C., private arbitration ceased to be voluntary and became public and compulsory. Judges were appointed to settle disputes. Each male citizen had to serve as a judge during the official year following that in which he reached the age of fifty-nine. Failure to serve was punishable by *atimia,* or loss of citizenship rights. The judges' sentences could be appealed before a higher court, the Council of the Areopagus, the first real court that judged the most important cases.

The city was the most vital aspect of Greek existence and allegiance, so various degrees of *atimia* were very serious and degrading punishments. Total and perpetual *atimia*, or civil death by permanent exile, was almost equivalent to execution. In the case of total *atimia*, anyone—including slaves—could, without fear of reprisal, kill an exiled offender who illegally returned. In this early system of justice, no distinction was made between matters of government and matters of sin and crime. Violations of religious, civil, and criminal customs were all simply "wrongs" that disrupted orderly and secure life in the city and surrounding area. Most matters were settled by orders for payment of restitution and fines, but slavery for debtors and their entire families, total or partial *atimia*, and the death penalty were also used. Interestingly, homicide was considered a matter for private revenge and was not punished by the collective.

Imprisonment was used occasionally for very serious offenders awaiting trial and for some debtors who did not pay their fines within the given time. If such debtors were not sold into slavery, they could remain imprisoned for their entire lives. If an offender was sentenced to death, being forced to drink poison (hemlock) and public stoning were the most common forms of execution. For very serious or treacherous acts that were harmful to all citizens, extremely barbarous methods were employed to achieve community revenge.

This early system of government and administration of justice operated on the basis of established customs. By the seventh century B.C., these customs were being implemented with great favoritism to wealthy aristocrats and their families. There was widespread arbitrariness, bribery, and corruption among magistrates and judges, and the traditions of administration of justice were becoming unclear and abusive to many, if not most, citizens. This was the situation when a man by the name of Draco was appointed to put the customary traditions in writing and thereby standardize the procedures and practices of justice in the first written code of ancient Greece.

Draco did little to reduce the preferential treatment of the rich and powerful families, especially concerning the enslavement of debtors. Also, his approach to standardization was to adopt the most severe punishment (i.e., death—either civil death by *atimia* or execution) for virtually all offenses, whether they were minor or serious, "including laziness, theft of fruits or cabbage, sacrilege, or homicide" (Drapkin, 1989, p. 183). This scheme made the quality of justice worse instead of better for the majority of Athenians. Still, Draco's Code did contain several advancements over prior customs. It established the right of any citizen to bring an alleged injury before court directly, instead of having to depend on members of the government to initiate actions on behalf of the entire community. It set up a procedure for higher governmental supervision of judges' decisions in order to ensure that the provisions of the code were followed. Also, it made homicide a community concern rather than a matter of purely private revenge, and it recognized different types of homicide, including "malicious" and premeditated (punishable by death); "impassioned" by love or anger (punishable by *atimia*); "involuntary" due to negligence and accident (punishable by *atimia*); and "justifiable" by self-defense or catching an adulterer in the act (not punishable).

Draco's Code went into effect in 621 B.C. It is remembered for its severity of punishments, but it was its strong favoritism to the social and economic benefit of aristocrats that forced its reform. It was particularly hard on farmers, artisans, and merchants who for any reason could not pay their debts to wealthy property owners within the specified time. Many were made slaves, or had to sell their children into slavery, in order to satisfy their debts. Within a period of about thirty years, the hostility of the majority of Athenian citizens toward the aristocrats became so strong that a new code had to be written to maintain community order.

Thus, it was in a situation of rapidly approaching breakdown of the total social, economic, and political system that a truly remarkable series of legislative reforms emerged in order to regain societal stability. These reforms were written and implemented by Solon, and they became known as Solon's Code in the period from 608 to 560 B.C. They were further refined by Cleisthenes from about 510 to 480 B.C. Taken together, these reforms constituted the Greek experiment with democracy. Although the experiment was sporadic and relatively short-lived, these codes established the lasting ideal concept of government run directly and equally by the citizens themselves.

Solon's Code diminished the aristocracy of families with large land holdings and also abolished the slavery to these families of debtors, their wives, and children. Slavery, especially the selling of children, was prohibited as a means for securing a loan or as punishment for nonpayment of debts. In fact, no citizen could be punished with slavery for any offense. Also, limits were set on the amount of land that any citizen or family could own. Although Solon's Code recognized four socioeconomic classes, and certain powers and privileges were retained for the upper classes, people could move from one class to another on the basis of accumulated wealth. A popular Assembly was established, along with a Senate of 400 members with equal representation from the different social classes. A system of courts was initiated, with judges hearing common matters and a high court for serious cases and appeals. The high court (the Heliaea) was made up of elected representatives of the general population and, according to Drapkin (1989), it may well have been "the first in which the accused was judged by his peers. Its sentences were final and immediately executed" (p. 188).

Solon's Code classified different types of offenses and punishments according to seriousness, and it set out details of legal procedures to be followed in the prosecution of cases. Contrary to Draco's approach, many different forms of punishment were instituted, ranging from minor fines based on the offender's ability to pay, to permanent *atimia* or execution. Under this code, legislation was proposed by the Senate, enacted by the Assembly, and implemented by the courts. All members of the community could attend the Assembly, and each citizen (except women and the very poor who paid no taxes) had an equal right to debate and vote on every piece of proposed legislation. Any citizen could start the prosecution of an alleged wrongdoer in the Assembly, and he could present an appeal of a lower court judge's decision. Thus, virtually all male citizens had the right to be personally involved in making and implementing the rules under which they had to live. This era was the beginning of government of the people, by the people— democracy in its ideal form, in which all citizens are direct participants in their own government and administration of justice.

THE ROMAN WINDS OF LEGALITY AND
THE NEED FOR EFFICIENT CORRECTIONS

If one thinks of Greek culture as the seeds of flowering civilization, one can consider the Romans as the strong wind that carried those seeds from Scotland to North Africa, and from Portugal to Arabia. Where the Greeks were innovative designers and thinkers, the Romans were practical managers and doers. More than knowledge and perfection, it was an orderly existence that was most important to the Roman citizen, and efficient administration of law was the key to order. In fact, the Roman Empire expanded more from the need to keep order along its boundaries than from a raw desire for conquest.

When Solon and Cleisthenes were developing their ideals of government and justice in legal codes (608–560 and 510–480 B.C., respectively), the Romans were just approaching the end of their primitive stage of cultural evolution. Their family and social life, religion, economy, and government were all combined in arbitrarily interpreted customs involving mystical beliefs, private and public vengeance, and brutal public punishments such as burning, drowning, beheading, crucifying, throwing into the abyss, fighting wild animals, and various forms of lesser mutilations. As in other primitive societies, homicide was altogether a matter of family revenge, often settled by arbitration and compensation.

As the city of Rome grew in size and complexity of life, a pressing need for a written legal code was recognized, once again for predictability and to protect the interests of middle- and lower-class citizens from arbitrary abuse by the nobility. Ten scribes were appointed to write the code, and in 450 B.C., about the height of the Greek era, the first set of Roman statutes was presented in the Twelve Tables. The Twelve Tables were written laws that clearly reflected the influence of Greek principles concerning the protection of all citizens' rights, but the interpretation of these statutes remained largely under aristocratic control. That is, the Romans established a bureaucratic republic of appointed and elected representatives of the people (who were mostly members of, or were controlled by, the nobility), rather than setting up a democracy of all the people. To them, order and efficiency in their lives held priority over equality of participation among all citizens.

All but two of the Twelve Tablets dealt with family, property, economic, and other civil matters. However, for the first time, religious matters were dealt with separately, and acts that would anger the gods were put in the hands of a high court of religious leaders, from which there was no appeal. The two tablets covering injuries to others dealt mostly with specific limitations and procedures for private vengeance. Criminal acts against the state were classified according to the severity of punishment rather than the severity of the offense; that is, offenses punishable by death, and offenses with lesser punishments. As might be expected, the death penalty was imposed for many offenses, and it could be applied to all members of an offender's family to prevent revenge and blood feud between families. Some of the forms of execution, like a number of crucifixions at one time and offenders fighting wild beasts, soon became notorious events of public spectacle and sport.

Perhaps the most progressive aspect of this early Roman code is the manner in which it dealt with juvenile offenders. Like all of the earlier codes discussed, this code held infancy to be an exemption from criminal liability. This phase generally ended at about age seven, although Hebraic law placed the age at thirteen with the ceremonial passage to adulthood (bar mitzvah). However, the Roman code

> divided minors into three categories with regard to responsibility: (a) children under seven were not responsible under any circumstances; (b) those from age seven up to the age of puberty were not responsible if the praetor was of the opinion that they lacked understanding of the nature of their acts; and (c) those from puberty up to twenty-five years of age were to have their youthfulness taken into consideration in the prescribing of punishment. (Barron, 1954, p. 12)

Overall, the punishments were lighter for juveniles than adults.

Also, under primitive Roman customs, the head of a family (*pater familias*) had virtually unlimited power over children for their entire lives. A child's disrespect, refusal to obey, or striking of the *pater familias* was severely punished and sometimes included death. This threat tended to maintain order within families, but it also fostered more than a few assassinations of heads of households by adult children seeking independence and power. Although the original Twelve Tablets were apparently destroyed about sixty years after their creation, and it is not known if they clearly specified this, later interpretations resulted in freeing adult children from lifelong parental dominance—in law, if not in custom. Also, the criminal corruption of children became a severely punishable criminal offense.

THE MIDDLE AGES, CHRISTIANITY, AND CORRECTIONS

One needs to understand that the emergence of Christianity was (and remains) a matter of great social, political, legal, educational, and even economic impact, as well as being a religious phenomenon. From the very beginning, it was taken as a vital ally, or a resolute enemy, of whatever system of government it encountered; there was seldom a middle ground of simple tolerance. In large part, this is due to two of its major tenets: (1) the intense dedication of many of its members to a missionary obligation (i.e., convincing nonbelievers that the Christian faith is not just the best, but the only, road to salvation); and (2) the threat of divine condemnation to the greatest conceivable punishment (eternal suffering) if this way of believing is not accepted and spiritual redemption for sins is not accomplished before death. It is a real paradox that, even with its strong teachings of the value of human life, charity, mercy, equality, and forgiveness, the force of the missionary doctrine and the infliction of atonement to avoid eternal punishment have probably brought to human beings more individual violence and suffering, more civil disorder, and more war among groups and nations in the world than any other single influence, with the exception of the human need for vengeance. All of this began with Roman life and law at the time that the Christian church was established.

By the fourth century, Christianity became the official religion of the Roman Empire, and the Catholic Church in Rome was established as the center of the faith. Understandably, it was structured on the Roman model of bureaucratic organization. Its leaders, from the pope, cardinals, and bishops, down to the local priests and missionaries, understood the practical value of good organization, management, and discipline, and the missionary dictum meant that they too had an empire to build and administer. Indeed, as the Roman Empire declined and broke apart, and the "dark age" of Western civilization from the seventh to the eleventh centuries commenced, the Roman Catholic Church became the major force behind cultural preservation and distribution—the guardian and governor of literature, art, architecture, music, and education, as well as religion. In general, however, it had little influence on criminal law and corrections, except where members of the clergy were involved.

Spiritual banishment (excommunication) and the prospect of eternal damnation were extremely strong leverages with those who believed, and, although church and state were philosophically separate, they worked very closely together in controlling crime (which was also sin), in maintaining social order (which was also religious order), and in supporting and defending Christendom (both financially and through the Crusades against the Muslims). Under feudalism, many bishops and abbots were "invested" with large estates by kings and lords, and they became powerful members of the nobility and the royal courts. In return, they communicated to the secular rulers a divine blessing upon their right to rule, and they did little to interfere with the policies and practices of administering justice.

Individuals could not impose atonements on themselves, since they could not know what God required. Therefore, the church fathers assumed this responsibility either directly, such as in cases of heresy and witchcraft, or indirectly, through the lord of the estate or king of the realm. If the offender resisted, this was a further crime, with the ultimate consequence being denial of absolution and, therefore, condemnation to eternal damnation. What was required for atonement was often an infliction of restitutions and physical sufferings that were more severe than the individual's offense. Even if the offender repented of his or her wrongdoing, it was necessary to make sure that the soul was "purged" and that reparation was made to God through the church, as well as accomplishing reparation to the victims, the community, and the ruler—all of whose "peace" had been violated by the offense. Thus, so long as the offender received absolution before death, the brutal punishments of the times satisfied several vastly different purposes (i.e., atonement for the church, vengeance for rulers, and entertainment for the masses).

For several centuries, the church had been opposed to forcing confessions from accused persons, and torture was expressly forbidden. However, when the Justinian Code was found and studied, its provisions for torture were adopted in Canon Law by the papal bull of 1252, and the inquisitors received instructions for the administration of the law. Solitary imprisonment with only bread and water was instituted as a form of penance for heretics, and the most severe form was a living entombment (Korn, 1959).

Another major aspect of the interaction between religion and corrections in the Middle Ages rests with the concept of spiritual "atonement." The pope, as God's representative on earth (and through him, the church leaders all the way down to local priests), could grant absolution or forgiveness for sins and crimes. However, individual verbal repentance and promise of good deeds was not enough. A person could be falsely repenting and, although God would know and ultimately judge and punish, the task of the church was to "save" the offender from the finality of such consequences. If at all possible, the church should help the offender to save himself or herself from God's vengeance. Thus there must be visible demonstration of expiation—purging the soul and mind of sinful thoughts and intentions (as well as reparation through payment of restitution and performance of good deeds). All of this added up to visible prayers for forgiveness, economic payment, and physical suffering as "atonement."

Of all the curses that the Inquisition brought, perhaps the greatest was that, until the closing years of the eighteenth century throughout the greater part of Europe, the inquisitional process, as developed for the destruction of heresy, became the customary method of dealing with all who were under accusation. The accused was treated as one having no rights, whose guilt was assumed in advance, and from whom confession was to be extorted by guile or force.

The number of people put to death is not known for certain, but the estimates of different authors range from 50,000 to as many as a million. It was possible to hold mass trials for witchcraft, since the usual rules of trial procedure were set aside "inasmuch as the proof of such crimes is so obscure and so difficult that not one witch in a million would be accused or punished if the procedure were governed by the ordinary rules" (Rennie, 1978, p. 12).

THE AGE OF ENLIGHTENMENT, THE STATE, AND CRIMINAL SANCTIONS

From 1650 to 1800, many new thinkers and philosophies emerged during the Age of Enlightenment. The most capable scholars of the time began thinking creatively instead of simply interpreting and reinterpreting ideas and writings from the past. They put existing information and ideas together in ways that generated new insights and explanations for virtually everything that was happening in the world around them. Not since the ancient Greeks had the intellectual spirit been so lively. It is to this time of change that the origin of modern concepts of criminal law and corrections can be traced.

The Classical School of Criminology: An Evolution in Thought

The most dramatic occurrence of enlightened thinking about the administration of criminal justice came in 1764, with a small publication in Italy entitled *Essays on Crimes and Punishment*. It was written by Cesare Beccaria (1738–1794), a young lawyer living in Austria who did not put his name on the original work for fear of reprisal by Austrian officials. In one short work, he managed to sift out, integrate, and concisely express the major principles of all of the liberal philosophies of the Enlightenment as they related to crime and punishment. He did not originate most of the ideas, but his presentation of them was remarkably clear and forceful, and the timing of his publication could not have been better. His book quickly spread throughout Europe, and instead of being condemned, it was read and praised by many scholars and intellectuals as well as several kings and emperors, including Joseph II of Austria, whose reprisal Beccaria had feared.

In England, Jeremy Bentham (1748–1832) was a prolific writer who was a strong advocate of utilitarian philosophy. He believed that the purpose of government is to promote the greatest good for the greatest number of persons, that all punishment is evil, and that "it ought only be admitted in as far as it promises to exclude some greater evil" (Bentham, 1780/1948, p. 70). He grounded his work on the hedonistic philosophy that all human behavior is governed by pleasure and pain. From this basis he developed a "hedonistic calculus," or set of principles for punishments that would slightly outweigh the rewards of various types of offenses, and therefore deter the prospective offender from offending and the punished offender from repeating his or her acts (Rennie, 1978).

Because their works influenced many other thinkers throughout the 1700s and 1800s, Beccaria and Bentham are both known as founders of the Classical School of Criminology. It was the culmination of thought that began with Deism and rationalism, and it was a major advancement in thought about criminal behavior because it allowed people to move away from superstition as an explanation for deviance.

Thought versus Reality: Corrections during the Age of Enlightenment

Despite all of the progressive thinking and good intentions of the eighteenth century, the Enlightenment's ultimate impact was far greater on systems of government and court procedures for protecting the innocent than on correctional practices for punishing the guilty. Once the "worthy" (honest, working) poor were excluded from public care in houses of corrections, the principle of least eligibility soon came into play for the criminal offenders remaining in those houses.

To the enlightened intellectuals of the late 1700s, the substitution of the forward-looking, preventive purpose of deterrence for the backward-looking purposes of private and collective vengeance was a great advancement in the civilization of criminal law. For offenders, the fact that legislators and judges thought differently about the reasons for punishment was not much relief. Although public exhibitions of torturous execution and corporal punishment were phased out in the late eighteenth century, these were replaced with an increase in longer terms of confinement in jails, transportation to penal colonies, and storage in "hulks" (old, rotting wooden ships). These "alternatives" involved years of intense suffering in unbelievably horrible conditions, all largely hidden from public view and concern.

Beginning in the late 1500s, the transportation of offenders to penal colonies in the New World was a way of reducing the overcrowded populations in the deplorable jails that evolved from bridewells and workhouses. Transportation was as much an economic enterprise as it was a correctional practice. Shipping companies profited from the transport of prisoners to the colonies, and the hauling of raw materials and merchandise on the return trip. Administrators of the penal colonies profited from the productivity and leasing out of convicts, and owners of farms surrounding the colonies profited from a seemingly endless supply of cheap labor.

In order to increase the profits all around, as many offenders as possible were transported with the least possible expense for their physical care. Many offenders died of starvation and disease or were injured or killed in the holds of the ships. For those who lived through the voyage, there awaited the chain gangs and frequently brutal punishments of their keepers. Skilled workers fared a little better, since they could often obtain employment in the community. Eventually, a policy was adopted in which unskilled workers, through good behavior, could earn a "ticket of leave" (the earliest form of parole) for employment by settlers. Any infraction of rules while working in the community would return offenders to the penal colony, where they would face severe punishment. Those who survived their sentences were given their freedom and simply turned out to seek employment in the surrounding settlements. Some became reputable citizens, and, of course, those who did not were subject to the local practices of punishment.

As towns and cities grew in the areas surrounding the penal colonies in the New World, citizens became increasingly resistant to the presence of convicts in their communities. The widespread reputation of penal colonies was hardly conducive to local cultural development, and, in time, the social and political problems grew to outweigh the economic benefits. Also, after the American Revolution, the new states refused to accept deported criminals. Although transportation continued to colonies in other parts of the world, the growing public resistance and political influence in these provinces brought the practice largely to an end by the late 1800s. After having deported more than 130,000 offenders to Australia in some ninety years, including juveniles and adults of both sexes, England abolished its practice of transportation to Australia in 1857.

Even though a large number of offenders were transported to penal colonies, England's jails became increasingly overcrowded. In the mid-1770s, old abandoned ships known as "hulks" began to be used to house prisoners to relieve the overflowing populations of jails. Hulks were wooden ships, with hulls rotted beyond economical repair. Their holds were leaking, dark, unventilated, unsanitary, and just about the least likely conditions imaginable for the support of human existence. As in the jails, offenders of all types, all ages, and both sexes were thrown together. They were simply herded into these holds with infrequent observation, let alone supervision, by their keepers. In addition, there were inflictions of corporal punishments and all manner of abuses by the keepers, who often became as degenerate as the worst of their charges. The use of hulks was meant to be a temporary measure, but the practice continued until 1859.

REFORMING CORRECTIONS: FROM ENLIGHTENMENT TO THE EARLY TWENTIETH CENTURY

While the ideas of the Classical School of Criminology certainly changed the way people thought about crime, change in the system of punishment and rehabilitation occurred at a much slower pace. One must also remember that these systems and modes of thought did not exist in a vacuum. Other events, movements, and individuals would bring change to the system, not only in thought but also in the actual physical structure of correctional institutions.

One such individual was John Howard (1726–1790), who, in 1773, became the sheriff of Bedfordshire, England. Although it appeared that no other officials were greatly disturbed by the inhumane conditions in the jails and hulks, Howard was appalled and angered. Some years earlier he had been held as a prisoner of war in France, and he knew firsthand the brutalities inflicted on inmates. When he made an inspection of the Bedfordshire jail, he found not only the deplorable conditions already described, but also several poor inmates who had served their sentences and were being held simply because they could not pay the fees that were charged for their food and housing. From this, he took it upon himself to make inspections all over the country.

In 1777, Howard published a report entitled *The State of Prisons in England and Wales.* He not only publicized the terrible plight of offenders, but he set forth a number of recommendations for reform. These proposals included (1) separation of females from males, children from adults, minor violators from hardened criminals, and persons awaiting trial from those serving sentences, with congregate work for each group, but separate rooms for sleeping; (2) abolition of fees for care; (3) provision of wholesome food, healthful living conditions, regular medical care, and chaplaincy services; and (4) employment of honest, respectable jailers and outside inspectors to maintain compliance with operating standards.

John Howard's proposals were, for the most part, adopted by the English Parliament in the Penitentiary Act of 1779, an act that also established the country's first penitentiary in Norfolk, England. However, the enactment of statutes does not always bring rapid change in customary practices, and until his death in 1790, Howard devoted his full effort to the improvement of jail and prison conditions. In the following decades, there was much that was yet to be accomplished, and the John Howard Society became (and remains) a widely recognized influence for prison and jail reform.

Building on Howard's work, Elizabeth Fry (1780–1845) took up the cause for women offenders in the early nineteenth century. She was a Quaker and, with other Quaker women, in 1817 formed an association for the benefit of females in London's Newgate Prison. Fry's group pressed for the standards of reform that John Howard had proposed, with the added provisions that female facilities should not only be separate from those for males, but should also be of a domestic nature and staffed by women. While helping to bring about a number of significant improvements at Newgate, Fry also visited other prisons and jails in England and Scotland. Her notes of these experiences were published in 1818, and in 1827 she published a work entitled *Observations in Visiting, Superintendence and Government of Female*

Prisons. These writings and her subsequent visits to many European countries were highly influential in the improvement of conditions for female offenders. Before her death in 1845, her works also became a leading force for the improvement of female corrections in the United States.

At about the time of Elizabeth Fry's death, a retired naval officer by the name of Alexander Maconochie (1787–1860) was put in charge of one of the English penal colonies in Australia. When he arrived in 1840, he was as shocked and repulsed by the cruelty of the conditions and practices he found as John Howard and Elizabeth Fry had been when they visited the jails and prisons of England in their respective times. He not only complained to his superiors, vigorously, but he went much further and proposed a radically different approach to the administration of penal colonies. He was promptly fired from his appointment. However, the governor of the province decided to let him experiment with his ideas at another penal settlement, located on Norfolk Island, which was used for the worst offenders. "The conditions there were so horrible that condemned prisoners expressed thanks to God when the Governor refused to grant a stay of their execution, and those who were given a reprieve from execution often wept bitterly" (Barry, 1957, p. 5).

Maconochie abolished the cruel punishments, improved the living conditions, and established the mark system. In the mark system, prisoners earned a certain number of marks for accomplishing specific work assignments and for good behavior. He translated prisoners' sentences in terms of years into a schedule of marks, in which 8,000 was the equivalent of a life sentence. When the required numbers of marks were accumulated, the prisoner would be freed. Instead of receiving corporal punishment for violations of rules, prisoners were required to pay fines from the marks they had earned. In effect, this system made each prisoner directly responsible for the length of his or her own sentence. Further, it held out to all prisoners, first-timers and repeaters, the same prospects of freedom as a reward for good behavior and hard work.

In a short time, word of Maconochie's experiment reached his superiors and administrators of other penal colonies on the mainland, and there were strong complaints against it. It was argued that the lack of severe punishment for the worst criminals would not deter them from repeating their crimes, nor would others be deterred from committing similar crimes, which in turn would seriously threaten the public safety of mainland communities. It was decided that Maconochie had to be replaced, but no one was eager for the job. He would remain until a new superintendent could be found and was in charge for four years, all told. Despite the fact that his system was working effectively, it was replaced with the cruel practices in use elsewhere. In the years after he left, there were so many riots by the prisoners that the Norfolk Island colony was finally abandoned in 1855.

After Maconochie returned to England in 1844, and until his death in 1860, he remained a strong advocate for improvement of penal practices. In 1854, Sir Walter Crofton adopted for the Irish penal system many of Maconochie's policies, to which he added a "ticket of leave" policy that provided for supervision of inmates in the community following their release from prison. The policy was set up so that local police would be responsible for "surveillance" of released inmates, and inspectors of released prisoners would be responsible for providing assistance and "supervision."

Later, some debate emerged about whether this division of responsibility was necessary, appropriate, and effective. Some correctional leaders argued that parole officers should conduct both surveillance and supervision, whereas others held that law enforcement on the one hand, and support and assistance on the other, were contradictory and mutually defeating objectives. Crofton's was the first fully developed parole program, and the argument still continues about the role of parole officers in surveillance and law enforcement, as well as in supervising and helping offenders to become established in legitimate community life.

The innovative crusaders discussed here (Howard, Fry, Maconochie, and Crofton), among others, had a great impact on thinking and legislation that ultimately improved living conditions for accused persons and offenders in confinement. Even with such improvements, however, the motives underlying the confinement of offenders remained essentially the same; that is, collective vengeance, with an intellectual veneer of deterrence. For the most part, criminals were still looked upon and dealt with as despised outcasts. They should be made to suffer—enough to keep them from committing further crimes, and to serve as preventive examples for potential offenders in the general public. The goals of improving offenders' behaviors and returning them to society as legitimate, productive citizens were viewed as "experimental ideals," and these ideals did not last for very long in most English and European penal facilities. The general public sentiments of "least eligibility," and the economic needs for cheap convict labor, made programs for the "benefit" of criminals very difficult to support, either politically or financially. While all of this was occurring in Europe, a quite different chain of events was taking place in the United States of America.

CONCLUSION

Even though no one truly knows when criminal law and corrections began to develop, several assumptions can safely be made. Most knowledgeable individuals would offer that it probably occurred at the point when people realized that collective vengeance should be substituted for private vengeance. It was probably when people realized that feuding was costing the group too much in terms of injuries and lives. Further, it was probably when some individual's behavior was first imagined to be harmful to the group as a whole, so that the entire group, or the leader(s) of the group, needed to take action against the offender.

It can also be assumed that most initial criminal and correctional codes were designed to control private vengeance and preserve public order. The underlying principle of justice in these codes was the law of Talion (i.e., the consequences for the offender should be equivalent to the injury sustained by the victim). A long history had taught groups that if the official punishment was much more or less than "getting even," private feuding would continue and more crime and social disorder would be promoted.

By the eighth century B.C., despite the lack of written statutes at this time, a system of courts had developed that served the interests of all citizens, in principle if not in practice. During this time, private arbitration ceased to be voluntary and became public and compulsory. Judges were appointed to settle disputes. The judges' sentences could be appealed before a higher court—the first real court that judges the most important cases. This early system of government and administration of justice operated on the basis of established customs.

As cities grew in size and complexity of life, a pressing need for a written legal code was recognized, if for no other reason than for predictability and to protect the interests of middle- and lower-class citizens from arbitrary abuse by the nobility. Generally, these written codes dealt with family, property, economic, and other civil matters. Religious matters were dealt with separately, and acts that would anger the gods were put in the hands of a high court of religious leaders, from which there was no appeal. Criminal acts against the state were classified according to the severity of punishment rather than the severity of the offense.

REFERENCES

Barron, M. L. (1954). *The juvenile in delinquent society*. New York: Knopf.

Barry, J. V. (1957). Captain Alexander Maconochie. *Victorian Historical Magazine, 27* (June).

Bentham, J. (1780/1948). *An introduction to the principles of morals and legislation*. New York: Hafner.

Bohannan, P. (1967). *Beyond the frontier*. Garden City, NY: Natural History Press.

Drapkin, I. (1989). *Crime and punishment in the ancient world*. Lexington, MA: Lexington Books.

Fox, V. (1985). *Introduction to corrections* (3rd ed.). Englewood Cliffs, NJ: Prentice-Hall.

Hayes, C. J. H., Baldwin, M. W., & Cole, C. W. (1962). *History of Western civilization*. New York: Macmillan.

Hoebel, E. A. (1954). *The law of primitive man*. Cambridge, MA: Harvard University Press.

Korn, R. R. (1959). *Criminology and penology.* New York: Holt.
Mays, G. L., & Winfree, L. T. (2002). *Contemporary corrections.* Belmont, CA: Wadsworth/Thompson Learning.
Rennie, Y. (1978). *The search for criminal man.* Lexington, MA: Heath.

3

A BRIEF HISTORY OF CORRECTIONS IN AMERICA

Gordon Crews and Wayne Gillespie

INTRODUCTION

Prior to the American Revolution, things were not much different in the colonies than in England. For the most part, corrections amounted to humiliations, severe corporal punishments, and executions. However, the alternative of long-term confinement at hard labor, in place of the traditional punishments, did start again just before the Revolution. It is reported by the Connecticut Historical Commission in Hartford, Connecticut, that the New Gate Prison at East Granby was opened in 1773. After the Revolution, it became the first state prison in the United States. It was built over an old copper mine, and prisoners were housed in spurs off of the vertical mine shaft. Their "hard labor" was largely busywork, since the mine had played out some years earlier. Although it was claimed to be an advancement over the brutalities of corporal and capital punishment, the living and working conditions were so miserable that its operation was plagued by inmate riots, and it was closed in 1825.

QUAKER REFORM AND THE RISE OF THE AMERICAN PENITENTIARY

The real beginning of the American prison movement came in Pennsylvania, and it was mainly, but not exclusively, through the efforts of the Quakers. It was here that the progressive, humanitarian ideas of persons such as John Howard and Elizabeth Fry were forged, over a period of some forty years (1788–1829), into a major public policy for criminal corrections—the philosophy and practice of reformation.

The basic assumptions of reformation were that (1) human beings are fundamentally good, harmonious, and productive; (2) criminal behavior is the result of evil influences in the offender's environment gaining dominance over the natural good in the offender's character; (3) given an environment that is free of evil contamination, and opportunities for productive labor, the natural goodness of even the worst offenders will surface and replace the evil tendencies; and (4) such an environment can be provided through long-term solitary confinement, in physically healthful conditions, with long hours of useful work, supported by religious counseling. It is important to note here that confinement, in the "care-prayer-work" model of reformation, is seen as something that is done "for" the offender, rather than "to" the offender. Also, rather than the offender's improvement being caused or brought about by another person or persons through the infliction of punishment, confinement for reformation simply aims to provide an environment in which the offender "reforms" himself or herself, and cannot avoid doing so.

William Penn was instrumental in shaping the Quaker reform movement of the late seventeenth century. In fact, he worked on the "Great Law," which was a series of statutes enacted in 1682 by the first state legislature in Pennsylvania (Pennsylvania State Archives, 2003). The Great Law covered many topics of law, including the establishment of courts, conduct of trials, and punishment. For example, the Great Law proclaimed that capital punishment was only to be used in cases were the defendant was guilty of premeditated murder. Penn, like many other Quakers, believed that criminals could redeem themselves through incarceration in "houses of correction" or "workhouses" (Pennsylvania State Archives, 2003).

The precepts of the Great Law were eventually abolished in 1718 by the majority in Pennsylvania. Harsh penalties for criminals were put back into effect, and many Pennsylvania Quakers became frustrated by these cruel practices. They believed that cruelty perpetuated crime rather than reduced it. Still, there was not much they could accomplish until the American Revolution provided the opportunity for sweeping political, legal, and social changes. In this climate of change, the writings of Cesare Beccaria and John Howard in particular became the working manuals for the formation of the Philadelphia Society for Alleviating the Miseries of Public Prisons, which was established in 1787.

The Quaker influence persisted with the development of the Walnut Street Jail, the first bona fide penitentiary in the United States. The remodeling of the Walnut Street Jail was completed in 1791, and the new building was named the "penitentiary house," after a term introduced by John Howard. The rationale for its construction was based on religious doctrine rather than scientific fact. This was a very apt name in this case, since there was no cell space provided for any type of work. All other inmates in the jail were given regular work assignments, but for the penitentiary inmates, self-reflection and "penitence" was the sole purpose of confinement. As shall be seen, this no-work policy for those in solitary confinement would become a serious problem for the Pennsylvania prison reformers in the next several decades. From its opening in 1791, the remodeled Walnut Street Jail with its internal "penitentiary" became the prison for the state of Pennsylvania. In the first few years of its operation, its board of inspectors (managers) made enthusiastic, eloquent, and quite exaggerated claims for its success. This approach to corrections was dubbed the Philadelphia or Pennsylvania system.

Almost as if these early Quaker reformers expected to overcome facts with words, the reports began flowing out (to the entire world) praising the new penitentiary system and its alleged benefits. Although the penitentiary idea had been born in Europe, and then put into practice in the United States, it was returned to Europe as if it were an American invention. In 1794, the French visitor Francois Alexandre Frederic La Rochefoucauld-Liancourt, after inspecting the Walnut Street Jail and talking with Caleb Lownes from the Philadelphia Society for Alleviating the Miseries of Public Prisons, proclaimed the excellence of the facility and program to the people of France. Some forty years later, his fellow citizens Gustave de Beaumont and Alexis de Tocqueville would still be praising the American penitentiary movement.

However, even from the beginning, things did not go all that well. The Walnut Street Jail was the only prison for the entire state of Pennsylvania, and it also housed vagrants, debtors, and those awaiting trial for the city of Philadelphia and the surrounding county. It soon began to feel the strains of overcrowding, and by 1803 the conditions became so bad that the Philadelphia Society for Alleviating the Miseries of Public Prisons sent a memorandum to the legislature asking for the construction of a new prison. The new prison—the Arch Street Jail—was approved, but fourteen years went by before it was opened, and by that time it was not of much help. During that period, the society persistently lobbied the legislature for much larger institutions, and in 1818 the plans were adopted for two new prisons—one in the eastern part and one in the western part of the state. The Eastern Penitentiary was to have solitary confinement with labor, and the Western Penitentiary would have solitary confinement without labor. Although history recalls penitentiaries as advancements in the treatment of prisoners, Johnson (1997) noted that "penitentiaries offered at best only a deceptive façade of humanity" (p. 33). He maintained that both physical and psychological pain were endemic inside penitentiaries of the nineteenth century.

THE PENNSYLVANIA SYSTEM

The Western Penitentiary, indicative of the Pennsylvania system, was built first, and it opened in 1826 with solitary cells for 200 inmates. By this time, however, penal reformers were becoming convinced that solitary confinement without labor was neither reformative nor economical. Although the prison operated in this manner for three years, the legislature, in 1829, finally mandated that both penitentiaries adopt a program of labor. Unfortunately, the cells at the Western Penitentiary were so small that they were too dark, and too unhealthy, for either continual confinement or work. An attempt was made to remodel the prison, but this proved to be almost impossible. In 1833, it was ordered that the institution be demolished and a new one built to provide better facilities for carrying out the principles of work in individual cells.

While all of this was occurring, the Eastern Penitentiary on Cherry Hill in Philadelphia was completed, and it opened in 1829. It was specifically and carefully designed for solitary living and work. The cells were larger than at the Western Penitentiary, and a small, completely private outside exercise area was attached to each cell. Although the customary sentence "at hard labor" was seen by the public as punishment, the real punishment was in the solitude rather than the work. For the most part, inmates welcomed the work as much needed relief from the overwhelming monotony of their lonely environment; especially since the reformation policy called for visits from craftsmen and chaplains to provide them with "instructions in labor, in morals and in religion" (Montgomery & Crews, 1998, p. 56). The physical design and program at the Eastern Penitentiary were highly publicized, and this combination quickly became the model for what has since been referred to as the Pennsylvania system of long-term confinement for the reformation of criminals.

THE AUBURN SYSTEM IN NEW YORK

In 1794, the Philadelphia Society for Alleviating the Miseries of Public Prisons had launched into an extensive campaign of correspondence with other states. Possibly as a direct result of the society's contact with Governor John Jay of New York, Jay sent a team to study the reforms at the Walnut Street Jail—namely, General Philip Schuyler, a Revolutionary War hero, and Thomas Eddy, a Quaker financier. Eddy and Lownes of the Philadelphia Society, both Quakers, quickly developed an agreeable relationship, and Lownes shared the philosophy and the experiences of the society in bringing about the changes at the jail. Convinced of the desirability of the "reformation" approach in dealing with criminals, Eddy and Schuyler returned to New York with recommendations for similar efforts there.

On March 26, 1796, the New York legislature reduced the long list of capital crimes to murder and treason, and substituted imprisonment for corporal punishment in all other offenses (Killinger & Cromwell, 1973). The act provided for the construction of two prisons, one at Albany and another in New York City. The plan for the Albany prison was soon abandoned, and only the New York City prison was built. The new prison, called Newgate, opened in 1797. Eddy was the first warden, and he operated the institution under firm but humane Quaker policies until 1804. Newgate soon became seriously overcrowded, and discipline became impossible to maintain. Unhappily, Newgate too closely copied the operation of the Walnut Street Jail in Philadelphia and thus developed the same problems. By 1816, the New York reformers, like those in Pennsylvania, were pressing the legislature for the construction of large new prisons. New York managed to pass the necessary legislation sooner than Pennsylvania, and by the winter of 1817, the new prison at Auburn was opened.

At the beginning, Auburn was set up to operate like the Walnut Street Jail, except for the "penitentiary house." That is, some prisoners lived in double quarters and others in dormitories, and they worked in common areas. The Auburn system became known as the congregate system. The program objectives were order and reformation, but there was no evidence that these were being achieved. Thus, an attempt at solitary confinement was made, based on the Pennsylvania model. The costs and inmate behavioral problems became worse instead of better, and "when this experiment failed, the future of the penitentiary hung in the balance" (Lewis, 1965, p. 56).

The Quaker belief in the Inner Light, or the essential goodness in every person, simply did not produce a prison program that worked for New York. The early experiences at Auburn more nearly fit the Calvinist doctrine of the basic "depravity of man," and Calvinism was better established than was Quakerism in the state of New York. So, the reaction was a program oriented toward harsh discipline that stressed submission and regimentation, combined with productivity and profit from convict labor. Inmates were separated at night, they were brought together for "hard labor in silence" during the day, and flogging was authorized for rule violations. The goal of reformation was dropped in favor of order, efficiency, and economy.

THE GREAT PRISON DEBATE

Out of the Quaker doctrine grew a reformation philosophy directed at moral recovery through separate confinement, work, and meditation. From the Calvinist heritage of New York grew a penal philosophy oriented toward maintenance of order and maximum economic benefit from prisoner labor. These two correctional approaches would be debated for the next several decades by their respective champions, the Philadelphia Society for Alleviating the Miseries of Public Prisons and the Prison Discipline Society of Boston. With the spread of the prison movement in the United States, these two systems (the Pennsylvania and the Auburn) would become the models that other states would study and emulate.

Rothman (1971) reported that the debate between the proponents of the two systems deeply concerned Americans. Annual reports of the two systems to state legislatures, and detailed discussions in popular journals, contained arguments on the merits of each approach. The advocates of the Auburn system believed that the practice of congregate work, in silence, was not further contaminating already contaminated souls. The supporters of the Pennsylvania system believed that complete isolation was necessary to avoid moral contamination and to bring out the essential goodness within each inmate.

The success and failure of these systems, however, proved to hinge on more practical considerations than who was most correct in their beliefs about inmates' souls. The Auburn-style prison turned out to be less expensive to build and operate, despite its foundation on pessimistic premises about the moral character of criminals. Also, it produced what many people judged to be a more positive effect on the behavior of prisoners. Eventually, the Auburn system prevailed, and it not only spread in the United States but was also transferred to Europe. According to the French observers Beaumont and Tocqueville (1833/1964), Pennsylvania was left standing "quite alone" in its insistence upon complete separate confinement.

Although Pennsylvania lost the competition for the model prison, the Quakers' belief in reformation and their concern with humanitarian improvement of conditions in institutions did not decline. They continued to work for prison improvements, but their main focus shifted from adults to juveniles.

Even though the Quakers advocated prison reform and human rights, certain groups were excluded from this noble endeavor. Johnson (1997) recalled that "women and minorities were barely considered human—most blacks at this time were slaves, most women confined to subservient domestic roles—and hence these groups were not considered fit candidates for the penitentiary's rehabilitative regime" (p. 32). Women who were incarcerated in penitentiaries often received less care than their male counterparts. Moreover, during the nineteenth century, most female institutions were located in the attics, kitchens, or back rooms of male prisons.

THE EMERGENCE OF PROBATION

Although the Auburn system was more widely adopted for the development of penitentiaries in the United States, the debate between the advocates of the Pennsylvania and New York systems continued through much of the nineteenth century. While this was going on, a radically different correctional movement emerged, one that would ultimately gain a major place in systems of corrections throughout the Western world. This was the concept of probation, a social service alternative to, rather than an improvement of, confinement and punishment for criminal offenders.

The idea for what was later to become known as probation began with the enlightened legal thought of some judges in Boston, Massachusetts, in the 1830s. Much of the fuel for debate about the Pennsylvania and Auburn systems came from an increasing recognition that neither approach was working very well. In general, confinement in jails and penitentiaries was not effectively achieving either the deterrent or the reformative influence on the behavior of offenders that had been originally hoped for, and initially claimed. Also, there were a number of offenders whose personal circumstances, type of violation, and demeanor in court suggested that they could change without being removed from the community. For these persons, the practice of suspending either the imposition or carrying out of their sentences, and releasing them with the promise of good behavior, was already being used. This approach, however, was not very satisfactory, since such offenders were left with the task of reforming themselves, without any sort of assistance or supervision. The Boston judges imagined that this problem might be legally overcome, but it remained for John Augustus, who was neither a lawyer nor a governmental official of any sort, to demonstrate how it could done—and with remarkable success.

John Augustus (1784–1859) was the prosperous owner of a small shoe-making business in Boston. He was a promoter of the temperance movement, which was aimed at eliminating the evil effects of alcohol on society in general, and on family life in particular. A major focus of the movement was on helping alcoholics to overcome their addiction and to rebuild their lives. Apparently, it was this concern that prompted Augustus to visit the Boston court one August day in 1841.

The legal procedure that Augustus and the court adopted in this first case—his payment of the offender's bail, a period of personal assistance and supervision, a later return to court for sentencing, and his payment of a one-cent fine and court costs for the offender—became an established process in the Boston court, for which Augustus coined the term *probation*. In preparing an account of his work in 1852, entitled *A Report of the Labors of John Augustus*, he found that he had provided probation services for 674 males and 428 females, both adults and children, charged with almost every type of bailable offense, at a personal expense of $19,464 in bail payments and $2,417.65 in fines and court costs. Out of the entire group of 1,102 persons, the bond was reportedly forfeited in only one case.

Before his death, some eight years after the above report, Augustus provided bail and probation services for almost 2,000 offenders. He and his wife also started and operated a house of refuge for prostitutes. He gave up his business and devoted his full time to social service, sometimes carrying a caseload as high as 150 persons, not all of whom were criminal offenders. His efforts were continuously criticized and ridiculed by officials such as the court clerk, jailers, and process servers, who lost the fees they would have earned from processing and maintaining the offenders that Augustus bailed and kept from returning to the court. According to Cromwell (1985), judges, media, and community leaders encouraged and supported Augustus's endeavors. His work was sufficiently successful that, despite the ongoing opposition and harassment from some quarters, it became an established part of the administration of justice in Boston until Augustus's death in 1859.

In 1879, twenty years after Augustus's death, the first state statute authorizing probation was enacted by the Massachusetts legislature. This act permitted the mayor of Boston to appoint to the police department the first full-time, publicly paid probation officer. In 1890, a statute was passed extending probation to the entire state, with the provision that it be removed from police jurisdiction. The popularity of probation spread throughout the nation, and by 1925 all states and the U.S. Congress had enacted some sort of probation legislation.

THE REFORMATORY MOVEMENT

As discussed in chapter 2, Sir Walter Crofton in Ireland was the person who preserved and further refined the "mark" and "ticket of leave" systems that Alexander Machonochie had experimented with in Australia. Crofton's program was one of several stages in which the prisoner earned marks to progress from solitary confinement to congregate work, to congregate living and training for future employment, and finally to early release on a ticket of leave. While in the community the offender had to report regularly to the police, and the ticket of leave could be revoked at any time for unacceptable behavior until the end of the originally prescribed sentence. Crofton's program is generally credited with being the beginning of parole—the conditional early release from imprisonment, with official monitoring or supervision.

Word of Crofton's program and its reported success reached the United States in the 1860s, and a movement began for its adoption in American prisons. Among the most enthusiastic supporters were Franklin Sanborn (1831–1917), the secretary of the Massachusetts Board of Charities; Enoch Wines (1806–1879), a strong humanitarian and advocate of prison reform; and Zebulon Brockway (1827–1920), administrator of the Detroit House of Corrections. These men recognized that the debate about the Pennsylvania and Auburn systems was stale, the existing prisons were repressive and grossly overcrowded, and attempts to deter criminal behavior through punishment were failing.

In most southern states, leasing out convicts as virtual slaves for farm labor was the prevalent practice. There were state prisons, but in their operations the Auburn-Pennsylvania debate was not as important as agricultural productivity, however it could be accomplished. Then, the destruction brought by the Civil War further impeded any development of prison reformation programs. The emancipation of slaves made leasing out convict labor even more economically desirable. Also, taking contracts for prison farm products and some manufactured goods was seen as a way to make the institutional operations self-supporting and to gain some resources for reconstruction. Concerns for improvement of prisoners' living conditions, for more humaneness in their punishment, and for their moral and behavioral reformation were simply not matters of high priority in southern correctional systems.

In 1870, a conference of leading prison administrators and penologists was held in Cincinnati, Ohio, to consider new ideas for correctional programming. At this conference, Brockway recounted the failures of the existing systems, and then presented an outline for what he believed to be "The Ideal Prison System for a State" (1912/1969, pp. 389–408). His system was modeled after Crofton's progressive-mark program in Ireland, and its underlying fundamental premise was that the state was the people's guardian or helper.

In particular, Brockway (1912/1969) delineated the following six aspects of the ideal prison system: a state police, primary schools, reform schools, district reformatories, a graduated series of reformatory institutions for adults, the house of reception, and separate reformatories for women. From this basic orientation, his proposals began with attention to children. Schooling was integral to his reforms. He envisioned primary schools for young, poor, and neglected children, where they could be trained as good citizens. Brockway also promoted compulsory schools for troublesome children who were expelled from public school, and he wanted reform schools for older, more advanced juveniles.

It should be noted here that this conference was taking place at a time when the industrial revolution was getting underway, when poor immigrants were pouring into the United States, when many of the younger children of these struggling newcomers were without adult supervision while both parents worked long hours, and when educational institutions (academic, but mainly vocational) were becoming popularized, not only as a vehicle for economic growth, but also as the solution to making "good" American citizens of rapidly increasing numbers of foreigners in the shortest possible time (Platt, 1977).

After proposing these schools for children, Brockway radically called for the elimination of jails. In their place he put separate facilities for accused persons awaiting court action, "with large, well-lighted, cheerful apartments, strong and secure against escape, entirely isolating the occupants from each other" (1912/1969, p. 397). Then, for adult misdemeanant offenders, he proposed district reformatories providing healthful physical care, military-type discipline, and programs of educational and moral training.

For male adults convicted of felonies and sentenced to long-term confinement, Brockway (1912/1969) set out a progressive-stage system of three separate types of institutions. The first was the house of reception, where prospects for reformation would be determined from the offender's history, and classification would be made for academic and vocational training. "Here the incorrigible must be detained in solitary or safe custody, and experimental treatment applied to all, for the purpose of finding those who can be properly transferred to the next grade" (p. 398). The second type of institution was the industrial reformatory, where inmates progressing from the house of reception would be given vocational training for future employment. In addition to their successful development of occupational skills, their progress in "perseverance and self-command" would be evaluated, so that "such of the prisoners as thrive under this training may be removed, with great hope and confident security to the last of the series for male prisoners" (p. 398). This was the intermediate reformatory. Although it would be a securely enclosed institution where inmates would be housed in separate rooms, they would work cooperatively in productive industrial and agricultural activities, and they would share such amenities as a dining hall operated like a restaurant, a library and reading rooms, and facilities for religious services and academic classes.

For female offenders, Brockway (1912/1969) prescribed entirely separate reformatories. These were to be under the exclusive management of women, and they were to be operated with "womanly affection," aimed at winning wayward women to virtue and training them in employable skills (p. 399).

Brockway's plan was that inmates would earn points through good behavior and hard work in order to gain privileges in these institutions, to progress through the different institutions, and to finally earn the prized reward of early release on parole. Thus, discipline, order, and productivity in the reformatories would be maintained by a busy schedule of varied activities and the giving or taking away of points. This system would eliminate any need for or use of the rule of silence, lockstep, chains, and corporal punishment, which had become standard practices in the predominant Auburn system. Brockway saw the legislative enactment of statutes authorizing indeterminate sentences as the vital key for the success of the reformatory approach. Ideally, there should be no minimum or maximum length of sentence set by statute or judicial decision. When an offender's institutional adjustment warranted parole and when successful reformation of the offender was finally accomplished were stages to be determined by professional correctional judgment, rather than legislative or judicial decision.

Brockway's presentation captured the imagination and emotions of even the most hardened prison wardens at the meeting, and it set a remarkably progressive tone for the duration of the conference. Brockway introduced strong proposals for indeterminate sentencing and lobbied vigorously for adoption of this provision by the conference members. Before the conference ended, the participants developed and signed a Declaration of Principles covering virtually every aspect of correctional administration; for example, correctional goals (training and reformation), types and designs of institutions, classification of inmates, general and specialized programs, training of personnel, indeterminate sentencing and pardon/parole procedures, centralization of state correctional administration, maintenance of records and statistical reports, elimination of political influence, and societal responsibility and public relations.

As might be expected, the first of the state correctional administrators was Brockway himself. In the years immediately following the 1870 conference, it was he who made the most notable attempt to implement the declaration's principles. In 1876, based on his years of experience as a correctional administrator at Albany, New York, and Detroit, Michigan, he was appointed general superintendent of a new "reformatory" at Elmira, New York. He promptly launched a sincere attempt to make this facility "the model" for modern institutional corrections.

From the beginning, there were major obstacles in his path, the first being that the institution was designed and built during the previous decade as an Auburn-type facility. Thus, the physical plant was not well suited to the operation of his ideal program. Nonetheless, he was able to implement many of his plans and to get started with a program of immediate renovation of existing facilities and long-term construction of new buildings. He limited the admission of inmates to youthful first offenders (ages sixteen to thirty), he established general education classes, and he began paying wages to inmates for their labor. He tried to get legislative and court approval for completely indeterminate sentences to the institution; however, the best he could achieve was agreement for sentences with no minimum time, but with a statutory maximum limit.

In corrections, major changes in established policies and procedures usually come slowly, and throughout the next decade Brockway worked hard at developing and improving the Elmira facility and program. Still, despite support from the legislature and much acclaim from progressive correctional leaders throughout the United States and Europe, the experience inside the institution did not go as well as he had initially envisioned (Foucault, 1995). Many inmates were not as inspired by the opportunity for education as he had thought they would be, and there was little he could do to prevent the industrial training from becoming drudgery. The worst of it was that his best intentions and efforts simply did not work with some recalcitrant inmates. Thus, under the pressing need to maintain order in the institution, and out of frustration about what else to do, he felt forced to compromise his own ideals and standards by resorting to solitary confinement, paddling, and flogging as disciplinary measures. Despite the difficulties, glowing annual reports of innovative programming and unusual successes persistently emanated from the Elmira Reformatory.

Overall, Brockway's experience at Elmira was the hallmark of what is generally referred to in correctional circles as the reformatory movement. Many correctional reformers throughout the United States and Europe promoted Brockway's ideals, and various aspects of his program were copied in a number of new and reconstituted "reformatories" in the decades extending into the mid-twentieth century. Still, Brockway's own recognition that his program was not really working began to show in his speech to the National Prison Association in 1887. In the course of several decades, others also found the approach to be generally ineffective.

The basic assumption about human behavior underlying the concept of reform was that, given training in a positive physical, moral, and educational environment, free from contaminating evil influences, the natural goodness in human nature would emerge to suppress and permanently replace the previously established antisocial tendencies of criminal offenders. However, even with the best efforts of progressive correctional administrators, this assumption could not be validated in the everyday operations of large institutions for the confinement of criminal offenders. It simply did not produce the hoped-for results of permanently redirecting offenders from illegal to socially conforming behaviors. Still, the reformatory movement did improve the humaneness of conditions and practices in more than a few correctional institutions, and it established many of the standards for programs of long-term confinement that remain in effect.

BEYOND REFORM:
THE RISE OF THE REHABILITATIVE IDEAL

The attempts at reform discussed above should not be confused with the concept of rehabilitation. Pollock (1997) offered a useful distinction between the two:

> *Reform* (as in Brockway's concept of the reformatory) monitors external behavior; success is defined as conformance of behavior to expectations. *Rehabilitation* implies internal change, meaning a permanent change in values, attitudes, morals, or ways of looking at the world. (p. 161)

Rehabilitation is based on resocialization. Individuals become functioning members of society through socialization. During this process, individuals learn how to live by society's rules and norms, communicate their needs, and obtain sustenance. However, socialization sometimes fails.

Kennedy and Kerber (1973) noted that "an individual is considered to be poorly socialized by the dominant society when his behavior does not comply with its norms" (p. 29). According to this perspective, criminals have simply not been appropriately socialized. Resocialization, then, may be defined in the following manner:

> Resocialization is that process wherein an individual, defined as inadequate according to the norms of a dominant institution(s), is subjected to a dynamic program of behavior intervention aimed at instilling and/or rejuvenating those

values, attitudes, and abilities which would allow him to function according to the norms of said dominant society. (Kennedy & Kerber, 1973, p. 39)

Rehabilitation is the primary resocialization procedure associated with the criminal justice system. During rehabilitation, offenders learn that obedient, conforming behavior provides more emotional and material rewards than defiant, oppositional behavior.

Correctional rehabilitation developed in tandem with the rise of the social sciences in the early twentieth century (Pollock, 1997). Academics began visiting prisons for the purpose of scientific research. Haynes (1948) noted that rehabilitation often had a medical orientation. Psychologists and psychiatrics began administering personality tests to inmates during reception and assessment in the early twentieth century. Prison sociologists were also hired to classify inmates according to their conduct and needs. A variety of counseling programs was initiated, including group therapy, behavior modification, and meditation (Pollock, 1997).

Rehabilitation was the dominant correctional philosophy for most of the twentieth century. However, the New York State Department of Corrections conducted an evaluation study of rehabilitative programs in the mid-1970s. Martinson (1974) was one of the researchers who concluded that rehabilitation did not reduce recidivism. That is, treatment and therapy programs designed to resocialized inmates were not working. Martinson's research initiated a debate that lasted into the 1980s and 1990s. Politicians and social conservatives used his conclusions to advance the punitive aspect of corrections, while researchers and liberals disputed his findings (Pollock, 1997). In recent years, however, the debate over rehabilitation has waned in light of more pressing correctional issues, such as rising prison populations, overcrowding, and budgetary cutbacks.

CONTEMPORARY CORRECTIONS: MIXED MESSAGES AND DIVERGENT PHILOSOPHIES

Today, the term *corrections* technically refers to actions taken by the state to deal with convicted offenders in their jurisdiction. However, the term is also used to cover many different areas and concepts, including all agencies, programs, and organizations at the local, state, and federal levels. Basically it means any type of effort at dealing with both those who have been accused of crimes and those who have already been convicted (Mays & Winfree, 2002). It must also be pointed out that the term *corrections* has replaced the older term *penology*. *Penology* came from the Latin word meaning "punishment," and it still is used to encompass an organized body of concepts, theories, and approaches centered on the prison and the institutional experience. It basically signifies the study of punishment. One of the things that is so interesting about the study of criminal justice is how many different definitions a single word can have. This is nowhere truer than with the term *corrections*.

Contemporary correctional efforts involve myriad methods and approaches, including punishment, treatment, and the improvement of academic and job skills for individuals. The objectives of such efforts generally focus on returning to society offenders who will lead productive lives and not reoffend. Although this seems like a simple objective, in reality it is quite controversial (Mays & Winfree, 2002).

In addition to rehabilitation, several other philosophies inform correctional policy. These include retribution, deterrence, restoration, and incapacitation. There are many who feel that the primary objective of corrections is retribution—the belief that one should pay back society and victims for offenses committed (Montgomery & Crews, 1998). Mackie (1982) described three forms of retribution. Positive retribution requires that one who is guilty be punished, whereas negative retribution mandates that those who are not guilty must not be punished. Permissive retribution is a medium between the two, and it simply states that guilty persons may be punished. Several contemporary criminal justice policies are consistent with retribution. "Three strikes" laws are perhaps the most prevalent; these require that offenders with a prior criminal history receive longer prison terms than would be required by statute. Retribution is associated with conservative social and political ideology.

The most widely offered and accepted objective of corrections is probably that of retribution. It is also probably the most controversial. The basic definition of *retribution* is that it is something given or exacted in recompense or for punishment for some act committed. It can also mean (1) requital according to merits or deserts, especially for evil; (2) something given or inflicted in such requital; and (3) the distribution of rewards and punishments in a future life. For the criminal justice system, retribution is generally referred to as a policy or theory that advocates the punishment of criminals in response to the harm they have inflicted. The problem then becomes, is retribution enough? And what in fact is the purpose of retribution?

One of the inherent purposes of corrections and punishment is to deter those who have offended from offending again and those who have not from doing so in the first place. Deterrence is the act of stopping crime by the capacity or threat of retaliating through punishment. Like retribution, deterrence is a complex concept that informs several related theories of punishment. Criminologists distinguish between general and individual deterrence. General deterrence is punishment or threat of punishment designed to serve as an example to the greater population. By witnessing the punishment of another, citizens are discouraged from participating in whatever behavior merited the punishment. Specific deterrence is designed to teach a lesson to the individual offender so his or her future behavior will conform to the expectations of society.

Deterrence is dependent upon the severity, speed, and swiftness of the punishment. The principle that the severity of punishment should fit the severity of the crime has been recognized in virtually every criminal code in the history of Western civilization. Although legally prescribed correctional practices have changed dramatically throughout history, the basic idea of deterrence has remained fairly constant to the present time. The problem with deterrence, from the very beginning, has not been in figuring out how severe the punishment should be. The difficulty comes in determining how harmful various behaviors actually are, when considered as offenses against the whole society. The primary purpose of deterrence is crime prevention. It is not designed to punish for purposes of just deserts or resocialization.

Reintegration is a relatively new concept for the purpose of corrections, in that the vast majority of offenders who are incarcerated will one day return to society. Therefore, if these individuals are unable to reintegrate, then they will probably return to a life of crime. Restorative justice offers an alternative to retribution or deterrence. Van Ness and Strong (1997) discussed the following tenets of restorative justice:

> Proposition 1: Justice requires that we work to restore victims, offenders, and communities who have been injured by crime.
> Proposition 2: Victims, offenders, and communities should have opportunities for active involvement in the restorative justice process as early and as fully as possible.
> Proposition 3: In promoting justice, government is responsible for preserving order and the community for establishing peace. (pp. 32–35)

Restorative justice is concerned with repairing or healing the harm caused by crime. Offenders are encouraged to take responsibility for their actions and account for the harm they caused. Reintegration is central to restorative justice. Reintegration calls for the reconciliation of offenders and victims. It also requires accepting offenders back into the community once they are released without stigmatizing them. The goal of these initiatives is to strengthen community ties and reduce recidivism in the long term.

Incapacitation is perhaps the least political objective associated with the correctional system. According to Brown, Esbensen, and Geis (2001), "incapacitation seeks to reduce or to eliminate the capacity of offenders to commit additional crimes" (p. 52). Whereas rehabilitation, retribution, and restoration all have an ideological aspect, incapacitation is simply confinement until the risk of further crime is appropriately reduced. Its purpose is not to inflict pain, resocialize, or restore the community. It is supposed to only remove the offender from the opportunities needed to engage in criminal behavior.

CONCLUSION

Reformation and rehabilitation are two themes that have dominated the history of corrections in the United States since its inception. Quaker reformers were appalled and angered by the inhumane conditions of confinement facilities in colonial America. Reformers sought changes such as (1) separation of females from males, children from adults, minor violators from hardened criminals, and persons awaiting trial from those serving sentences, with congregate work for each group, but separate rooms for sleeping; (2) abolition of fees for care; (3) provision of wholesome food, healthful living conditions, regular medical care and chaplaincy services, and (4) employment of honest, respectable jailers and outside inspectors to maintain compliance with operating standards.

Others sought to abolish the cruel punishments, improve the living conditions, and establish new practices. Another push for reformation centered on the basic assumptions that (1) human beings are fundamentally good, harmonious, and productive; (2) criminal behavior is the result of evil influences in the offender's environment gaining dominance over the natural good in the offender's character; (3) given an environment that is free of evil contamination and has opportunities for productive labor, the natural goodness of even the worst offenders will surface and replace the evil tendencies; and (4) such an environment can be provided through long-term solitary confinement, in physically healthful conditions, with long hours of useful work, supported by religious counseling. These practices and reformations continue to be topics of discussion and debate in the twenty-first century.

The contemporary correctional system is fragment by mixed messages and divergent philosophies. Many prison administrators now endorse the principles of retribution and incapacitation. Their focus is on control rather than treatment or resocialization. However, the tenacity of the rehabilitative ideal persists. Most prisons have programs for inmates that address their educational abilities, job skills, or substance abuse problems. Prison programs are inextricably linked with the idea of resocialization and personal change. As the prison population in the United States begins to exceed two million, administrators will undoubtedly continue to face the tensions between these competing correctional objectives.

REFERENCES

Augustus, J. (1852/1972 reprint). *A Report of the labors of John Augustus.* Montclair, NJ: Patterson Smith.

Beaumont, G. de, & de Tocqueville, A. (1833/1964). *On the penitentiary system in the United States and its application in France.* Carbondale, IL: Southern Illinois University Press.

Beccaria, C. (1764/1963). *Essay on crimes and punishments.* Indianapolis, IN: Bobbs-Merrill.

Bentham, J. (1780/1948). *An introduction to the principles of morals and legislation.* New York: Hafner.

Brockway, Z. (1912/1969). *Fifty years of prison srvice.* Montclair, NJ: Patterson Smith.

Brown, S. E., Esbensen, F. A., & Geis, G. (2001). *Criminology: Explaining crime and its context.* (4th ed.). Cincinnati, OH: Anderson.

Cromwell, P. F. (1985). *Penology: The evolution of corrections in America.* St. Paul, MN: West.

Foucault, Michel. (1995). *Discipline and punishment: The birth of the prison.* New York: Vintage Books.

Haynes, F. E. (1948). The sociological study of the prison community. *Journal of Criminal Law & Criminology, 39,* 432–440.

Johnson, R. (1997). Race, gender, and the American prison: Historical observations. In J. M. Pollock (Ed.), *Prisons: Today and tomorrow* (pp. 26–51). Gaithersburg, MD: Aspen.

Kennedy, D. B., & Kerber, A. (1973). *Resocialization: An American experiment.* New York: Behavioral Publications.

Killinger, G. G., & Cromwell, P. F. (1973). *Penology: the evolution of corrections in America.* St. Paul, MN: West.

Lewis, W. D. (1965). *From Newgate to Dannemora.* Ithaca, NY: Cornell University Press.

Mackie, J. L. (1982). Morality and the retributive emotions. *Criminal Justice Ethics, 1* (1), 3–10.

Martinson, R. (1974). What works? Questions and answers about prison reform. *The Public Interest, 35,* 22–54.

Mays, G. L., & Winfree, L.T. (2002). *Contemporary corrections.* Belmont, CA: Wadsworth/Thompson Learning.

Montgomery, R. H., & Crews, G. A. (1998). *A history of prison violence.* Lanham, MD: American Correctional Association.

Pennsylvania State Archives (2003). *The 'Great Law,' December 7, 1682* [On-line]. Available: http://www.docheritage.state.pa.us/documents/greatlaw.asp.

Platt, A. (1977). *The child savers: The invention of delinquency,* (2nd ed.). Chicago: University of Chicago Press.

Pollock, J. (1997). Rehabilitation revisited. In J. M. Pollock (Ed.), *Prisons: Today and tomorrow* (pp. 158–216). Gaithersburg, MD: Aspen.

Rothman, D. (1971). *The discovery of the asylum: Order and disorder in the new republic.* Boston: Little, Brown.

Van Ness, D., & Strong, K. H. (1997). *Restoring justice.* Cincinnati, OH: Anderson.

Part II

Contemporary Correctional Issues

4

THE CONTEXT OF IMPRISONMENT

Wayne Gillespie

INTRODUCTION

The study of prison life stretches back to the early twentieth century. For example, in 1913, Thomas Osborne volunteered to spend a week in Auburn Prison as an inmate for academic study (Haynes, 1948). Clemmer (1940) also was a pioneer of this line of scholarship. He described prison as a community with a pecking order and value system that exists apart from and often contradicts that of the outside world. Sykes (1958) further described prison as a society of captives, formed as a consequence of the deprivations or lack of privileges that confinement imposes on inmates. Thus, some of the early investigations of life behind bars focused on the prison as a unique social system. Even today, those involved with corrections stress that any type of person and most things outside prison may be found on the inside as well.

RESOCIALIZATION INSIDE TOTAL INSTITUTIONS

A salient analogy for the context of imprisonment is a community or a society. A context is an environment that typically affects the individual who is subjected to it. For example, the classroom is a context for learning, and the sports field is a context for athleticism. However, the purpose of the correctional context is not so straightforward.

Goffman (1961) claimed that prisons are total institutions. A total institution has a character that is "symbolized by the barrier to social intercourse with the outside and to departure that is often built right into the physical plant, such as locked doors, high walls, barbed wire, cliffs, water, forests, or moors" (Goffman, p. 4). Goffman described the following four characteristics that are common to total institutions in general but may not be found in each and every institution:

First, all aspects of life are conducted in the same place and under the same single authority. Second, each phase of the member's daily activity is carried on in the immediate company of a large batch of others, all of whom are treated alike and required to do the same thing together. Third, all phases of the day's activities are tightly scheduled, with one activity leading at a prearranged time into the next, the whole sequence of activities being imposed from above by a system of explicit formal rulings and a body of officials. Finally, the various enforced activities are brought together into a single rational plan purportedly designed to fulfill the official aims of the institution. (p. 6)

These qualities vary in the extent to which they apply to the specific institutions. Goffman used the method of the ideal type to discern characteristics common to total institutions; his description represents total institutions in their most abstract form.

Another common element to these institutions is the handling of human needs en masse by the bureaucratic organization. In simplest terms, two groups of people can be found within total institutions. Goffman (1961) noted, "In total institutions there is a basic split between a large managed group, conveniently called inmates, and a small supervisory staff" (p. 7). Inmates spend their daily lives inside the institutions, whereas staff work there and remain part of the outside world. Goffman further remarked, "Social mobility between the two strata is grossly restricted; social distance is typically great and often formally prescribed" (p. 7). Thus, the barriers within total institutions are both physical and social. The correctional context reflects these ever-present barriers and tensions. Goffman obviously emphasized the pathological aspects of prisons.

However, other scholars defend these total institutions as worthwhile and necessary enterprises designed to transform criminals into law-abiding citizens. Kennedy and Kerber (1973) suggested that imprisonment involves a process of resocialization. They define resocialization as follows:

Resocialization is that process wherein an individual, defined as inadequate according to the norms of a dominant institution(s), is subjected to a dynamic program of behavior intervention aimed at instilling and/or rejuvenating those values, attitudes, and abilities which would allow him to function according to the norms of said dominant institution(s). (p. 39)

Those who are illiterate, high school dropouts, criminals, the unemployed, those on welfare, and lifelong dependents are all examples of individuals with inadequate socialization.

Rehabilitation is the primary resocialization procedure associated with the criminal justice system. It was also the dominant goal of incarceration during the first wave of scholarship on imprisonment. Von Hirsch (1985) recounted, "The judge was supposed to fashion the disposition to promote the offender's resocialization" (p. 660). Thus, it was believed that prison

would be a context in which criminals were resocialized. Various prison programs, such as vocational training, academic instruction, psychological counseling, religious services, and alcohol and drug treatment, were considered
integral to this resocialization process.

However, in the mid-1970s, the logic of resocialization and rehabilitation
was challenged. Several research studies questioned the effectiveness of correctional rehabilitation programs (Allen, 1981). After a review of correctional
research, Martinson (1974) concluded that "these data, involving over two
hundred studies and hundreds of thousands of individuals as they do, are
the best available and give us very little reason to hope that we have in fact
found a sure way of reducing recidivism through rehabilitation" (p. 49).
Furthermore, scholars suggested that, rather than promoting change in a
positive direction, imprisonment actually changed offenders in a negative,
antisocial manner.

THE CONVICT CODE AND THE INMATE SUBCULTURE

A process first documented by Clemmer (1940) called prisonization is a
form of resocialization that involves negative personal change. Prisonization
involves the extent to which prisoners adopt norms or beliefs that are representative of an inmate subculture. Gordon (1947/1997) defined a subculture as

> a sub-division of a national culture, composed of a combination of factorable
> social situations such as class status, ethnic background, regional and rural or
> urban residence, and religious affiliation, but *forming in their combination a
> functioning unity which has an integrated impact on the participating individual.*
> (p. 41)

Subcultures form when individuals with similar problems begin to interact
with one another (Cohen, 1955/1997). Thus, when individual prisoners
experience the problem of incarceration simultaneously, an inmate subculture
arises. This shared frame of reference is directed at the problems inmates face.

The inmate subculture maintains a subterranean, social order inside prison.
Clemmer (1940) described the specific characteristics of the inmate subculture:

> Habits, behavior systems, traditions, history, customs, folkways, codes, the laws
> and rules which guide the inmates and their ideas, opinions and attitudes to-
> ward or against homes, families, education, work, recreations, government,
> prisons, police, judges, other inmates, wardens, ministers, doctors, guards,
> ballplayers, clubs, guns, cells, buckets, gravy, beans, walls, lamps, rain, clouds,
> clothes, machinery, hammers, rocks, caps, bibles, radios, monies, stealing,
> murder, rape, sex, love, honesty, martyrdom, and so on. (pp. 294–295)

Inmate subculture also involves schemes of power and interchange, expectations, values, and behavioral outcomes.

Life inside prison involves a distinct social organization that is often at odds with the outside world. Goffman (1961) provided the following insight:

> Total institutions do not substitute their own unique culture for something already formed. . . . They create and maintain a particular kind of tension between the home world and the institutional world and use this persistent tension as strategic leverage in the management of men. (p. 13)

Total institutions are juxtaposed against conventional society and function as constant reminders of the relations and luxuries that inmates are denied inside prison. In this sense, the inmate subculture is independent of life outside prison; at the very least, it is semi-autonomous.

Furthermore, a single code is at the core of this inmate subculture. Ohlin (1956) remarked, "The code represents an organization of criminal values in clearcut opposition to the values of conventional society, and to prison officials as representatives of that society" (p. 28). During the mid-twentieth century, this convict code was based primarily upon a collective opposition to prison officials. Sykes and Messinger (1960) studied the code more thoroughly and updated it with several pertinent tenets. In particular, the inmate code revolves around the maxim "Never rat on a con." Other important tenets are "Be tough" as well as "Have a connection."

The values that underlie the inmate code involve violence, strength, and sexual proclivity (Wilder, 1965). Ohlin (1956) described these values and beliefs as follows:

> These criminal beliefs and attitudes place a high premium on physical violence and strength, on exploitative sex relations, and predatory attitudes toward money and property. They place a strong emphasis on in-group loyalty and solidarity and on aggressive and exploitative relations with conventionally oriented out-groups. (p. 29)

Although not every prisoner is active in the inmate subculture, most are aware of and respect it. This system of values and beliefs developed over time from individuals with similar problems of adjustment.

Origins of the Convict Code

Academics who study prison life proposed two theories to account for the origin of the convict code and the inmate subculture in general. The first explanation was called indigenous influence theory, or the deprivation model. According to this perspective, the inmate subculture arose in order to compensate for the deprivations of prison life. Sykes (1958) used the phrase "pains of imprisonment" to describe the harsh reality of the New Jersey State Prison. He wrote,

> The deprivations or frustrations of prison life today . . . viewed as punishments which the free community deliberately inflicts on the offender for violating the law . . . that can be just as painful as the physical maltreatment . . . [and] appear as a serious attack on the personality, as a threat to the life goals of the individual, to his defensive system, to the self-esteem, or to his feelings of security. (p. 64)

The specific frustrations include, but are not limited to, the deprivation of liberty, the deprivation of goods and services, the deprivation of heterosexual relations, the deprivation of autonomy, and the deprivation of security. Sykes stressed that this anguish is extremely painful for inmates. Furthermore, he suggested that *all* prisoners experience these problems caused by confinement.

Because all inmates experience these deprivations, the inmate subculture is a collective response to alleviate the pains associated with imprisonment. Thomas and Petersen (1977) explained the mechanism of subcultural formation as follows:

> Once such a response occurs, an inmate society begins to take form, a society that includes a network of positions which reflect various types and levels of subcultural norms as well as adaptive reactions to the problems of confinement, a system of rewards and sanctions that encourage compliance to the normative expectations associated with these positions, and a socialization process which is directed toward the goal of increasing the level of appreciation for and responsiveness to the prescriptions and proscriptions of the inmate code. (p. 49)

Thus, the deprivation model proposes that a variety of pains, stresses, and problems associated with incarceration and the criminal justice system in general labels inmates and confronts them with problems of adjustment that require a collective solution.

Irwin and Cressey (1962) also noted that the inmate subculture provides convicts with "patterns to be used to help solve the problem" of imprisonment (p. 147). However, they also suggested that thieves were the dominant criminal type in most state penitentiaries. The inmate code and the patterns of which Irwin and Cressey wrote were not formed through collective action inside prison. Rather, the rules that compose the convict code were imported by thieves from the street.

The second explanation of the inmate culture is called cultural drift theory, or the importation model. This point of view does not hold that the subculture arose in response to pains of imprisonment. Instead, the importation model supposes that the convict code developed from the street culture to which prisoners belonged prior to incarceration.

In fact, Irwin (1980) proposed that the convict code was itself a version of the thieves' code. He noted that thieves were commonly imprisoned in the Big House. Irwin described the thieves' code as follows:

> The central rule in the thieves' code was "thou shalt not snitch." In prison, thieves converted this to the dual norm of "do not rat on another prisoner" and "do your own time." Thieves were also obliged by their code to be cool and tough, that is to maintain respect and dignity; not to show weakness; to help other thieves; and to leave most other prisoners alone. (p. 12)

This thieves' code dominated social relations inside the correctional institutions of the early twentieth century. Thieves had an extensive communication network, thus ensuring that their beliefs would be imported from the outside into prison.

Rather than submitting that the genesis of the convict code and the inmate subculture lie in the deprivations or pains of imprisonment, Irwin (1980) suggested that these constructs of prison life were nothing more than the institutionalized mechanisms for criminal behavior on the outside. In other words, the inmate subculture drifted inside prison from the outside. The inmate subculture did not originate inside prison. It did not come to pass vis-à-vis the deprivations of prison life. Thieves and other convicts relied upon the skills and beliefs obtained during their socialization on the outside to deal with the problem of imprisonment.

Although at first blush these two explanations may seem contradictory, the importation and deprivation models have been integrated to offer a more comprehensive account of the context of life inside prison. Schwartz (1971) charged that both theories are inadequate when stated in terms that deny one another. Thomas and Petersen (1977) stated that "the deprivation model identifies certain structural conditions that may be viewed as a sufficient condition for the emergence of *some type* of adaptive response, but these conditions are not sufficient to predict the nature of the response" (p. 51). The extent to which a prisoner will participate in the inmate subculture depends on his or her preprison socialization experiences. Regardless, both theories of subcultural formation are relevant for understanding the process of prisonization.

PRISONIZATION

Clemmer (1940) was also the first academic to fully describe prisonization. He studied inmates' letters, biographies, and stories to better understand what goes on inside prison. In assessing Clemmer's work, Irwin (1980) wrote, "In spite of the shortcomings and in spite of the middle-class moral cast that dulls or distorts some of his analysis, it is still the most complete study of the prison" (p. 32). Clemmer was able to identify prisonization as a bona fide social process that occurs inside prison.

Prisonization is socialization that involves "a slow, gradual more or less unconscious process during which a person learns enough of the culture of a social unit into which he is placed to make him characteristic of it" (Clemmer, 1940, pp. 298–299). Clemmer (1958) fully defined prisonization as "the taking on in greater or lesser degree of the folkways, mores, customs, and general culture of the penitentiary" (p. 299). Thus, prisonization includes adoption of the convict code in greater or lesser degree.

Moreover, Clemmer (1950) outlined seven universal features of prisonization in the following noteworthy passage:

> Acceptance of an inferior role, accumulation of facts concerning the organization of the prison, the development of somewhat new habits of eating, dressing, working, sleeping, and the adoption of local language, the recognition that nothing is owed to the environment for the supplying of needs, and the eventual desire for a good job are aspects of prisonization which are operative for all inmates. (p. 316)

He also speculated that prisonization may disrupt the personalities of inmates and make their adjustment on the outside next to impossible. Clemmer's inmate subjects confirmed that a highly prisonized convict would have difficulties adjusting to life outside prison.

Prisonization involves both enculturation into the inmate subculture and a process of disculturation that strips inmates of prior identities. Enculturation is an anthropological concept that is similar in meaning to socialization. As Herskovits (1949) noted, enculturation involves the learning of customs and culture through both conscious and unconscious conditioning. For the convict, Goffman (1961) observed,

> If the inmate's stay is long, what has been called "disculturation" may occur— that is, an "untraining" which renders him temporarily incapable of managing certain features of daily life on the outside, if and when he gets back to it. (p. 13)

Imprisonment strips an inmate of the supports of his or her home world or life on the outside. Prisoners are cut off from their families, friends, jobs, communities, and so forth. A number replaces the inmate's name. Moreover, their identities often become distorted inside prison. All other social roles (e.g., husband, wife, son, daughter, worker) become subordinate to that of convict. Goffman referred to this as the mortification of self.

The Antecedents of Prisonization

As mentioned earlier, scholars agree that both the deprivation and importation models are important for fully understanding the causes of prisonization (Akers, Hayner, & Gruninger, 1977; Thomas, 1971; Thomas & Petersen, 1977). The individual characteristics of prisoners affect socialization into the inmate subculture. Preprison characteristics coupled with situational deprivations influence the degree of prisonization. The determinants of socialization in correctional facilities have been well documented by extant scholarship. The micro-, or inmate-level, antecedents of prisonization include time served (e.g., Clemmer, 1940; Haynes, 1948); proportion of time served (e.g., Atchley & McCabe, 1968; Wellford; 1967; Wheeler, 1961); primary group contacts (e.g., Clemmer, 1940; Haynes, 1948; Stratton, 1967; Wheeler, 1961); prior incarcerations (e.g., Morris & Morris, 1962; Tittle & Tittle, 1964; Wheeler, 1961); social role adaptations (e.g., Garabedian, 1963; Schrag, 1961; Sykes, 1958); the number of outside contacts (e.g., Morris & Morris, 1962); self-concept (e.g., Faine, 1973; Tittle, 1972); age (e.g., Jensen & Jones, 1976; Schwartz, 1971); and other preprison, sociodemographic characteristics (e.g., Schwartz, 1971).

The antecedents of prisonization have an interconnected nature. Haynes (1948) provided some insight when he enumerated the following list of antecedents:

> Whether or not complete prisonization occurs depends on a number of determining factors. It depends: (1) on the man himself, his personality; (2) the kind and extent of relationships which he had outside; (3) his affiliations with prison groups; (4) chance placement in work gang, cellhouse, and with cellmate; (5) acceptance of the dogmas or codes of the prison culture. (pp. 439–440)

He also noted that prisonization was related to demographic characteristics such as age, criminality, nationality, race, and regional conditioning. That is, persons of different ages, races, and nationalities were likely to have varying degrees of prisonization.

Clemmer (1940) also discussed seven interrelated factors that influence the extent of prisonization. First, he noted that long prison sentences seem to cause a higher degree of prisonization than short terms. An unstable personality also contributes to prisonization. Furthermore, inmates who lack contact with persons outside prison typically have a high degree of prisonization. The inmate who has a lot of friends inside prison is more likely to become prisonized than those who have few buddies on the inside. In addition, a high degree of prisonization is also linked to going along with the rules of prison groups and gangs. Chance also affects prisonization; an inmate is more likely to be prisonized if he is placed with others of a similar orientation. Finally, a high degree of prisonization is associated with gambling and sexual behavior inside prison. Clemmer believed that the opposite conditions would result in low prisonization.

In addition to the connectedness of the precursors of prisonization, the phenomenon also seems to vary across time. Wheeler (1961) examined the relationship between prisonization and time served as well as phase of incarceration. He was particularly interested in determining if prisonization was more related to time served or some phase of incarceration. He divided a group of 237 subjects by their phase of incarceration and examined their obedience to prison staff workers. Wheeler (1961) described three main phases:

> (a) Those who have served less than six months in the correctional community and are thus in an *early phase* of their commitment; (b) those who have less than six months remaining to serve—the *late phase* inmates; and (c) those who have served more than six months and have more than six months left to serve—the *middle phase* inmates. (p. 706)

Specifically, he discovered a U-shaped relationship between the inmates' institutional conformity and their phase of incarceration. That is, inmates in earlier and later phases of incarceration conformed more to custodial authority than did inmates who were in the middle phase of incarceration.

Although Wheeler's (1961) work represented a sophistication of the concept of prisonization, attempts to replicate his findings have been mixed. Atchley and McCabe (1968) used a sample of 403 inmates incarcerated in a federal prison. Yet when they divided the sample by phase of incarceration and examined the degree of conformity to custodial authority, no relationship was observed. Atchley and McCabe were unable to duplicate Wheeler's findings. In short, they found no statistically significant relationships between prisonization and a number of predictors such as time served, phase of incarceration, and frequency or intensity of contact among inmates.

However, Wheeler's (1961) findings were validated by other researchers. For example, Wellford (1967) also examined the effect of time served on prisonization. He used a random sample of 120 inmates from a correctional facility in the District of Columbia. Wellford compared the effects on prisonization of both time served and phase of incarceration. There was no significant relationship between the amount of time served and the degree of prisonization. However, Wellford did observe a weak but significant effect of phase of incarceration on prisonization. In sum, Wellford's study provided some support for Wheeler's finding that an inmate's phase of incarceration was related to his degree of prisonization.

Tittle and Tittle (1964) also looked at situational antecedents of socialization into the inmate subculture. They interviewed subjects in a hospital for narcotic addicts. Tittle and Tittle found that, as time served increased, so did prisonization. Incidentally, Tittle and Tittle reaffirmed that "the pains of imprisonment do decrease with greater integration into the prisoner social organization, as indicated by the subscription to the prison code" (p. 218). Previous incarcerations also enhanced the degree of prisonization.

The concept of prisonization also seems to hold up cross-nationally. In their study of the Pentonville Prison in London, Morris and Morris (1962) suggested that prisonization was dependent upon the following factors:

1. The extent of previous exposure to prison culture, both in terms of the number and duration of sentences.
2. The nature of the relationship maintained with the outside.
3. The degree to which the prisoner consciously accepts the dogmas and codes of the inmate culture.
4. The nature of the prisoner's relationships with the outside. (p. 348)

However, they noted that the effects of these antecedents on prisonization were not uniform. In particular, prisonization was high among troublesome or resistant inmates with dissimilar problems of adjustment.

Several advancements in prisonization research were also made during the 1970s. Schwartz (1971) compared the effects of both pre-institutional and situational influences on prisonization in a sample of 194 delinquent boys. The situational factors included integration into prison primary groups, staff orientation, family contact, and length of confinement. Conformity to the convict code was related to staff orientation and length of confinement. Preprison variables were numerous and involved race, residence, migration, age at commitment, family status, family relationships, number of siblings, number of brothers, age rank, IQ, achievement, school grades, school status, truancies, suspensions, number of arrests, number of arrests for violent offenses, age at first arrest, and prior commitments. However, only race, migration, age at commitment, number of arrests, number of arrests for violent offenses, and prior commitments were significantly associated with conformity to the inmate code. Thus, Schwartz demonstrated that preprison attributes were as strongly related to prisonization as situational deprivations.

Although most of this research focused on male prisoners, Jensen and Jones (1976) studied prisonization among female inmates. They applied the findings from prior research on prisonization among male inmates to a sample of female convicts. They examined situational variables such as time spent in the institution, contact with outside friends and relatives, contact with staff, participation in special programs, and inmate interactions. Jensen and Jones also investigated the effects of noninstitutional characteristics such as race, age, education, urban experience, previous incarceration, and legal status. Their findings supported Wheeler's (1961) finding about the phase of incarceration and prisonization. In particular, inmates in the middle phase of imprisonment were most likely to embrace attitudes contrary to staff expectations. However, age was most strongly and persistently related with nonconformist attitudes toward staff and the institution. Jensen and Jones (1976) concluded that "younger inmates, educated inmates, and inmates with urban backgrounds are more hostile towards the institution and its staff than older, less educated, nonurban inmates" (p. 594). Their research supports the contention that the antecedents of prisonization are similar for both male and female inmates.

A major advance in prisonization research involved Alpert's (1979) longitudinal analysis of 198 inmates. Longitudinal research looks at phenomena over time. Alpert found that individual characteristics such as race, criminal record, and years in prison were significantly related to prisonization. For example, whites and nonwhites seemed to experience prisonization at different rates. Prisoners with long criminal records also exhibited higher degrees of prisonization. Finally, Alpert determined that prisoners who had been incarcerated for over three years were more prisonized than inmates who had been incarcerated for less than three years. Thus, Alpert's study was consistent with Clemmer's (1940) finding that length of sentence is related to prisonization. Alpert's work can also be interpreted as moderately supportive of Wheeler's (1961) hypothesis that prisonization varies by phase of institutional career.

Another line of research was directed at the macro, or prison, level. It attempted to uncover the macro antecedents of prisonization, or the features of correctional institutions that influence adoption of the convict code by individual inmates. This research on the macro antecedents of prisonization almost exclusively focused on the organizational structure of prisons. Thomas and Petersen (1977) provided the following list of correctional features:

> The physical structure of the institution, the manner in which available resources are allocated, the rigid organizational hierarchy, lines of communication, the distribution of decision-making power, the routinization of organizational activities, the means by which organizational participants other than inmates are evaluated, and related characteristics and activities and characteristics of the organization. (p. 37)

Likewise, many structural analyses of prison life have investigated two particular goals of correctional institutions, namely treatment and custody (see Adamek & Dager, 1968; Akers et al., 1977; Berk, 1966; Grusky, 1959; Mathiesen, 1971; Street, 1965; Street, Vinter, & Perrow, 1966; Wilson, 1968; Zald, 1962).

Grusky (1959) examined an experimental prison camp that stressed treatment goals. He found that inmate leaders in this treatment-oriented facility expressed positive attitudes toward the institution. Berk (1966) extended Grusky's findings. In particular, he investigated the relationship between the organizational goals of three minimum-security prisons and the inmate subculture. He found that positive prisoner attitudes toward the institution were related to the facility's support for treatment goals. Berk (1966) commented,

> Inmates who had spent longer time in the custodially oriented prison were more likely to hold negative attitudes than those who had only been there a few months, whereas the reverse was true at the treatment-oriented prison where inmates who had spent a long time in the prison were more likely to hold positive attitudes than negative ones. (p. 525)

Berk also found that the individual characteristics of offenders could not explain these contextual or institutional effects. For instance, he noted that more serious offenders did not have more negative attitudes toward the facility than less serious offenders.

Street (1965) looked at inmate groups in four correctional facilities for juvenile males. Two institutions focused on custodial goals and two were treatment oriented. He found that juveniles in the custodial facilities showed negative attitudes toward the institution and appeared to be more prisonized. Conversely, Street remarked, "Inmates in the treatment-oriented institutions more often expressed positive attitudes toward the institution and staff, nonprisonized views of adaptation to the institution, and positive images of self change" (p. 49). He also included individual variables (e.g., age, race, IQ, prior record, family status, urban-rural background, and social class) in the model to determine if the attitudinal differences were simply a reflection of individual variation. However, the institutional orientation still significantly affected prisonization when individual characteristics were taken into account.

The effect of institutional goals on prisonization applies cross-nationally as well. Akers et al. (1977) conducted a cross-national study that was designed to examine the influence of institutional goals (i.e., treatment versus custody) on the aggregated rate of prisonization. They looked at twenty-two penitentiaries in the United States, Mexico, England, Germany, and Spain. Akers et al. distinguished between treatment-oriented and custodial facilities by rating the institutions on specific organizational dimensions such as prison architecture, classification policy, use of inmate labor, ratios and quality of personnel, policy on freedom of outside contact for inmates, prison programs, and so forth. In general, Akers et al. found that custodial institutions intensified feelings of degradation and punishment and were associated with high rates of prisonization in all countries.

The Effects of Prisonization

Socialization into the inmate subculture may negatively affect inmates in prison as well as on the streets after their release. Clemmer (1950) suggested that "the culture of a prison influences the people participating in it, in the same way as culture anywhere plays a part in shaping the lives of men" (p. 313). He proposed that imprisonment might actually increase criminality among inmates. Inside prison, convicts may learn new or sophisticated methods of breaking the law. Clemmer was also one of the first scholars to relate prisonization to parole violations and recidivism.

Parole success is strongly related to employment obtained by parolees (Dale, 1976; Knox, 1981). Homant (1984) suggested that inmates may initially lack self-esteem due to the degradation ceremonies associated with entry into a total institution. Through participating in the inmate subculture, inmates regain their self-esteem and counteract the pains of imprisonment. Convicts may come to depend upon the subculture to sustain their self-esteem. Once prisonization occurs, inmates are less likely to seek out job training in prison that would help them get a job after release. Moreover, if released, a prisonized inmate does not have the subculture from which to draw self-esteem and is ill-prepared to enter the workforce. A highly prisonized inmate may turn to crime to survive on the outside. Thus, prisonization ultimately may decrease the likelihood that an ex-offender will secure employment upon release and increase the chances of parole violations.

Zingraff (1975) suggested that prisonization has three potential ramifications, including opposition to the formal organization of the institution and denial of the legitimacy of the legal system in general. He also confirmed that prisonization was actually associated with negative postrelease expectations. Zingraff remarked that "the greater the degree of normative assimilation and the more negative the postrelease expectations of the inmate, the greater the probability that the effects of confinement will be negative" (p. 375). He concluded that prisonization inhibits effective resocialization in prison.

Prisonization also undermines therapy inside prison. Peat and Winfree (1992) discovered that inmates in treatment were likely to be incarcerated for a nonviolent crime. These inmates also report lower levels of prisonization. Peat and Winfree (1992) noted,

> Prisonization and the traditional inmate subculture are antithetical to the goals of rehabilitation, including those proposed in most therapeutic communities. . . . Instead of participation in prison treatment and "self-improvement" programs, it mandates avoidance; instead of cooperation with prison officials, it mandates manipulation; instead of respect for middle-class values, it mandates derision. (p. 209)

Highly prisonized inmates chose not to participate in treatment or therapy inside prison. Thus, in addition to inhibiting effective resocialization, prisonization also impedes the delivery of therapeutic services to inmates.

Furthermore, Cohen (1976) suggested that the deprivations of imprisonment affect prison violence. Deprivations are also related to prisonization. In order to counteract the pains of imprisonment, prisoners become involved in the subculture to obtain material comforts such as food, alcohol, drugs, money, clothing, work assignments, and sex. Since most of these items are contraband in prison, the pursuit of illicit goods in prison may result in the following quandary:

> If they [illicit goods] give rise to conflict and disputes as commerce (as we call it on the outside) and hustles (as we call it on the inside) invariably do, they cannot be settled by the invoking of services of legally constituted authority. (Cohen, 1976, p. 18)

The inmate subculture has its own ways of securing justice, revenge, discipline, the collection of debts, and the enforcement of contracts.

These informal methods often involve violence or the threat of violence. Cohen (1976) remarked, "Within the prison, likewise, the 'criminalization' of activities for which the demand nonetheless persists has the consequence of insuring the unauthorized use of force, that is, of violence" (p. 18). Thus, misconduct and violence inside prison may result from the pains of imprisonment and the subcultural response.

DEPENDENCY

From a psychological point of view, dependency is a personality orientation (Bornstein, 1993). An orientation implies some general or lasting quality, but it is a quality that may change direction. The definition of an orientation differs from that of a trait, which is a stable quality that may be inheritable and is usually quite difficult to change. Hirschfeld, Klerman, Gough, Barrett, Korchin, and Chodoff (1977) defined interpersonal dependency as "a complex of thoughts, beliefs, feelings, and behaviors which revolve around the need to associate closely with, or interact with, and rely upon valued other people" (p. 610). Highly dependent individuals also exhibit problem behaviors such as depression, alcoholism, psychopathology, physical illness, and poor achievement-related behavior in school (Bornstein, 1995; Bornstein & Kennedy, 1994; Fenichel, 1945).

Bornstein, Riggs, Hill, and Calabrese (1996) approached the issue of interpersonal dependency by expanding four components of dependency initially described by Hirschfeld et al. (1977). In regard to interpersonal dependency, Bornstein et al. (1996) suggested the following:

> Dependency is best conceptualized as consisting of four separate but related components: (a) motivational (i.e., a marked need for guidance, approval, and support from others); (b) cognitive (i.e., a perception of the self as powerless

and ineffectual, along with the belief that others are powerful and in control of the outcome of situations); (c) affective (i.e., a tendency to become anxious and fearful when required to function independently, especially when the products of one's efforts will be evaluated by others); (d) behavioral (i.e., a tendency to seek help, approval, guidance, and reassurance from others). (p. 638)

In fact, cognitive, motivational, and affective tendencies interact in order to determine the behavior of an individual in different situations and settings (Bornstein, 1993). The subsequent behavior is associated with compliance, suggestibility, and help-seeking. This behavioral pattern is typical of an individual with a dependent personality orientation.

The American Psychiatric Association (1994) classified this behavioral outcome as dependent personality disorder. It is defined in the association's *Diagnostic and Statistical Manual of Mental Disorders* as

pervasive and excessive need to be taken care of that leads to submissive and clinging behavior and fears of separation. This pattern begins by early adulthood and is present in a variety of contexts. The dependent and submissive behaviors are designed to elicit caregiving and arise from a self-perception of being unable to function adequately without the help of others. (p. 665)

However, Bornstein et al. (1996) noted that subjects with dependent personality orientations do not always behave as expected (i.e., passively or submissively). They suggested that dependent personality disorder is not simply an involuntary impulse, but is affected by contextual influences. Thus, it seems as if interpersonal dependency is not static and does, in fact, vary across different scenarios.

Unlike interpersonal dependency, institutional dependency is not some peculiarity of personality. Rather, institutional dependency is a learned behavior or a product of socialization. In many ways, this distinction is similar to sociologists' insistence that social facts are external and coercive to the individual. In other words, social phenomena constrain individual behavior. Lehmann (1993) even implied that social phenomena actually penetrate the individual psyche and inhibit behavior. Thus, the two approaches (sociological versus psychological) offer quite contrary sources for dependency behavior. By employing the notion of a dependent personality orientation, psychologists locate the source of dependency behavior internal to the individual. Sociologists, on the other hand, locate the source of dependency behavior in the external, coercive nature of social phenomena; thus, individuals react to contextual features with various behavioral responses.

The model of institutional dependency is related to the phenomenon of prisonization. In particular, institutional dependency takes as its starting point one of the universal features of incarceration as outlined by Clemmer (1950): the recognition that nothing is owed the environment for the supplying of basic needs. Moreover, Straus (1974) identified a behavioral problem that may result from this feature of prison life as

> dependency on institutional living [that] encompasses every aspect of human adaptation; it involves elementary biological functioning, human adaptations to time and space, personality development and status, and the socialization of the individual and his adequacy for fulfilling expected social roles. (p. 8)

Given Clemmer's claim that this characteristic of imprisonment is universal, it appears as though every inmate has an equal chance of developing institutional dependency.

However, Aday and Webster (1979) discovered that long prison sentences and lack of outside support predict which inmates will develop institutional dependency. Aday (1994) determined that older inmates are also at a much greater risk of developing institutional dependency than younger prisoners. In particular, older inmates who have spent a majority of their adult lives behind bars are extremely likely to exhibit signs of institutional dependency. The robustness of this finding is well documented (Baier, 1961; Goetting, 1983; Jensen, 1977; Krajick, 1979; Reed & Glamser, 1979; Teller & Howell, 1981). In fact, the age-dependency link may explain Wheeler's (1961) U-shaped relationship between prisonization and length of sentence. Perhaps initially, inmates learn and imitate the values associated with the criminal subculture (i.e., resistance to the authority of prison staff). However, as they spend more time in prison, they are conditioned to conform to the authority of prison staff and thus begin to develop dependency behavior.

THE MODERN PRISON MILIEU

In her 1997 textbook about prisons, Pollock divided extant scholarship on life inside prison into two time frames. During the first phase of research, scholars examined the social processes associated with the inmate subculture. Pollock remarked, "Between the 1940s and 1960s prison researchers were concerned with the definition of, and socialization to, the prisoner subculture" (p. 246). During this time frame, sociologists in particular developed theories that explained the origin of the convict code and the inmate subculture. They also explored how prisoners were socialized in prison, how they became institutionalized, and how some developed dependency. This classical work on life inside prison was primarily centered on three concepts: the convict code, the inmate subculture, and prisonization.

However, as Pollock (1997) suggested, "Even as researchers were utilizing various research modalities to study the prison world, it was changing rapidly and inevitably in response to events both outside and inside the prison walls" (p. 246). She attributes change in correctional research agendas to several historical incidents, such as public unrest in the 1960s, the black awareness movement, and increased racial minorities, gangs, and drugs in prison. Whatever the cause, contemporary scholarship on imprisonment from 1960 to 1990 focused on a variety of issues, including drugs in prison, prison gangs, and violence.

Drugs in Prison

The linkage between crime and substance use is well documented (e.g., see Goldstein, 1998; Leukefeld, Araujo, & Farabee, 1997; Menard, Mihalic, & Huizinga, 2001; Parker & Auerhahn, 1998). Leukefeld and Tims (1993) reviewed results from the Drug Use Forecasting system and reported that about 60 percent of arrestees from twenty-two large cities tested positive for drugs other than alcohol at the time of their arrests. They noted, "Our nation's jails provide a reservoir for drug abusers" (p. 78). A substantial proportion of the inmate population continues to use drugs inside prison (Swann & James, 1998).

However, it is not known exactly how many inmates use drugs during their confinement. Thomas and Cage (1977) reported that only 22 percent of their sample of 273 adult male felons used drugs while in prison. Inciardi, Lockwood, and Quinlan (1993) found that 60 percent of their small sample of forty-four inmates in therapeutic drug treatment communities admitted to using drugs inside prison. Likewise, Edwards, Curtis, and Sherrard (1999) determined that of the 376 prisoners involved in their sample, 58 percent confessed to injecting drugs during incarceration. Based on these studies, the proportion of prisoners who use drugs during confinement appears to range from one-fifth to upwards of two-thirds of the total inmate population.

Indeed, the patterns of drug-related behavior found inside prison are similar to those on the street. According to Keene (1997), "Although there is a reduction in the use of all substances, the drug use patterns in the community are reflected in custody" (p. 348). During incarceration, inmates use a variety of drugs, including marijuana, Valium, amphetamine, LSD, ecstasy, cocaine, heroin, and even steroids. Kassebaum and Chandler (1994) found that alcohol, marijuana, cocaine, and crystal methamphetamine are the most popular drugs among newly admitted inmates. Keene's research showed that marijuana is the most prevalent drug in prison, but LSD and ecstasy are common as well. Inciardi et al. (1993) also reported that the most common drugs in prison are marijuana, cocaine, and alcohol. However, they noted that inmates admitted to using LSD, PCP, methamphetamine, intravenous cocaine, and crack cocaine.

Drug use inside prison is nothing peculiar per se in the life-course of addicts; rather, it is an expression of their habit and addiction. For example, Keene (1997) compared three groups of inmates at different phases of incarceration. In the first group of 134 prisoners, 74 percent admitted to using drugs in their communities before they were incarcerated. In another group of 119 inmates, 75 percent were using drugs during imprisonment. Furthermore, of 119 ex-convicts, 82 percent disclosed using drugs in their communities after release. Keene concluded, "Custodial drug use can be seen to reflect continuing use before and after prison in similar populations" (p. 350). It is in this sense that prison becomes simply another context in which the user must manage his or her habit.

Inciardi et al. (1993) related that "the use of cocaine, heroin, and other drugs does not necessarily initiate criminal careers, it tends to intensify and perpetuate them" (p. 120). Through systematic interviewing in the Delaware correctional system, they described drug-related behavior in prison and found that both visitors and correctional officers supply inmates with illegal drugs. Once inside, drugs are most often concealed on the person rather than hidden in their cells. Prisoners also produce alcohol on the inside by fermenting fruit, sugar, and bread. Furthermore, Inciardi et al. discovered that both inmates and correctional officers sell drugs inside prison. They also noted that prisoners use drugs in their cells, in the yard, in the shower, or on work assignments. Additionally, inmates congregate in small groups of two to four inmates and typically use drugs together. Intravenous drug users commonly share injection equipment with one another. In sum, although illicit drugs are only available in limited quantities and at considerable cost inside prison, inmates still manage to engage in a wide range of drug-related behavior (i.e., production, use, sale, and possession of illicit drugs).

Moreover, the management of drug-related behaviors inside prison requires inmates to make decisions and choices during their incarceration. Cope (2000) suggested that inmates use strategic thinking to meet short-term goals. For example, prisoners may stop using drugs if they desire transfer or parole and realize that a urinalysis will be involved. Short-term changes such as this one led Cope (2000) to contend that "inmates are to some extent in control of the trajectory of their drug career in prison" (p. 360). In fact, she goes on to say that the self-control demonstrated by inmates in regard to their drug-related behavior inside prison may be the result of the monitored correctional context. That is, the highly controlled prison environment forces an inmate to constantly monitor his or her own behavior.

Prison Gangs

Inmates are unlikely to agree on many issues nowadays. The contemporary inmate subculture cannot be characterized as one single consensus. Rather, it comprises many sociocultural subsystems vying for power, goods, and services. Hunt, Riegel, Morales, and Waldorf (1993) argued that new forms of social organization have replaced the traditional inmate subculture. These subcultures are now called gangs, and these gangs often have norms that may be different from the tenets of in-group loyalty and opposition to custodial authority that represented the traditional convict code.

Stevens (1997) developed a model of prisonization that takes the gang phenomenon into consideration. In fact, he suggested that inmates, once incarcerated, still undergo a prisonization process. However, prisoners are now socialized into gangs rather than the convict subculture. Stevens noted, "Subsequent incarceration promotes the social agents of gang participation through prisonization" (p. 25). Moreover, he proposed that juvenile detention actually contributes to further criminality and adult gang involvement.

Stevens (1997) proposed that "juveniles confined in closed institutions might share place-intensity experiences and gang affiliation agents through tip encounters when they are subjected to substandard environments and poor living conditions" (p. 25). A tip is a group of individuals from the same town or neighborhood who engage in similar types of delinquency (Irwin, 1980). In short, Stevens maintained that a process of prisonization (i.e., juvenilization) begins at juvenile training facilities and expedites adult entry into the world of gangs. To borrow an example from medicine, youth confined in juvenile detention centers become infected with a social pathogen (i.e., norms consistent with adult gangs) that develops into a full-blown disease (i.e., violent gang alliances) if they become imprisoned as adults.

According to Pollock (1997), gangs dominate the prison social world. Examples of prison gangs include the Aryan Brotherhood, the Disciples, the Rangers, the Vice Lords, the Black Guerrilla Family, the Mexican Mafia, the Latin Kings, and the Nuestra Familia. Often, these groups differentiate themselves on the basis of race. In fact, Hawkins and Alpert (1989) use the term *super gang* to describe groups of organized, racially homogeneous inmates that have members in multiple prisons. Of course, prison gangs are involved in deviant behavior inside prison such as the trafficking of contraband and strong-arming or extortion.

Pollock (1997) also suggested that the growing prison population is related to hard-line drug policies enacted in the United States during the last few decades. Likewise, Irwin and Austin (1994) noted that America's new drug laws proscribe more punitive sentencing for drug offenders. Specifically, more drug offenders are being convicted and sentenced to prison. Increased prison populations often result in overcrowded institutions.

Crowding in Prison

Although findings are not entirely consistent, research tends to indicate that prison crowding is associated with several pathologies. Megargee (1977) used archival data from incident reports to link prison misconduct with population density. Specifically, density was significantly associated with the number and the rate of disciplinary reports filed. Farrington and Nuttall (1980) also examined prison crowding in relation to institutional misconduct and recidivism. They used archival data to illustrate a negative relationship between overcrowding and effectiveness. Farrington and Nuttall made the following insightful comment: "It may be that prisoners are more likely to become contaminated by other prisoners in over-crowded conditions, or that the experience of living in an overcrowded prison produces stress and aggression" (p. 230). In their view, prison crowding is a source of strain that produces feelings of deprivation that can induce violence during confinement.

Cox, Paulus, and McCain (1984) also discovered problems created by prison crowding. First, they determined that increases in prison populations without increased housing were associated with deaths, suicides, disciplinary infractions, and psychiatric commitments. Also, double cells resulted in negative housing ratings, increased disciplinary infraction rates, and more complaints of illness. Likewise, negative psychological reactions and increased complaints of illness were both associated with large open dormitories. Multiple-occupant units were also related to low space per person, no privacy, and double bunking.

The problems associated with prison crowding will likely intensify if correctional trends (i.e., repressive policies and growing prison populations) continue on their current course. From 1990 to 1999, the population of incarcerated individuals in the United States grew by 74 percent. However, the number of beds in state and federal prisons grew only 41 percent during the 1990s (Bureau of Justice Statistics, 1997). The disparity between the number of incarcerated individuals and bed space indicates the potential for future crowding problems in America's prisons.

CONCLUSION

The prison environment definitely influences the individuals who find themselves incarcerated behind the walls. Early studies of imprisonment brought academics to prison to better understand how men and women cope with confinement. In the 1940s, the prisonization hypothesis was developed, and much research focused on the convict code and the inmate subculture. However, due to social and cultural changes in the 1960s and 1970s, salient issues in correctional research involved race relations, prison gangs, drug use in prison, and prison crowding.

Social scientists now stress the influence of context on inmate behavior (Haney, 1997; Wooldredge, Griffin, & Pratt, 2001). For instance, Toch (1984) insisted that many researchers ignore individual and group differences when studying prison life. Different prison conditions influence how groups of inmates react and adapt to living inside prison. Likewise, Bonta and Gendreau (1990) advocated a "situation-by-person" approach to corrections. In particular, researchers should explore individual adaptations and examine more closely the moderating and contextual antecedents of inmate adjustment. Haney's comments also seemed to favor contextual analyses of prison life:

> Notwithstanding the tendency among researchers to talk about prison as if it were some sort of Weberian ideal type, conditions of confinement can vary dramatically along critical dimensions that render one prison a fundamentally different place in which to live from another. Indeed, the effects of confinement in, say, a relatively well run Canadian prison cannot be generalized to those suffered in a dangerously overcrowded or brutally mismanaged U.S. prison. (p. 531)

Both psychologists and sociologists working in corrections now recognize the importance context has for behavior and advocate explanatory models with both contextual and individual variables.

Wooldredge et al. (2001) conducted one of the first truly contextual studies of prison life to date. They developed a multilevel model of inmate misconduct that was sensitive to both the characteristics of individual prisoners and the features of correctional institutions. Multilevel research of this nature is quite new. It makes use of the similar experiences that inmates share in the same prison, and these shared experiences tend to shape the individual behavior of inmates over time. More multilevel or hierarchical studies of prison life are currently under way.

REFERENCES

Adamek, R. J., & Dager, E. Z. (1968). Social structure, identification and change in a treatment-oriented institution. *American Sociological Review, 33,* 931–944.

Aday, R. H. (1994). Aging in prison: A case study of new elderly inmates. *International Journal of Offender Therapy and Comparative Criminology, 38*(1), 79–91.

Aday, R. H., & Webster, E. L. (1979). Aging in prison: The development of a preliminary model. *Offender Rehabilitation, 3*(3), 271–280.

Akers, R. L, Hayner, N. S., & Gruninger, W. (1977). Prisonization in five countries: Type of prison and inmate characteristics. *Criminology, 14,* 527–554.

Allen, F. A. (1981). *The decline of the rehabilitative ideal.* New Haven, CT: Yale University Press.

Alpert, G. P. (1979). Patterns of change in prisonization: A longitudinal analysis. *Criminal Justice and Behavior, 6,* 159–174.

American Psychiatric Association. (1994). *Diagnostic and statistical manual of mental disorders* (4th ed.). Washington, DC: Author.

Atchley, R., & McCabe, M. (1968). Socialization in correctional communities: A replication. *American Sociological Review, 33,* 312–323.

Baier, G. F. (1961). The aged inmate. *American Journal of Corrections* (March–April), 4–34.

Berk, B. B. (1966). Organizational goals and inmate organization. *American Journal of Sociology, 71,* 522–534.

Bonta, J., & Gendreau, P. (1990). Reexamining the cruel and unusual punishment of prison life. *Law and Human Behavior, 14,* 347–372.

Bornstein, R. F. (1993). *The dependent personality.* New York: Guilford.

Bornstein, R. F. (1995). Active dependency. *Journal of Nervous and Mental Disorders, 183*(2), 64–77.

Bornstein, R. F., & Kennedy, T. D. (1994). Interpersonal dependency and academic performance. *Journal of Personality Disorders, 8,* 240–248.

Bornstein, R. F., Krukonis, A. B., Manning, K. A., Mastrosimone, C. C., & Rossner, S. C. (1993). Interpersonal dependency and health service utilization in a college student sample. *Journal of Social and Clinical Psychology, 12,* 262–279.

Bornstein, R. F., Riggs, J. M., Hill, E. L., & Calabrese, C. (1996). Activity, passivity, self-denigration, and self-promotion: Toward an interactionist model of interpersonal dependency. *Journal of Personality, 64*(3), 637–673.

Bureau of Justice Statistics. (1997). *Census of state and federal correctional facilities.* Washington, DC: U.S. Department of Justice.

Clemmer, D. (1940). *The prison community.* Boston: Christopher.

Clemmer, D. (1950). Observations on imprisonment as a source of criminality. *Journal of Criminal Law & Criminology, 41,* 311–319.

Clemmer, D. (1958). *The prison community* (rev. ed.). New York: Rinehart.

Cohen, A. K. (1955/1997). A general theory of subcultures. In K. Gelder & S. Thornton (Eds.), *The subcultures reader* (pp. 44–54). London: Routledge.

Cohen, A. K. (1976). Prison violence: A sociological perspective. In A. K. Cohen, G. F. Cole, & R. G. Bailey (Eds.), *Prison violence* (pp. 3–22). Lexington, MA: Lexington Books.

Cope, N. (2000). Drug use in prison: The experience of young offenders. *Drugs: Education, Prevention, and Policy, 7,* 355–366.

Cox, V. C., Paulus, P. B., & McCain, G. (1984). Prison crowding research: The relevance for prison housing standards and a general approach regarding crowding phenomena. *American Psychologist, 39,* 1148–1160.

Dale, M. (1976). Barriers to the rehabilitation of ex-offenders. *Crime and Delinquency, 22,* 322–337.

Edwards, A., Curtis, S., & Sherrard, J. (1999). Survey of risk behaviour and HIV prevalence in an English prison. *International Journal of STD & AIDS, 10,* 464–466.

Faine, J. R. (1973). A self-consistency approach to prisonization. *The Sociological Quarterly, 14,* 576–588.

Farrington, D. P., & Nuttall, C. P. (1980). Prison size, overcrowding, prison violence, and recidivism. *Journal of Criminal Justice, 8,* 221–231.

Fenichel, O. (1945). *The psychoanalytic theory of neurosis.* New York: Norton.

Garabedian, P. G. (1963). Social roles and processes of socialization in the prison community. *Social Problems, 11,* 139–152.

Goetting, A. (1983). The elderly in prison: Issues and perspectives. *Journal of Research in Crime and Delinquency, 20,* 291–309.

Goffman, E. (1961). *Asylums.* New York: Anchor Books/Doubleday.

Goldstein, P. J. (1998). The drugs/violence nexus: A tripartite conceptual frame-
    work. In J. A. Inciardi & K. McElrath (Eds.), *The American drug scene* (pp.
    243–253). Los Angeles: Roxbury.
Gordon, M. M. (1947/1997). The concept of the sub-culture and its application.
    In K. Gelder & S. Thornton (Eds.), *The subcultures reader* (pp. 40–43). Lon-
    don: Routledge.
Grusky, O. (1959). Organizational goals and the behavior of informal leaders.
    American Journal of Sociology, 65, 59–67.
Haney, C. (1997). Psychology and the limits to prison pain: Confronting the coming
    crisis in Eighth Amendment law. *Psychology, Public Policy, and Law, 3,* 499–
    588.
Hawkins, R., & Alpert, G. (1989). *American prison systems: Punishment and justice.*
    Englewood Cliffs, NJ: Prentice-Hall.
Haynes, F. E. (1948). The sociological study of the prison community. *Journal of
    Criminal Law & Criminology, 39,* 432–440.
Herskovits, M. J. (1949). *Man and his works: The science of cultural anthropology.*
    New York: Knopf.
Hirschfeld, R.M.A., Klerman, G. L., Gough, H. G., Barrett, J., Korchin, S. J., &
    Chodoff, P. (1977). A measure of interpersonal dependency. *Journal of Per-
    sonality, 41*(6), 610–618.
Homant, R. J. (1984). Employment of ex-offenders: The role of prisonization and
    self-esteem. *Journal of Counseling, Services, & Rehabilitation, 8,* 5–24.
Hunt, G., Riegel, S., Morales, T., & Waldorf, D. (1993). Changes in prison culture:
    Prison gangs and the case of the "Pepsi generation." *Social Problems, 40,* 398–
    409.
Inciardi, J. A., Lockwood, D., & Quinlan, J. A. (1993). Drug use in prison: Patterns,
    processes, and implications for treatment. *Journal of Drug Issues, 23,* 119–129.
Irwin, J. (1980). *Prisons in turmoil.* Boston: Little, Brown.
Irwin, J., & Austin, J. (1994). *It's about time: America's imprisonment binge.*
    Belmont, CA: Wadsworth.
Irwin, J., & Cressey, D. R. (1962). Thieves, convicts and the inmate culture. *Social
    Problems, 10,* 142–155.
Jensen, G. F. (1977). Age and rule-breaking in prison: A test of sociocultural inter-
    pretations. *Criminology, 14*(4), 555–568.
Jensen, G. F., & Jones, D. (1976). Perspectives on inmate culture: A study of women
    in prison. *Social Forces, 54,* 590–603.
Kassebaum, G., & Chandler, S. M. (1994). Polydrug use and self-control among
    men and women in prisons. *Journal of Drug Education, 24,* 333–350.
Keene, J. (1997). Drug use among prisoners before, during and after custody.
    Addiction Research, 4, 343–353.
Kennedy, D. B., & Kerber, A. (1973). *Resocialization: An American experiment.*
    New York: Behavioral Publications.
Knox, G. (1981). Differential integration and job retention among ex-offenders.
    Criminology, 18, 481–499.
Krajick, K. (1979). Growing old in prison. *Corrections Magazine* (March), 33–46.
Lehmann, J. M. (1993). *Deconstructing Durkheim.* New York: Routledge.

Leukefeld, C. G., Araujo, G. M., & Farabee, D. (1997). Drugs, crime and HIV. *Substance Use and Misuse, 32,* 749–756.

Leukefeld, C. G., & Tims, F. R. (1993). Drug abuse treatment in prisons and jails. *Journal of Substance Abuse Treatment, 10,* 77–84.

Martinson, R. (1974). What works? Questions and answers about prison reform. *Public Interest, 35,* 22–54.

Mathiesen, T. (1971). *Across the boundaries of organizations: An exploratory study of communication patterns in two penal institutions.* Berkeley, CA: Glendessary Press.

Megargee, E. I. (1977). The association of population density, reduced space, and uncomfortable temperatures with misconduct in a prison community. *American Journal of Community Psychology, 5,* 289–298.

Menard, S., Mihalic, S., & Huizinga, D. (2001). Drugs and crime revisited. *Justice Quarterly, 18,* 269–299.

Morris, T., & Morris, P. (1962). The experience of imprisonment. *British Journal of Criminology, 2,* 337–360.

Ohlin, L. E. (1956). *Sociology and the field of corrections.* New York: Russell Sage.

Parker, R. N., & Auerhahn, K. (1998). Alcohol, drugs, and violence. *Annual Review of Sociology, 24,* 291–311.

Peat, B. J., & Winfree, L. T. (1992). Reducing the intra-institutional effects of "prisonization": A study of the therapeutic community of drug-using inmates. *Criminal Justice and Behavior, 19,* 206–225.

Pollock, J. (1997). The social world of the prisoner. In J. Pollock (Ed.), *Prisons: Today and tomorrow* (pp. 218–269). Gaithersburg, MD: Aspen.

Reed, M. B., & Glamser, F. D. (1979). Aging in total institutions: The case of older prisoners. *Gerontologist, 19*(4), 354–360.

Schrag, C. (1961). Some foundations for a theory of correction. In D. Cressey (Ed.), *The prison: Studies in institutional organization and change* (pp. 309–358). New York: Holt, Rinehart, and Winston.

Schwartz, B. (1971). Pre-institutional vs. situational influence in a correctional community. *Journal of Criminal Law, Criminology, & Police Science, 62,* 532–541.

Stevens, D. J. (1997). Origins and effects of prison drug gangs in North Carolina. *Journal of Gang Research, 4,* 23–35.

Stratton, J. (1967). Differential identification and attitudes toward the law. *Social Forces, 46,* 256–263.

Straus, R. (1974). *Escape from custody.* New York: Harper & Row.

Street, D. (1965). The inmate group in custodial and treatment settings. *American Sociological Review, 30,* 40–55.

Street, D., Vinter, R. D., & Perrow, C. (1966). *Organization for treatment: A comparative study of institutions for delinquents.* New York: Free Press.

Swann, R., & James, P. (1998). The effect of the prison environment upon inmate drug taking behaviour. *Howard Journal of Criminal Justice, 37,* 252–265.

Sykes, G. M. (1958). *The society of captives.* Princeton, NJ: Princeton University Press.

Sykes, G. M., & Messinger, S. (1960). The inmate social system. In R. Cloward (Ed.), *Theoretical studies in the social organization of the prison* (pp. 6–10). New York: Social Science Research Council.

Teller, F. E., & Howell, R. J. (1981). The older prisoner: Criminal and psychological characteristics. *Criminology, 18*(4), 549–555.

Thomas, C. W. (1971). *Determinants of prisonization: A test of two analytical perspectives on adult socialization in total institutions.* Unpublished doctoral dissertation, University of Kentucky.

Thomas, C. W., & Cage, R. J. (1977). Correlates of prison drug use: An evaluation of two conceptual models. *Criminology, 15,* 193–210.

Thomas, C. W., & Petersen, D. M. (1977). *Prison organization and inmate subculture.* Indianapolis, IN: Bobbs-Merrill.

Tittle, C. R. (1972). Institutional living and self-esteem. *Social Problems, 20,* 65–77.

Tittle, C. R., & Tittle, R. P. (1964). Social organization of prisoners: An empirical test. *Social Forces, 43,* 215–221.

Toch, H. (1984). Quo vadis? *Canadian Journal of Criminology, 26,* 511–516.

Von Hirsch, A. (1985). *Past or future crimes: Deservedness and dangerousness in the sentencing of criminals.* New Brunswick, NJ: Rutgers University Press.

Wellford, C. F. (1967). Factors associated with adoption of the inmate code: A study of normative socialization. *Journal of Criminal Law, Criminology, and Police Science, 58,* 197–203.

Wheeler, S. (1961). Socialization in correctional communities. *American Sociological Review, 26,* 679–712.

Wilder, H. A. (1965). The role of the "rat" in the prison. *Federal Probation, 29,* 44–60.

Wilson, T. P. (1968). Patterns of management and adaptations to organizational roles: A study of prison inmates. *American Journal of Sociology, 74,* 146–157.

Wooldredge, J., Griffin, T., & Pratt, T. (2001). Considering hierarchical models for research on inmate behavior: Predicting misconduct with multilevel data. *Justice Quarterly, 18,* 203–231.

Zald, M. N. (1962). Organizational control structures in five correctional institutions. *American Journal of Sociology, 68,* 335–345.

Zingraff, M. T. (1975). Prisonization as an inhibitor of effective resocialization. *Criminology, 13,* 366–388.

5

WOMEN AND PRISON

Wayne Gillespie

INTRODUCTION

Crime and punishment are gendered concepts. The types of crime in which women and men engage are dissimilar, and their rates of offending vary considerably. Female offenders seem to experience each stage of the criminal justice system differently than do men. During arrest, female offenders are treated chivalrously by male officers (Visher, 1983). Women are dealt with differently in criminal court, and sentencing disparities between the sexes exist. The chivalry hypothesis may also explain some of the differences in sentencing (Johnson & Scheuble, 1991). Women are often handled differently from men by the correctional system, and it is incorrect to assume that the experience of imprisonment is identical for both women and men. Prisons for women are unlike institutions for men, and women adapt to the prison environment differently than do men.

There are several reasons for studying women's prisons separately from men's. Carlen (1994) proposed that, for the past hundred years, female convicts have been housed separately from male inmates throughout North America and Europe. This fact sets the context of imprisonment for women apart from that of men. Moreover, scholars of the early twentieth century did not write about or campaign for women prisoners or their institutions. As a consequence, the gender-specific needs of female prisoners were somewhat neglected by researchers (Carlen, 1994; Rafter, 1983). This chapter begins to rectify that problem, and it should serve as a comparison to the experience of male imprisonment that is described throughout this book. This chapter also addresses female imprisonment as one of the current issues in prison management identified by Rausch (1996).

HISTORY OF WOMEN'S IMPRISONMENT

Before the nineteenth century, all convicted criminals were housed together regardless of their sex or age. In fact, one of the first recommendations of early penal reformers was the segregation of prisoners by age and sex (Howard, 1777). Prison administrators eventually separated women convicts from male inmates. Often, these women were moved to other parts of a predominantly male penal institution. Women prisoners were frequently relegated to an attic because there were so few of them (Rafter, 1983). Unfortunately, these incarcerated women were often ignored by prison officials and given tasks traditionally associated with women's work such as sewing or cooking. Eventually, nineteenth-century prison administrators established separate buildings for women inmates in male prisons (Grana, 2002; Rafter).

The first women's prisons opened during the 1800s in the United States. In 1835, the first correctional facility exclusively for women was opened in New York; it was named Mount Pleasant Female Prison (Grana, 2002). And it was not until the 1870s that the first large-scale, completely separate, and independent penitentiary for women was opened in the United States—the Indiana Reformatory Institution (Grana; Muraskin, 2003). The openings of these institutions coincided with a popular social movement of the late nineteenth century.

The Progressive movement of the nineteenth century was concerned with prison reform, among many other things. Platt (1977) described that the impetus for these social reforms was rooted in the emerging system of corporate capitalism:

> Corporate reformers launched a movement to rescue and regulate capitalism through developing a new political economy, designed on the one hand to stabilize production and fiscal planning, and on the other hand to co-opt the rising wave of popular militancy. (p. xix)

Corporate reformers recognized the need for economic, political, and social reforms. Part of their vision called for increased state regulation of social institutions.

Women from the middle class played an important role in this grand scheme. As Platt (1977) noted, "Middle-class women were now better educated and had more leisure time, but their choice of careers was limited" (p. 76). Consequently, the women of the middle class felt a void in their lives. Platt suggested that philanthropic charity work filled this void created by capitalism. Of those women who began working for prison reform, some chose to work with youth, and others decided to reform women convicts.

The reformation of women offenders was associated with the Progressive movement. Middle-class female reformers, such as Elizabeth Fry, attempted to resocialize criminal women into respectable, law-abiding citizens. Often, this process involved educating female offenders about the "ladylike" virtues of womanhood (e.g., chastity, altruism, self-sacrifice, motherhood). Today, many women's prisons continue to operate based on these principles and, particularly, the belief that the most acceptable role for women is wife and mother (Feinman, 1986; Grana, 2002).

THE EXTENT OF FEMALE IMPRISONMENT

In 1998, there were 74,941 women imprisoned in state correctional institutions throughout the United States and 9,186 incarcerated in the federal system (Bureau of Justice Statistics, 2002). That is, over 84,000 women were imprisoned in the United States at the end of the twentieth century. California imprisoned more women than any other state or the federal government, with 11,527 female inmates; Texas followed closely with 10,332; then Florida with 3,526; and New York with 3,502 women in prison (Bureau of Justice Statistics).

Of course, when compared with the 1,214,969 male prisoners in 1998, the number of women in prison may seem relatively small. In fact, there were fourteen times as many male inmates as there were female inmates in the United States that year. Yet a comparison of the sexes based on raw numbers is misleading. The salient issue here is the growth rate in female imprisonment, not the sheer quantity of women in prison. Bloom and Chesney-Lind (2003) traced the growth in the U.S. female incarceration rate and remarked, "The increase in women's imprisonment has outstripped the male increase every year since the mid-1980s" (p. 175). When comparing female and male rates of incarceration, Bloom and Chesney-Lind discovered that "since 1985 the annual rate of growth of female prisoners averaged 11.2 percent higher than the 7.9 percent average increase in male prisoners" (p. 176).

Bloom and Chesney-Lind (2003) also echoed a contention made earlier by Irwin, Schiraldi, and Ziedenberg (2000) that women currently make up more of the total prison population in the United States than ever before. In fact, Irwin et al. described the current problematic trend in female imprisonment:

> Ironically, women represent both the fastest growing and the least violent segment of prison and jail populations. Women made up three percent (12,927) of state prisoners in 1978 (Mauer and Huling, 1995), a figure that grew to 6.3% (79,624) by 1997. (p. 137)

Thus, in the span of twenty years, the female imprisonment rate in the United States grew by over 500 percent, with the majority of that growth coming from women sentenced for nonviolent offenses.

Snell and Morton (1994) conducted a detailed analysis of women prisoners based on secondary data. They found that increasing incarceration rates for women were due in large part to the growing number of women who have been sentenced to prison for drug offenses. In fact, from 1986 to 1991, drug offenders made up more than 50 percent of the total rise in the female incarceration rate, whereas women sentenced for violent crimes only accounted for 20 percent of the growth. Furthermore, about half of the women in prison committed their crime under the influence of drugs and/ or alcohol.

Bloom and Chesney-Lind (2003) also acknowledged the fact that the seriousness of women's offending cannot explain the growth in female imprisonment. They suggested that women offenders actually had become less violent in recent years. The growth in women prisoners is due to the commission of nonviolent crimes. In particular, Bloom and Chesney-Lind made the following observation about women's imprisonment for drug-related offenses:

> Over two decades ago (1979), one in ten women in U.S. prisons was serving time for drugs. Now it is one out of three (32.8 percent), and while the intent of "get tough" policies was to rid society of drug dealers and "kingpins," over a third (35.9 percent) of the women serving sentences for drug offenses in the nation's prisons are serving time for "possession." (p. 177)

In short, women became the targets of heightened policing and prosecution associated with the government's War on Drugs.

CHARACTERISTICS OF WOMEN PRISONERS

A demographic profile of female inmates includes extralegal characteristics such as their race, age, education, and employment status. According to the Bureau of Justice Statistics (2002), in 1998, 46.17 percent of female inmates in state and federal prisons throughout the United States were African American, and 44.75 percent were white. The race of the remaining 9 percent was unknown, or neither white nor African American. The majority were also mothers, age twenty-five to thirty-four years, and unmarried (Snell & Morton, 1994). Over 40 percent of imprisoned women reported that they were unemployed at the time of their arrest, and 43 percent indicated that they had a high school diploma or a GED. However, only 16 percent had attended college (Greenfeld & Snell, 1999). Consequently, a sizable minority (30 percent) of incarcerated women was dependent upon welfare assistance at the time of arrest (Greenfeld & Snell).

In addition, half of all female prisoners were chemically dependent or abusing drugs or alcohol at the time of their offense. Sheridan (1996) analyzed secondary data collected on eighty-one inmates in a mid-Atlantic state and found several differences in the life experiences of male and female inmates. Women used significantly more drugs than did men when they were out on the street, and females reported mixing alcohol and drugs more than did male inmates. However, a greater percentage of women than men got inpatient substance-abuse treatment on the street. Furthermore, more women than men revealed that their parents abused drugs or alcohol. Women's families were altogether more dysfunctional than men's. Females reported significantly more childhood sexual abuse than did males. As adults, women also experienced significantly more physical, sexual, and emotional abuse than men did. Thus, the life experiences of female inmates appear to differ from those of their male counterparts.

Moreover, a third of the women committed the crime that resulted in their incarceration to get money for their drug dependency. Greenfeld and Snell's (1999) analysis revealed that female inmates also had health problems related to their lifestyle. About 23 percent of women prisoners received medication for an emotional disorder. Roughly 3.5 percent of the female inmate population tested positive for HIV, the virus that causes AIDS.

In addition to demographics, legal variables such as criminal background, sentence length, and recidivism are also necessary to understand the female inmate. According to Greenfeld and Snell (1999), nearly 60 percent of women in state prisons had at least one prior conviction as an adult. Only 19 percent reported a juvenile record. Over 93 percent of female prisoners were serving a sentence of more than a year (Bureau of Justice Statistics, 2002). In terms of recidivism, Greenfeld and Snell reported that "A 3-year followup for a sample representing 109,000 persons (6,400 females among them) discharged from prisons in 11 states in 1983 found that 52% of women were rearrested" (p. 11). They also noted that prior criminal history was an influential predictor of postprison recidivism.

RELATIONSHIPS AND ADAPTATION TO PRISON

Several feminist scholars working outside the realm of criminology and penology have suggested that the key to understanding women involves appreciating the social relationships into which they enter. For example, Gilligan (1979) suggested, "Woman's place in man's life cycle has been that of nurturer, caretaker, and helpmate, the weaver of those networks of relationships on which she in turn relies" (p. 440). She claimed that the moral reasoning of women cannot and should not be compared with that of men, because women value relationships above ethical maxims and rules.

Noddings (1984) also asked, "For what ethical need have women for God?" She suggested that women have no need for a God wrought in the image of man. Noddings claimed that "all the love and goodness commanded by such a God can be generated from the love and goodness found in the warmest and best human relations" (p. 97). If women's spirituality and morality are tied to relationships, then isolation from their primary social relations outside prison must be especially painful for women prisoners.

In fact, separation from family and friends on the outside is the most acute deprivation reported by female inmates (Jones, 1993; Ward & Kassebaum, 1964). In prison, women prisoners may cope with this particular deprivation in several ways. First, they may maintain contact with the outside world through visits, letters, and the telephone. Although visits are the preferred method of maintaining contact with the outside world, letters are the most prevalent means of keeping in contact with family and friends on the outside. According to Jones, maintaining contact demonstrates love and caring interrupted by imprisonment. Maintaining contact also provides inmates with a sense of support and encouragement. Conversely, a prisoner may come to believe that the outside world has cast her away if there is a lull in the contact received from family and friends.

Two recent studies looked at the phenomenon of visitation in women's prisons. In his qualitative study of thirty-one female inmates, Jones (1993) noted that 50 percent of the participants revealed that family members were the most frequent visitors. Only 15 percent of his subjects reported monthly visits from friends. However, in their quantitative study of 180 female inmates, Casey-Acevedo and Bakken (2002) discovered, "Of the women who received visits, the most frequent visitors were friends (evenly divided between males and females), not family members" (p. 67). This finding contradicts the earlier work of Jones, but perhaps can be explained by the difference in research methodologies selected by the researchers.

Visitation of women serving time in prison is hampered by several factors. Most states only have one prison for women. Often the costs of transportation or travel to and from the facility are prohibitively high for the families of incarcerated women. The time and dates for visitation may also conflict with work schedules on the outside. Furthermore, according to Jones (1993), the husbands and boyfriends of imprisoned women may also be incarcerated or on parole.

In many cases, women inmates are unable to maintain contact with the outside world. If this happens, the convict is likely to adapt in several ways. Women prisoners who are unable to maintain contact with their families and friends may take on roles inside prison or form close relationships with other inmates. Groups of inmates sometimes mimic a family, and female prisoners assume the roles of mother, father, and child. However, inmates engage in a variety of other roles. Giallombardo (1966) enumerated an extensive list of the roles that develop among women inside prison. She further differentiated the roles inside women's prisons between those that are nonsexual (e.g., jive bitches, rap buddies) and the sexual ones (e.g., femmes, stud broads). Additionally, Ross and Richards (2002) used the term *connet* to describe a female prisoner.

Van Wormer and Bates (1979) focused on leadership roles in an Alabama prison for women. They discovered that both female inmates convicted of a violent crime and those involved in homosexual relationships in prison displayed high leadership (i.e., willingness to speak for the group in registering a complaint, and the know-how to get what one wants, for oneself and others). Van Wormer and Bates's work implied that social relationships help female inmates survive in prison. However, in a later report, Van Wormer (1987) claimed that role-playing in prison and taking part in pseudofamilies are ultimately detrimental for women inmates. These activities create a fantasy world in which women escape the deprivations of prison life. They also may inhibit rehabilitation or personal growth because they prevent women from addressing the real problems in their actual lives.

Homosexuality in women's institutions was a theme on which early researchers of female imprisonment focused. Ward and Kassebaum (1964) found that homosexuality was also a common way for women to adapt to the deprivations of prison life. The women inmates in their study estimated that about 50 percent of the total prison population engaged in homosexual relations. However, like Giallombardo (1966), Ward and Kassebaum conceived homosexuality among female inmates as a temporary solution to the deprivation of heterosexual relations. They made the following statement about prison homosexuality among women:

> The folklore of the female prison community provides rationalizations for homosexuality by emphasizing that women involved in prison affairs are not homosexual but bisexual, by referring to those who do not play as "prudes," by emphasizing the alleviation of loneliness that such involvements can bring, by alleging greater satisfactions than can be found in heterosexual affairs, and by repeating stories about the women who return to men upon release. (p. 174)

If an inmate makes these rationalizations, she is likely to adapt to incarceration by forming a homosexual relationship inside prison. Ward and Kassebaum admitted that inmates may also adapt to incarceration by withdrawing psychologically, engaging in fantasies, becoming rebellious, fighting, or accepting institutional life as a satisfactory existence. However, they maintained that homosexuality was the most prevalent adaptation by women inmates to the deprivations of prison life. In their analysis, homosexuality was functional.

Research by Leger (1987) supported the claims of previous studies about homosexuality among female prisoners. He found that, when compared with women who engaged in institutional homosexuality, women who were homosexual before prison had longer sentences, had served more time, were arrested at an earlier age, and had more previous confinements. Leger made the following conclusion about homosexuality in women's prisons:

> Within the lesbian group, women who "came out" at an early age were also the most frequent participants in homosexual behavior, the most criminalistic and most feministic—that is, these women, out of everyone at the institution,

were the ones who engaged in behavior that was the least consistent with the stereotypical female role. (p. 464)

Women who identified themselves as homosexual before incarceration were labeled true homosexuals, or lesbians (Giallombardo, 1966; Leger; Ward & Kassebaum, 1964). In fact, these women were often viewed as sick and shunned by other inmates. Likewise, Leger implied that these true homosexuals were antisocial and more difficult to manage than other female prisoners.

Ellis and Austin (1971) looked at the relationship between aggression and another aspect of women's sexuality. They tracked the menstrual cycles of forty-five inmates at the North Carolina Correctional Center for Women to determine if menstruation was linked with aggressive behavior. Ellis and Austin concluded that "the subjects of this study, normally menstruating women who happen to be in prison, do indeed tend to be nastier toward others during the pre-menstrual and menstrual phases of the menstrual cycle" (p. 392). They suggested that prison officials require female inmates to keep a daily menstrual log and place aggressive, menstruating women in jobs and accommodations that require little interpersonal contact.

In recent years, scholars have called into question this focus on female sexuality in early studies of women's imprisonment. Researchers tended to sexualize women's incarceration and negatively evaluate aspects of female sexuality among women inmates. In particular, Freedman (1996) suggested that the "aggressive lesbian" became a stereotype that was eventually treated as a threat to social order. Correctional personnel, politicians, and scholars exaggerated the risk from prison lesbians. Moreover, Freedman examined this phenomenon against the broader backdrop of race relations between whites and African Americans from 1915 through 1965. During this time frame, the image of the aggressive prison lesbian became intertwined with the aggressive African-American female. This new, expanded stereotype of the aggressive African-American lesbian served to justify the fact that lesbians serve longer prison sentences than nonlesbians and that they are treated by prison officials more harshly than other inmates.

There are additional reasons to believe that nonwhite inmates experience discrimination in prison. French (1977) claimed that African Americans make up a significant proportion of the female inmate population. Furthermore, he found that African-American women were more likely than white females to be incarcerated for drug-related charges. He attributed this discrepancy to discrimination at different stages of the judicial process. In reference to the African-American female offender, French (1977) made the following insightful observation:

The white male police officer may arrest her or not. The typical white male prosecutor then has the legal discretion to prosecute or not and to reduce charges or not. The typically white male judge has the discretion to assign reasonable bail or to deny bail altogether. (p. 488)

His analysis of the treatment of African-American female offenders is consistent with a school of thought in the social sciences called critical race theory. Critical race theory focuses on identifying the ways that race influences the identification, interpretation, and resolution of social and legal problems (Russell, 2000).

Kruttschnitt (1983) also provided evidence that correctional staff may be stricter with African-American inmates than with whites. In her study of fifty-three women prisoners at the Correctional Institution for Women in Shakopee, Minnesota, she examined three categories of inmate perceptions: racial discrimination by staff, racial integration among inmates, and race relations among inmates. She determined that both whites and nonwhites disagreed with the idea that a prisoner is treated the same by all correctional staff regardless of the officer's race. Moreover, although Kruttschnitt uncovered some bias by prison workers, she was unable to find any racial conflict among inmates.

American scholars proposed that relationships alleviate the feelings of isolation and deprivation that many women encounter in prison. Mawby (1982) questioned the cross-national generalizability of these findings. He conducted a study of women in British prisons and suggested that not all women adapt to imprisonment in the same fashion. He found that quasi-familial structures and lesbian relationships were not as prevalent in British prisons as American penitentiaries. Mawby concluded the following:

Women in British prisons include a higher proportion of first offenders, and more offenders whose crimes are relatively minor, and the inmates' contacts with family and friends appear to be more frequent than is the case in America. (p. 38)

Thus, he suggested that a woman's response to incarceration depends upon the type of person she is as well as the amount of contact she maintains with the outside world.

However, in a relatively recent study about women's responses to prison, Kruttschnitt, Gartner, and Miller (2000) found that friendships are still critical to the way female inmates do their time. Trust is a primary concern among female prisoners; consequently, most women's friendship networks consist of only one or two other inmates. Kruttschnitt et al. also noticed that the age of the correctional institution seemed to affect the intensity of the relationships among female inmates. In particular, women in a new correctional facility were less likely to form and depend upon prison friendships than women in an old prison.

MOTHERING FROM PRISON

About 70 percent of women prisoners have children under the age of eighteen years, and 64 percent of all female inmates had been caring for their children prior to their incarceration (Greenfeld & Snell, 1999). Inmate mothers reported, on average, having a family on the outside with 2.38 children under eighteen. Greenfeld and Snell estimated almost 250,000 children have mothers who are incarcerated in prison or jail. Incarceration obviously disrupts the relationships that these women have with their children. However, Snell and Morton (1994) reported that over 50 percent of imprisoned mothers said their children resided with a grandparent during their incarceration. In a little more than 25 percent of the cases, the father cared for the children in the mother's absence. Roughly 11 percent of incarcerated mothers revealed that their children had been placed in foster homes, agencies, or institutions. Research has shown that family members provide better care than do foster homes to infant or toddler children when the mother is incarcerated (Gaudin & Sutphen, 1993). Snell and Morton also reported that half of all female inmates received at least one visit from their children during their incarceration. However, in contrast, Casey-Acevedo and Bakken (2002) found that 61 percent of the women in their sample who were mothers never received a visit from their children.

Several researchers have explored the impact of imprisonment on the family life of women inmates (e.g., see Browne, 1989; Gaudin & Sutphen, 1993; LeFlore & Holston, 1989; Martin, 1997; Pelka-Slugocka & Slugocki, 1980; Sharp & Marcus-Mendoza, 2001). Using a sample of Polish inmates, Pelka-Slugocka and Slugocki studied the influence of imprisonment on the matrimonial life of women prisoners. They examined several variables, including family bonds during imprisonment, reestablishment of conjugal life with their husbands upon release, and evaluation of the effect of imprisonment on ex-prisoners' marriages. Overall, they found that women ex-convicts who return to their own families adjust well to life outside prison. In fact, about 82 percent of the female inmates in their study started families after they were released from prison.

Martin (1997) studied mothering among incarcerated women at the Minnesota Correctional Facility in Shakopee. She developed the concept of connected mothers to describe women inmates who demonstrated three integral aspects of mothering: legal custody, an emotional connection with their children, and a mature understanding of the needs of their children. The prison in which these women were incarcerated was a child-centered institution. Martin described the prison as follows:

> Shakopee provided a warm and active place for inmate mothers. There were children at nearly every meal and they dominated the dining room on weekends. Each cottage became the second home to many of the children. Trikes

> and plastic swimming pools were on the grounds in the summer, and there were sleds and snowmen in winter. (p. 18)

This particular facility in Minnesota allowed children to stay with their mothers at the prison three weekends a month. It also provided inmate mothers with child and parenting programs. Shakopee actually committed staff members to parenting programming. For example, a parenting director was on staff, and experts in early childhood development instructed mothers in parenting skills. Martin kept track of these women after they were released from prison and found that this type of intensive visitation was associated with postprison success. The programs at Shakopee clearly benefited both the mothers and their children.

However, imprisonment in the absence of such programs often creates hardships for the children of inmate mothers. Some of the problems faced by these children include financial distress, weak family bonds, poor school performance, juvenile delinquency, and emotional difficulties (Sharp & Marcus-Mendoza, 2001). Current criminological research also suggests that a lack of parental supervision may be linked with a lack of self-control in children. Gottfredson and Hirschi (1990) proposed that low self-control results from ineffective child rearing. Effective child rearing teaches self-control when parents are able to monitor their child's behavior, recognize deviant behavior when it occurs, and punish such behavior. People who have low self-control are self-centered, indifferent, or insensitive to the suffering and needs of others. According to Gottfredson and Hirschi, these characteristics often are associated with criminal behavior. Thus, imprisoning mothers and not allowing them to take part in effective child rearing may result in criminal behavior being passed down from one generation to the next. It may create a cycle of delinquency and criminality.

Sharp and Marcus-Mendoza (2001) also explored the relations among incarcerated women and their families in Oklahoma. The inmate mothers in their study feared that their children would have school-related problems such as bad grades, expulsion, and dropping out as a result of the incarceration. Some mothers noticed that their children were also emotionally depressed. Sharp and Marcus-Mendoza noted that inmates who are pregnant when they enter the criminal justice system are faced with a particularly difficult situation.

In fact, the case of a pregnant inmate in prison is especially problematic for both the woman and the institution. It is believed that about 6 percent of women are pregnant when they enter prison (Snell & Morton, 1994). In her review of nineteenth-century women convicts, Dodge (1999) discovered that as early as 1855, prison inspectors in Illinois were troubled by the issue of pregnant inmates, and their primary concern was the expense imposed on the institution, not the welfare of the mother. To rectify this problem, Dodge noted that a de facto policy was established in Illinois that allowed most pregnant women prisoners to be pardoned and released.

Today, however, the policy regarding pregnant convicts has changed. In the following passage, Ross and Richards (2002) described the childbearing experience for women inmates:

> When a prisoner goes through childbirth, she's handcuffed and transferred to a civilian hospital. The cuffs aren't taken off while she goes through labor and during delivery. With luck, the baby will be taken in by a relative. More likely, the baby is turned over to foster care or put up for adoption. (p. 150)

A jailer in Tennessee disclosed his frustration with a pregnant inmate (J. Rose, personal communication, May 29, 2003). The woman had been sentenced to prison, but the Tennessee Department of Corrections claimed that it did not have space for her in Nashville, where the state's only institution for women is located. As such, the woman was housed in the county jail during most of her pregnancy. She went into false labor twice, and was taken to the local hospital each time. In this case, the jailer was frustrated because the county was responsible for the expenses incurred by this inmate during her trips to the hospital. He was convinced that a space would open up for her at the state prison *after* the baby was delivered.

MANAGING FEMALE INMATES

As early as 1845, correctional personnel regarded women prisoners as more trouble than male inmates (Dodge, 1999). In fact, females were considered to be disruptive, hard to manage, and difficult in correctional contexts. They were described as impulsive, individualistic, unreasonable, and excitable. Dodge suggested that correctional personnel of the time may have regarded female inmates as more unmanageable because they often violated the middle-class standards of femininity such as subservience, modesty, hygiene, and sobriety. Also, during this time frame, the conventional wisdom was that female inmates needed individualized care and attention.

Indeed, the idea that women prisoners require more individualized supervision remains a prominent feature of correctional management to this day. Because female inmates are often described as emotional, sensitive, and communicative, Farr (2000) recently proposed, "The women do best with a management style that emphasizes staff responsiveness to inmates' openness about personal feelings and situations" (p. 8). She also recommended shifting current classification procedures for female offenders from risk-based measures to needs-based assessments. A needs-based classification policy for female inmates might focus on the treatment needs of incarcerated women such as parenting, custody, substance abuse, mental health, counseling for prior abuse, health care, and education and job training.

When applied to women, risk-based classification systems designed for men may overclassify women and thereby place too many of them in restrictive custody (Farr, 2000; Harer & Langan, 2001). However, recent research by Harer and Langan indicated that a risk classification instrument used in federal prison predicts violent behavior equally well for male and female inmates. Yet, due to the low prevalence of violence among women, dynamic measures of risk prediction might enhance a risk-based classification system. Such dynamic risk measures include educational attainment at prison admission, substance abuse, work skills and habits, relationship skills, peer associations, and attitudes (Harer & Langan). These factors could be used to lower the classification level of female offenders and thereby allow them to take part in programs that are not restrictive such as education, substance-abuse treatment, job training, and contact with children.

Another issue confronting correctional management involves specialized training for staff working with female inmates. Rasche (2003) used the phrase "male inmate preference" to describe "the pervasive tendency among correctional workers to dislike working with female offenders or to avoid working at women's prisons, and to view such duty as undesirable" (p. 450). Male correctional officers may experience difficulties supervising inmates of the opposite sex; they may feel the need to change their speech or behavior. Female correctional officers prefer to supervise male prisoners because they are more respectful and appreciative of women officers than are female inmates. However, many male and female officers believe that women prisoners demand more, complain more, and are more defiant than men are. Correctional workers learn these negative attitudes about female inmates from on-the-job inculcation into an officer subculture (Rasche).

Male correctional officers may also fear that women inmates will accuse them of a sexual offense (e.g., rape, sexual assault, unlawful touching). Yet, according to Henriques and Gilbert (2003), "The traditional response to charges of sexual assault brought against prison employees is to subject the female inmate to punishment (e.g., administrative, disciplinary, or protective confinement)" (p. 263). As larger numbers of women are incarcerated, the potential for sexual assault by male officers becomes a greater concern. However, the sexual assault of women inmates by male officers is extremely difficult to study. No one knows the extent of this problem, but some states (e.g., New Jersey, Connecticut, Delaware, New York) have passed laws that make sex between inmates and correctional employees a crime of rape.

New correctional officers are typically informed of these statutes during preservice training. However, the standard training for correctional officers in the United States focuses on operations (e.g., policies, rules, regulations) and mechanics (e.g., firearms training, housing and body searches, riot control tactics). There is little specialized training for staff working with women inmates. Most state correctional systems treat all inmates and all prisons the same in terms of rules, supplies, and assignments (Pollack-Byrne, 1990; Rasche, 2003). Rasche encouraged additional training that explains the differences in demographic characteristics, needs during incarceration, and personality between male and female inmates.

Farkas and Rand (1999) also argued that prison management should take the differences between men and women into account when forming correctional policies. In particular, they discussed the effect of cross-gender searches on female inmates. In 1993, the Ninth Circuit Court ruled that the practice of male officers searching female inmates violated the Eighth Amendment to the U.S. Constitution because it potentially could cause severe psychological injury, emotional pain, and suffering. This ruling hinged on the gender-specific experiences of many women inmates before incarceration. Specifically, a sizable minority (43 percent) of women inmates in state prisons reported physical or sexual abuse before incarceration; only 12 percent of male inmates reported a history of abuse (Snell & Morton, 1994). Due to the past mistreatment suffered by women prisoners at the hands of men, the Ninth Circuit Court felt that allowing male officers to search female inmates amounted to cruel and unusual punishment. Farkas and Rand endorsed same-sex searches of inmates and remarked, "The applicable legal standard should consider women inmates' different histories, needs, incarceration experience, and adaptations" (p. 52). A focus on the gender-specific needs of incarcerated women is a consistent theme throughout much of the policy-based research on female imprisonment.

In a study of women inmates in Britain, Mawby (1982) discovered that women need educational services in prison. In fact, some women rely upon education to cope with the deprivations of prison life. Unfortunately, educational programs for female inmates in the United States have not always been a priority among prison management. *Glover v. Johnson* (1979) was a landmark U.S. court case about education in women's prisons. It was alleged that the educational and vocational programs provided to women in Michigan's prison system were not equivalent to those for male inmates. The case revolved around issues of equal protection and due process. Ultimately, the court decided that the state of Michigan must provide female inmates with the same educational opportunities that are provided to incarcerated men. The verdict also required the prison system to offer vocational programs, postsecondary education, and legal education for female inmates (Muraskin, 2003). This court case is quite germane in light of the benefit that women derive from educational programs in prison.

However, Sheridan (1996) cautioned against adopting gender-based standards for prison programming. Many current correctional programs and services provided to inmates are already gender stereotyped. For instance, female inmates are significantly more likely than males to see a mental health professional, and incarcerated women are twice as likely to receive prescriptions for psychotropic drugs than are their male equivalents. This practice results in the overmedication of women and the neglect of men. Likewise, Sheridan remarked that "although the majority of incarcerated parents are fathers, the vast majority of parenting programs are offered in women's facilities" (p. 432). This is an example of gender-based programming. He recommended that male and female correctional institutions should have equivalent programs and services that are tailored to the needs of the individual correctional client and not provided on the basis of gender stereotypes.

CURRENT ISSUES IN FEMALE IMPRISONMENT

In general, the field of corrections has grown less rehabilitative and more punitive over the past thirty years. Several notable examples of punitive public policy with implications for corrections include three-strikes laws, boot camps, and capital punishment. Indeed, Danner (2003) described current criminal justice policy in the following passage:

> The use of a baseball analogy—"three strikes and you're out"—to refer to the policy of mandatory life sentences for those persons convicted of three felonies illustrates the exclusion of women from the crime debates. Although it's called the national pastime, women don't identify with baseball much, have no significant presence in the sport, and reap few of its economic benefits (facts true of most professional sports). Yet it is in this sense that baseball represents an excellent analogy to the crime bills since women remain largely invisible from the debates surrounding criminal justice reforms. (p. 211)

Usually, public debate and legislative initiatives on the subject of crime and punishment regard women only as victims. However, criminal justice policies affect women with both unintended consequences and hidden costs.

According to Danner (2003), the three-strikes analogy may be interpreted as three ways in which women will be harmed by and required to pay for reform in the criminal justice system. First, in order to fund expansion of the criminal justice system in an era of balanced budgets, money will most likely be taken from social programs for women and children. Women workers in public-sector social service agencies will also lose their jobs. Second, any additional jobs that are created in the criminal justice system will be primarily for men, due to harassment and the masculine work culture associated with this field. Third, women will shoulder the responsibility for care of children, the elderly, or disabled adults who are left behind when their family members are incarcerated. A recent example of this get-tough policy involved a case in Florida in which a woman was sentenced to thirty months in prison for not stopping a party held in her home by her teenage son where other teenagers used drugs and alcohol (*John Walsh Show*, 2002). This family had already experienced hardship with the recent murder of the father, and with the mother now in prison, the teenage children were left in the care of their grandmother.

Lauen (1997) also warned that the punitive three-strikes policies sometimes result in the inappropriate use of incarceration for women offenders.
Consider the following case:

> Rose Medina is locked up in a Colorado prison. She is about forty years old.
> Her sentence: life without parole. Unless the courts overturn her sentence or
> the governor commutes her sentence, she will die in prison. Her last offense
> of conviction: forgery. Her offense of conviction before that one: forgery. Her
> offense before that one: forgery. Rose was caught, charged, and convicted un-
> der a habitual offender law. During her last trial, her defense attorney was ne-
> gotiating with the District Attorney for a sentence that was mutually agreeable
> to both sides. The best deal he got from the District Attorney was a twenty-
> year sentence. Rose thought twenty years in prison for forgery was ridiculous.
> She turned it down. With no agreement, the District Attorney persuaded the
> court to go for the maximum allowable sentence, life without parole. A young,
> insecure sentencing judge attempting to "make her mark" in a very conserva-
> tive community agreed with the District Attorney's recommendation. Need-
> less to say, there is a lot of room for a change of policy regarding prison use.
> (Lauen, p. 9)

These policies have resulted in a 24 percent increase in the average length
of stay in state prisons for persons found guilty of nonviolent crimes. Sentence lengths for violent crimes have increased by as much as 90 percent as
a result of new punitive public policies.

Another corrective method for dealing with young, nonviolent female
offenders involves shock incarceration programs commonly known as boot
camps. Prison boot camps combine a militaristic atmosphere and hard labor
with treatment and therapy. The intensity of shock incarceration is designed
to deter offenders from future criminality and instill in them the discipline
required for conformity to the laws of society. However, boot camps have
been criticized because offenders who would normally receive probation are
sometimes sentenced to these residential programs instead, widening the
criminal justice system's net of control.

MacKenzie and Donaldson (1996) looked at six prison boot-camp programs for women. At the time of their research, twenty-five states operated
thirty-nine correctional boot camps. However, only thirteen states had
women in their programs. MacKenzie and Donaldson noted several problematic aspects of boot-camp programs for women. First, the requirements
seemed too physically strenuous for female inmates. Inmates with physical
health problems were unable to participate and often dropped out prema-
turely. Furthermore, participants who suffered prior abuse reported that the
confrontational nature of boot camps reminded them of their dysfunctional,
abusive relationships. Moreover, few of the boot-camp programs offered
counseling for abuse or treatment for substance abuse problems. Since many
female inmates have histories of domestic violence coupled with patterns of

substance abuse, the absence of services to address either problem remains a serious drawback of boot camps for women.

Capital punishment is the most punitive of any sentence imposed by courts in the United States today. However, only about 1.9 percent of death sentences have been imposed on women (Death Penalty Information Center, 2003). Table 2 shows the names of these women, the states in which the executions took place, the methods of execution, and the execution dates.

Since August 8, 1962, only eleven women have been put to death in the United States as punishment for their crimes. Yet, almost two-thirds of these executions took place since the year 2000. This suggests that the rate of executions for women inmates convicted of capital crimes is increasing in the United States.

Since 1976, 143 female offenders have been sentenced to death (Death Penalty Information Center, 2003). As Schulberg (2003) noted, "The United States holds the dubious distinction of housing more women condemned to death than any other country in the world, although this population remains virtually invisible unless a woman is scheduled for imminent execution" (p. 284). Unfortunately, due to the small population of women on death row and their "invisibility," researchers have not given much attention to executions of female offenders. A lack of research limits the development of gender-centric explanations for women's involvement in capital crimes.

However, Farr (1997) examined aggravating and differentiating factors in the cases of white and minority women on death row. She included thirty-five female murderers in her study: twenty whites and fifteen women of color (African American or Latina). More white women were on death row for the murder of their husbands or lovers than were minority women. Most of the murders were intraracial. That is, white women tended to kill white victims, and minority women murdered minority victims. Farr noticed an interesting difference in the media and prosecutorial treatment of women from different races. White women were depicted as rational and manipulative, cold-hearted killers with a seductive side. However, African-American and Hispanic women were portrayed as hotheaded, explosive, vengeful, and likely to strike out in rage. Women of color were also more often sentenced to death, although their crimes were less aggravated than the offenses of white women. Farr suggested that these cases involved stereotypes of women marginalized by race or sexual orientation.

CONCLUSION

The experience of imprisonment itself varies considerably between the sexes. Female offenders are more likely than men to enter prison with familial issues, histories of abuse, and problems related to drugs or alcohol. Women adapt to prison differently than do their male equivalents, often relying upon friendships and contacts with the outside world. The needs of incarcerated

Table 2
Women Executed in the United States, 1962–2002

Name of Inmate	State of Execution	Method of Execution	Date of Execution
Elizabeth Ann Duncan	California	Gas Chamber	August 8, 1962
Velma Barfield	North Carolina	Lethal Injection	November 2, 1984
Karla Faye Tucker	Texas	Lethal Injection	February 3, 1998
Judy Buenoano	Florida	Electrocution	March 30, 1998
Betty Lou Beets	Texas	Lethal Injection	February 24, 2000
Christina Riggs	Arkansas	Lethal Injection	May 2, 2000
Wanda Jean Allen	Oklahoma	Lethal Injection	January 11, 2001
Marilyn Plantz	Oklahoma	Lethal Injection	May 1, 2001
Lois Nadean Smith	Oklahoma	Lethal Injection	December 4, 2001
Lynda Lyon Block	Alabama	Electrocution	May 10, 2002
Aileen Wournos	Florida	Lethal Injection	October 9, 2002

Source: Death Penalty Information Center, 2003

women seem to cluster around educational and job-training services, parenting, and treatment for abuse and chemical dependency. Correctional management should take these differences between the sexes into account when following and forming policy.

Most offenders who are incarcerated in a correctional facility in the United States will eventually be released and reintegrated with society. This is true for both men and women. However, women may need more comprehensive services after incarceration. Richie (2001) looked at the challenges incarcerated women face as they return to their communities. In particular, she suggested four approaches that might facilitate the process of reintegration into the community. Richie noted, "Most services that are successful in helping women reintegrate into the community have hired (or are otherwise influenced by) women who have been similarly situated" (p. 385). Women ex-convicts benefit from comprehensive programs that offer assistance with multiple needs. Community development linkages also increase the quality of life for women returning to their neighborhoods after prison. This approach incorporates policy-level work, community organizing, and social change strategies. Empowerment and consciousness-raising initiatives enable formerly imprisoned women to become empowered to overcome the social stigma that they face. These initiatives involve women with self-help networks. Finally, female ex-convicts need a network of peers or mentors to assist with the restructuring of a stable life.

REFERENCES

Bloom, B., & Chesney-Lind, M. (2003). Women in prison: Vengeful equity. In R. Muraskin (Ed.), *It's a crime: Women and justice* (3rd ed., pp. 175–195). Upper Saddle River, NJ: Prentice-Hall.

Browne, D.C.H. (1989). Incarcerated mothers and parenting. *Journal of Family Violence, 4*(2), 211–221.

Bureau of Justice Statistics. (2002). *Correctional populations in the United States, 1998* (NCJ-192929). Washington, DC: U.S. Department of Justice.

Carlen, P. (1994). Why study women's imprisonment? Or anyone else's? An indefinite answer. *British Journal of Criminology, 34,* 131–140.

Casey-Acevedo, K., & Bakken, T. (2002). Visiting women in prison: Who visits and who cares? *Journal of Offender Rehabilitation, 32*(3), 67–83.

Danner, M.J.E. (2003). Three strikes and it's *women* who are out: The hidden consequences of criminal justice policy reforms. In R. Muraskin (Ed.), *It's a crime: Women and justice* (3rd ed., pp. 209–219). Upper Saddle River, NJ: Prentice-Hall.

Death Penalty Information Center. (2003). *Women and the death penalty* [On-line]. Available: http://www.deathpenaltyinfo.org/article.php?did=230&scid=24# executed

Dodge, L. M. (1999). "One female prisoner is more trouble than twenty males": Women convicts in Illinois prisons, 1835–1896. *Journal of Social History, 32*(4), 907–930.

Ellis, D. P., & Austin, P. (1971). Menstruation and aggressive behavior in a correctional center for women. *Journal of Criminal Law, Criminology, and Police Science, 62*(3), 388–395.

Farkas, M. A., & Rand, K.R.L. (1999). Sex matters: A gender-specific standard for cross-gender searches of inmates. *Women & Criminal Justice, 10*(3), 31–55.

Farr, K. A. (1997). Aggravating and differentiating factors in the cases of white and minority women on death row. *Crime & Delinquency, 43*(3), 260–278.

Farr, K. A. (2000). Classification for female inmates: Moving forward. *Crime & Delinquency, 46*(1), 3–17.

Feinman, C. (1986). *Women in the criminal justice system.* New York: Praeger.

Freedman, E. B. (1996). The prison lesbian: Race, class, and the construction of the aggressive female homosexual, 1915–1965. *Feminist Studies, 22*(2), 397–423.

French, L. (1977). An assessment of the black female prisoner in the south. *Signs: Journal of Women in Culture and Society, 3*(2), 483–488.

Gaudin, J. M., & Sutphen, R. (1993). Foster care vs. extended family care for children of incarcerated mothers. *Journal of Offender Rehabilitation, 19*(3/4), 129–147.

Giallombardo, R. (1966). Social roles in a prison for women. *Social Problems, 13*(3), 268–287.

Gilligan, C. (1979). Woman's place in a man's life cycle. *Harvard Education Review, 49*(4), 431–446.

Gottfredson, M. R., & Hirschi, T. (1990). *A general theory of crime.* Palo Alto, CA: Stanford University Press.

Grana, S. J. (2002). *Women and (in)justice: The criminal and civil effects of the common law on women's lives.* Boston: Allyn & Bacon.

Greenfeld, L. A., & Snell, T. L. (1999). *Women offenders* (NCJ-175688). Washington, DC: U.S. Department of Justice.

Harer, M. D., & Langan, N. P. (2001). Gender differences in predictors of prison violence: Assessing the predictive validity of a risk classification system. *Crime & Delinquency, 47*(4), 513–536.

Henriques, Z. W., & Gilbert, E. (2003). Sexual abuse and sexual assault of women in prison. In R. Muraskin (Ed.), *It's a crime: Women and justice* (3rd ed., pp. 258–272). Upper Saddle River, NJ: Prentice-Hall.

Howard, J. (1777). *State of prisons.* London: Dent.

Irwin, J., Schiraldi, V., & Ziedenberg, J. (2000). America's one million nonviolent prisoners. *Social Justice, 27*(2), 135–147.

John Walsh Show. (2002). *Paying the price for your kids' actions* [On-line]. Available: http://www.johnwalsh.tv/cgi-bin/topics/today.cgi?id=209

Johnson, D. R., & Scheuble, L. K. (1991). Gender bias in the disposition of juvenile court referrals: The effects of time and location. *Criminology, 29*, 677–699.

Jones, R. S. (1993). Coping with separation: Adaptive responses of women prisoners. *Women & Criminal Justice, 5*(1), 71–97.

Kruttschnitt, C. (1983). Race relations and the female inmate. *Crime & Delinquency, 29*(4), 577–592.

Kruttschnitt, C., Gartner, R., & Miller, A. (2000). Doing her own time? Women's responses to prison in the context of the old and the new penology. *Criminology, 38*(3), 681–717.

Lauen, R. (1997). *Positive approaches to corrections: Research, policy, and practice.* Lanham, MD: American Correctional Association.

LeFlore, L., & Holston, M. A. (1989). Perceived importance of parenting behaviors as reported by inmate mothers: An exploratory study. *Journal of Offender Counseling, Services, & Rehabilitation, 14*(1), 5–21.

Leger, R. G. (1987). Lesbianism among women prisoners: Participants and nonparticipants. *Criminal Justice and Behavior, 14,* 448–467.

MacKenzie, D. L., & Donaldson, H. (1996). Boot camp for women offenders. *Criminal Justice Review, 21*(1), 21–43.

Martin, M. (1997). Connected mothers: A follow-up study of incarcerated women and their children. *Women & Criminal Justice, 8*(4), 1–23.

Mauer, M., & Huling, T. (1995). *Young black Americans and the criminal justice system: 5 years later.* Washington, DC: Sentencing Project.

Mawby, R. I. (1982). Women in prison: A British study. *Crime and Delinquency, 28*(1), 24–39.

Muraskin, R. (2003). Disparate treatment in correctional facilities: Looking back. In R. Muraskin (Ed.), *It's a crime: Women and justice* (3rd ed., pp. 220–230). Upper Saddle River, NJ: Prentice-Hall.

Noddings, N. (1984). *Caring: A feminine approach to ethics and moral education.* Berkeley: University of California Press.

Pelka-Slugocka, M. D., & Slugocki, L. (1980). The impact of imprisonment on the family life of women convicts. *International Journal of Offender Therapy and Comparative Criminology, 24*(3), 249–259.

Platt, A. M. (1977). *The child savers: The invention of delinquency* (2nd ed.). Chicago: University of Chicago Press.

Pollack-Byrne, J. M. (1990). *Women, prison, and crime.* New York: Greenwood.

Rafter, N. (1983). Prisons for women, 1790–1980. In M. Tonry & N. Morries (Eds.), *Crime and justice: An annual review of research* (Vol. 5). Chicago: University of Chicago Press.

Rasche, C. E. (2003). The dislike of female offenders among correctional officers: The need for specialized training. In R. Muraskin (Ed.), *It's a crime: Women and justice* (3rd ed., pp. 450–465). Upper Saddle River, NJ: Prentice-Hall.

Rausch, S. P. (1996). Current issues in prison management. *Criminal Justice Review, 21*(1), 1–3.

Richie, B. E. (2001). Challenges incarcerated women face as they return to their communities: Findings from life history interviews. *Crime & Delinquency, 47*(3), 368–389.

Ross, J. I., & Richards, S. C. (2002). *Behind bars: Surviving prison.* Indianapolis, IN: Alpha Books.

Russell, K. K. (2000). Racial hoaxes: Applied critical race theory. In S. S. Simpson (Ed.), *Of crime and criminality: The uses of theory in everyday life* (pp. 47–59). Thousand Oaks, CA: Pine Forge Press.

Schulberg, D. E. (2003). Dying to get out: The execution of females in the post-Fuhrman era of the death penalty in the United States. In R. Muraskin (Ed.), *It's a crime: Women and justice* (3rd ed., pp. 273–288). Upper Saddle River, NJ: Prentice-Hall.

Sharp, S. F., & Marcus-Mendoza, S. T. (2001). It's a family affair: Incarcerated women and their families. *Women & Criminal Justice, 12*(4), 21–49.

Sheridan, M. J. (1996). Comparison of the life experiences and personal functioning of men and women in prison. *Families in Society: The Journal of Contemporary Human Services, 77*(7), 423–434.

Snell, T. L., & Morton, D. C. (1994). *Women in Prison* (NCJ-145321). Washington, DC: U.S. Department of Justice.

Van Wormer, K. W. (1987). Female prison families: How are they dysfunctional? *International Journal of Comparative and Applied Criminal Justice, 11,* 263–271.

Van Wormer, K. W., & Bates, F. L. (1979). A study of leadership roles in an Alabama prison for women. *Human Relations, 32*(9), 793–801.

Visher, C. A. (1983). Gender, police arrest decision, and notions of chivalry. *Criminology, 21,* 5–28.

Ward, D. A., & Kassebaum, G. G. (1964). Homosexuality: A mode of adaptation in a prison for women. *Social Problems, 12*(2), 159–177.

6

PRISONERS' RIGHTS AND STATES' RESPONSIBILITIES

Wayne Gillespie

INTRODUCTION

Life inside prison is, for the most part, a combination of contradictory ideas and goals; it is an oxymoron. This is especially true concerning the issue of prisoners' rights. For example, the process of incarceration is a punishment designed to deprive lawbreakers of freedom, access to goods and services, heterosexual relations, autonomy, and security (Sykes, 1958). Although imprisonment entails the deprivation of many basic liberties, inmates do not lose all their rights. Despite the fact that prisoners may be lawbreakers, they are still guaranteed certain liberties under the U.S. Constitution, the Civil Rights Act, and international accords such as those suggested by the United Nations (UN) Congress on the Prevention of Crime and the Treatment of Offenders. Thus, the oxymoron of prisoners' rights occurs because imprisonment involves a punishment based on the deprivation of certain liberties (e.g., freedom) that must simultaneously protect other rights (e.g., safeguards against cruel and unusual punishment).

The oxymoron of prisoners' rights is most likely a historical artifact that was generated by an evolution in both society and culture. Emile Durkheim (1933), one of the founding fathers of sociology, studied the transition of primitive cultures to modern societies. Using historical and anthropological evidence, he noted that the law in primitive societies was primarily repressive in nature. According to Durkheim, law in primitive cultures functioned to reinforce social and religious values. He noted that the violation of either written or unwritten laws in primitive societies often resulted in harsh penal sanctions. However, he believed that modern law would transcend the repressive legal codes associated with primitive cultures. In particular, Durkheim predicted that the law in modern societies would primarily be restitutive in nature. That is, he suggested that the restitutive law of modern societies would need to accommodate a more complex division of labor. Harsh penal sanctions for lawbreaking would be untenable, since in a truly modern society the citizenry would be bound by the different economic roles that each person plays. Hence, modern law would become administrative or civil in nature. Lawbreakers would not receive harsh sentences, but instead would be required to pay restitution or perform other works that would not interrupt the complex interdependences of modern social life.

The modern social world is markedly different from ancient society. Scholars stress that modern social life sustains a high degree of rationality and is less entrenched in magic and mysticism (Sheleff, 1997). Scientists have replaced wizards, and tribal councils are now governmental bureaucracies. Other scholars studying the modern social world have emphasized related aspects, including the shift from an agricultural way of life to an industrial mode of production, the concentration of people living in cities and towns, and the increased use of transportation and communication. Methods of dealing with criminals have kept pace with the broader societal changes over time.

In premodern times, punishment was often synonymous with torture. Indeed, the punishment of criminals was often a public spectacle such as flogging, quartering, or hanging. Imprisonment surely existed in ancient times, but it was employed less frequently, and it was often simply used to detain the offender until physical punishment or execution. In fact, Johnson (1996) noted, "confining dangerous people is an old if not venerable practice that, though generally carried out on a small scale, dates back to at least Biblical times" (p. 4). However, Foucault (1995) suggested that a "rupture in history" occurred after the birth of the prison system in the Middle Ages. By this he meant that the transition from torture to incapacitation shifted the object of punishment from the body of the criminal to his or her soul and psyche. Incapacitation vis-à-vis imprisonment is the ideal mechanism by which to exact psychological punishment.

Furthermore, during the Enlightenment, citizens pressured rulers to make punishment both rational and predictable. Imprisonment became seen as a *civilized* method of punishment (Johnson, 1996). The transition from torture to imprisonment ultimately legitimized the sovereign powers of modern governments (Beccaria, 1963; Foucault, 1995). It created a social contract between rulers and citizenry. The population at large implicitly agreed to conform to the civil law and resist revolution, while the sovereignty consented to abandon arbitrary and capricious physical torture (Beccaria, 1963).

Foucault (1995) drew upon the idea of a panopticon in order to make a broader statement about modern social life. The panopticon was an ideal type of prison with a centralized watchtower surrounded by enclosures of prisoners. Hypothetically, the prisoners could not see inside the tower to determine if they were being watched. The possibility of being watched without the capability to see who was watching instilled a sense of guilt and responsibility in the prisoners. Foucault claimed that the panopticon design also created powerlessness among prisoners. In fact, he went on to say that the principles associated with the panopticon have not been limited to prisons alone; they have penetrated other areas of social life (e.g., schools, businesses, factories). In essence, modern society has become a prison, with the general public constrained by its own sense of guilt and responsibility. According to Foucault, the powerlessness that accompanies these feelings of guilt ultimately benefits the ruling class by reifying the status quo. Thus, prisons are among those social institutions that perpetuate the inequalities that exist in modern society.

Contemporary methods of punishment are distinct from those of prior eras. Regardless of the rationale behind this transformation, the fact remains that imprisonment has replaced torture and corporal punishment as the favored method of punishment throughout most of the modern "civilized" world. These historical changes set the stage for the oxymoron of prisoners' rights that exists in the United States today. Prior to the twentieth century, inmates retained no rights once imprisoned. In fact, in *Ruffin v. Commonwealth* (1871), prisoners in the United States were ruled to be slaves of the state. In the absence of concern for prisoners' rights, punishment was certain, swift, and severe. Punishment was absolute, and its effects could be seen on the prisoners' bodies in the form of physical scars. The familiar dictum "an eye for an eye" was practiced with some regularity prior to the modern age.

The oxymoron of prisoners' rights did not exist in premodern times because prisoners' rights did not exist. The notion of prisoners' rights eventually developed as a result of changes in society that were spurred by economic and social developments, class interests, reason, and enlightenment. Although punitive methods evolved, the goals of punishment did not keep pace. The antiquated ideas of retribution and revenge remain strong goals of punishment in the modern world and particularly in the American criminal justice system. It is this mismatch of punishment's means and goals that has generated contradictions concerning the issue of prisoners' rights. Perhaps the most fundamental question relating to prisoners' rights is this: How do we punish fairly and humanely?

HUMANE TREATMENT OF PRISONERS

Concern over the humane treatment of prisoners is a touchstone in the development of prisoners' rights. The transition of a prisoner's status from that of a slave of the state to a person worthy of basic civil rights is directly tied to broader sociohistorical events. The two world wars generated the impetus for concern over humane treatment of prisoners. In particular, it was the Nazi regime's inhumane and barbaric treatment of concentration camp prisoners that led to international provisions on humane treatment. In fact, the expression "humanely treated," as it applies to prisoners, can be traced to the Hague Regulations and the two 1929 Geneva Conventions.

The Diplomatic Conference of Geneva of 1949 revised the 1929 guidelines relative to the treatment of prisoners of war. The procedures set forth in 1949 consist of 143 articles and five annexes. In particular, Article 13 pertains to the general protection of prisoners of war:

> Prisoners of war must at all times be humanely treated. Any unlawful act or omission by the Detaining Power causing death or seriously endangering the health of a prisoner of war in its custody is prohibited, and will be regarded as a serious breach of the Convention. In particular, no prisoner of war may be subjected to physical mutilation or to medical or scientific experiments of any kind which are not justified by the medical, dental or hospital treatment of the prisoner concerned and carried out in his interest. Likewise, prisoners of war must at all times be protected, particularly against acts of violence or intimidation and against insults and public curiosity. Measures of reprisal against prisoners of war are prohibited. (International Committee of the Red Cross 1949/2001)

Although not entirely relevant to domestic prisoners, the guidelines set forth at the Geneva Conventions laid the groundwork for the rights of all prisoners.

In 1955, the First UN Congress on the Prevention of Crime and the Treatment of Offenders was also held in Geneva, Switzerland, and set forth specific guidelines for the humane treatment of prisoners and the management of domestic institutions. These *Standard Minimum Rules for the Treatment of Prisoners* were approved by the UN's Economic and Social Council and put into effect in 1957. The *Rules* consist of two parts: Part I deals with the overall management of correctional facilities and applies to all prisoners, and Part II covers special categories dealt with in the various sections of Part I.

Part I of the *Rules* outlines recommendations that are particularly germane to prisoners' rights and concern over the humane treatment of inmates. A basic tenet governing Part I requires all provisions to be applied impartially regardless of race, color, sex, language, religion, political or other opinion, national or social origin, property, birth, or other status. The Part I rules cover myriad topics, including prisoners' registration, separation of categories, accommodation, personal hygiene, clothing and bedding, food, exercise, medical services, discipline and punishment, restraint, information to and complaints by prisoners, contact with the outside world, books, religion, personal property, notification of death, illness, transfer, and removal of prisoners (Office of the UN High Commissioner for Human Rights, 1957/2001). It also contains guidelines on institutional personnel and inspection.

A brief review of these provisions is necessary in order to fully appreciate the impact they have had on life inside prison. The UN noted that records should be kept on each prisoner. In essence, prisoners should be registered, and the information therein should contain the prisoner's identity, the reasons for his or her commitment and the authority therefore, and the day and hour of this admission and release. The *Rules* also specify a separation of categories, or the segregation of prisoners based upon specific characteristics. For example, it is suggested that institutions take the sex, age, criminal record, and the legal reason for their detention into account when making housing decisions. Ideally, this means that men and women should be kept in separate institutions, that untried prisoners should be set apart from convicted inmates, and that young prisoners should be segregated from adult convicts.

The UN also specified guidelines concerning accommodations for prisoners. For example, the *Rules* call for inmates to be housed in individual cells, which each prisoner could occupy by himself or herself at night. If dormitory-style housing is used, then inmates must be supervised at night. The provisions also require accommodations to meet all requirements of health that pertain to lighting, floor space, heating, and ventilation. For instance, the *Rules* suggest that windows should allow prisoners to read or work by natural light and should be constructed as to enable air circulation in the absence of artificial ventilation. Toilet, bath, and shower installations should also be adequate. Finally, in regard to accommodations, cooking utensils (e.g., pans) should be properly sanitized. Many of these humane provisions prevent outbreaks of communicable diseases such as tuberculosis.

Related to the toilet and bath, prisoners should be required to maintain personal hygiene and cleanliness. As such, inmates should be provided with water and basic toiletries that are necessary for health and cleanliness. The *Rules* also stipulate that prisoners should be allowed to keep a good appearance and thereby preserve their self-respect. It is to this end that institutions must provide barber facilities for hair and beard maintenance. Male prisoners must also be allowed to shave regularly. In regard to clothing, uniforms or a suitable outfit of clothing must be provided to prisoners if they are not permitted to wear their own garments. Uniforms should not degrade or humiliate the inmates. According to the *Rules,* underclothing must be changed and washed often in order to preserve personal hygiene. The provisions also require correctional facilities to provide inmates with separate beds and sufficient bedding.

On a more fundamental level, the UN advised that prisoners should receive drinking water and food. The food must be nutritional and good in its quality, in addition to being well prepared and served. The *Rules* also provide stipulations concerning exercise and sport, such that prisoners should have at least one hour of suitable exercise per day in the open air. Installations and equipment should be provided at correctional facilities for adequate physical and recreational training.

In order to ensure the humane treatment of its prisoners, the state must oversee the health of all inmates and provide for their basic medical services. All prisoners should be examined immediately after admission and thereafter as needed. Inmates afflicted with a contagious disease should be segregated. Sick prisoners should receive the proper medical care even when this means transferring ailing inmates to specialized medical institutions or civil hospitals. According to the *Rules,* at least one member of the prison's medical staff should be trained in psychiatry, and psychiatric services should be available for the diagnosis and treatment of mental illness among the inmate population. In addition, medical staff are expected to inspect the quantity, quality, and preparation of food; the hygiene and cleanliness of the institution and the inmates; the sanitation, heating, lighting, and ventilation of the facility; the cleanliness and suitability of the prisoners' clothing and bedding; and the observance of the rules concerning physical exercise. Finally, prenatal and postnatal treatment must be available to pregnant female prisoners. There are several other specialized rules that apply to childbirth inside prison.

The UN also set forth guidelines concerning discipline and punishment. First, the *Rules* concede that discipline and order must be upheld with firmness. However, there must be no unnecessary restriction except for what is required to maintain safe custody and well-ordered institutional life. Likewise, disciplinary offenses must be brought before an administrative authority and should always be determined by a legal proceeding. Prisoners may be punished only in accordance with the law and never twice for the same crime. The UN prohibited any type of corporal punishment, isolation in a dark cell, or any cruel, inhumane, or degrading punishments for disciplinary offenses. Close confinement or reduction in diet are also not appropriate punishments, unless the medical doctor has examined the inmate and certified in writing that he or she is able to withstand it.

Related to issues of discipline, the instruments of restraint (e.g., handcuffs, chains, irons, straitjackets) should never be applied as punishment. The UN does not condone the use of chains or irons as restraints. Moreover, other methods of restraint should only be used during transfers, for medical reasons, or by order of the warden when other means of control fail.

The *Rules* also cover the issue of information to and complaints by prisoners. For example, according the UN's provisions, prisoners are entitled to written information as it pertains to the regulations governing the treatment of prisoners, the disciplinary rules of the prison, and the proper way to seek information and make complaints. This information should be read to the prisoner if he or she is illiterate. Furthermore, all prisoners should have the chance to make requests or complaints to prison administration at least once per day during the week. Prisoners should be permitted to make a request or complaint without restriction provided that they use approved channels. Requests and complaints that are not frivolous or groundless should be addressed in an expedient manner.

The humane treatment of prisoners is also promoted by allowing inmates contact with the outside world. Such contact takes several forms, but the main goal is to keep the lines of communication open for all prisoners. The *Rules* hold that prisoners should be allowed to receive visits and correspondence from upstanding friends and family members. In addition, foreign nationals should be allowed the opportunity to consult with their diplomatic representatives. Prisoners must also be granted access to newspapers, periodicals, and wireless transmissions (e.g., television, radio) in order to keep abreast of important news events. Both recreational and instructional books should be available for inmates; every correctional institution must have a library to which all prisoners have access.

Not surprisingly, the UN also set forth provisions concerning religion. Freedom of religion should be allowed, and a qualified religious agent (e.g., priest, rabbi, shaman) should be appointed to hold regular religious services if a sufficient number of prisoners of one religion are incarcerated at the same correctional facility. The *Rules* also stipulate that a qualified religious leader should not be refused to any inmate and that every inmate should be permitted to freely attend the religious services in the prison. Inmates should also be allowed to have religious texts and personal property throughout their imprisonment.

Further, the UN's provisions pertain to the retention of prisoners' property. Specifically, prison officials are expected to secure all money, valuables, clothing, and other items that are not allowed inside the institution. Such objects should be inventoried, and the inventory should be signed by the inmate. Upon release, all items should be returned to the ex-convict except the monies that he or she used during imprisonment. A receipt should be used to document the return of these goods.

The *Rules* also cover the removal of prisoners from correctional institutions. In the event that a prisoner is transferred from one institution to another, proper safeguards must be in place to protect inmates from public view, ridicule, insult, or publicity. Correctional personnel should also inform the immediate family of any prisoner about transfers. During transport, inmates must receive adequate light and ventilation and never be subjected to uncalled-for hardship. The state must assume all expenses involved in the transfer of prisoners.

In addition to transfers, the UN's *Rules* cover notification of death or illness. In particular, correctional officials should notify the immediate family of any prisoner who dies or becomes seriously ill. Likewise, inmates should be informed without delay of the death or serious illness of any close relative. Although international provisions do not cover funeral visitation, many prisons in the United States allow inmates to attend funeral services of next of kin.

In an ideal world, all countries associated with the UN would abide by these minimum standards governing the humane treatment of prisoners.

However, this is not an ideal world. Although the provisions have constituted international and diplomatic agreement since 1957, they were largely
ignored by the United States. For example, Anderson (2000) recounts one
inmate's description of the living conditions at the Kentucky State Reformatory (KSR) in 1978:

> [The] place was nasty. . . . There were roaches and rats. The building leaked
> when it rained, and you nearly froze to death in cold weather. We were stacked
> like cordwood, with no room to move. Half the toilets didn't work, and there
> weren't enough of them to begin with. I wasn't raised under these conditions,
> and it made me mad when I realized what the state was subjecting me to. People
> treat their livestock better than we were treated. The whole place was really a
> mess. The way I felt, for them to have killed me would have been an act of
> mercy. (p. 2)

The unsanitary and inhumane conditions at KSR eventually led this inmate
to file a lawsuit in federal court. Incidentally, the case, *Thompson v. Commonwealth of Kentucky* (1979), was not based on international statutes, but rather
on extant U.S. law.

ISSUES RAISED BY CORRECTIONAL LAWSUITS

In the 1960s and 1970s, prisoners throughout the United States began
to challenge the manner in which they were treated by the state. They called
for better prison conditions, improved medical care, more rehabilitative programs, and the right to refuse psychiatric medications (Dick, 1978). In fact,
a specific part of the U.S. Code (i.e., Civil Rights Act of 1871, Title 42,
Chapter 21, Subchapter 1, Section 1983) allows inmates to make legal claims
that the conditions of imprisonment violate the Constitution. Commonly
known as Section 1983, it reads as follows:

> Every person who, under color of any statute, ordinance, regulation, custom,
> or usage, of any State or Territory or the District of Columbia, subjects, or
> causes to be subjected, any citizen of the United States, or other person within
> the jurisdiction thereof to the deprivation of any rights, privileges, or immuni-
> ties secured by the Constitution and its laws, shall be liable to the party injured
> in an action at law, suit in equity, or other proper proceeding for redress, ex-
> cept that in any action brought against a judicial officer for an act or omission
> taken in such officer's judicial capacity, injunctive relief shall not be granted
> unless a declaratory decree was violated or declaratory relief was unavailable.
> For the purposes of this section, any Act of Congress applicable exclusively to
> the District of Columbia shall be considered to be a statute of the District of
> Columbia. (Legal Information Institute, 2001)

In *Cooper v. Pate* (1964), the U.S. Supreme Court ruled that, under Section 1983, state inmates could sue prison administrations. This statute al-

lows state prisoners to seek redress if their constitutional rights have been violated. However, the plaintiff must establish that the defendant exhibited deliberate indifference to or gross negligence of the prisoner's risk of injury.

Prisoners usually base civil rights lawsuits regarding unsanitary and inhumane conditions of confinement on the Eighth Amendment. The Eighth Amendment decrees that "excessive bail shall not be required, nor excessive fines imposed, nor cruel and unusual punishment inflicted." The criteria most often used for establishing cruel and unusual punishment involve the notion of evolving standards of decency. *Holt v. Sarver* (1970) is the most important case dealing with U.S. prison conditions because it established a precedent for subsequent litigation. McLaren (1997) enumerated the following list of constitutional violations in the *Holt* case:

1. a virtual absence of professional staff to supervise the inmate population;
2. a prison system administered primarily by inmate trustees;
3. an atmosphere of hatred and mistrust maintained by brutal use of physical force;
4. an open barracks system that invited physical assaults;
5. unsanitary isolation cells;
6. a complete absence of rehabilitation or training programs;
7. inadequate diet and medical care; and
8. access to prison records, prescription drugs, contraband alcohol and drugs, weapons, and vehicles by some inmate trusties. (p. 348)

This case originated in Arkansas and was not settled by one lawsuit. The judgment handed down from the court was not initially implemented by correctional officials. Only after continued litigation did the prison conditions improve in Arkansas.

Although allegations of inadequate medical care were raised in *Holt*, the U.S. Supreme Court directly addressed the issue of sufficient medical treatment for prisoners in *Estelle v. Gamble* (1976). Drawing upon the doctrine of deliberate indifference, the court ruled that a prisoner's right of protection against cruel and unusual punishment under the Eighth Amendment is violated when his or her serious medical needs are purposefully neglected by correctional personnel.

Inmates have also filed lawsuits based on alleged violations of the Eighth Amendment regarding corporal punishment. Until the late 1960s, corporal punishment was frequently used to subdue prisoners and make them comply with the administration. For example, inmates in Kentucky were regularly whipped with a leather strap eighteen inches long, two inches wide, and attached to a wooden handle. The strap was often soaked in water and dragged through sand before it was used. In 1894, a survey of state correctional facilities revealed that Kentucky used lashing 300 times more often than any other state (Kentucky Department of Corrections, 2001). In *Jackson v. Bishop* (1968), a court ruled for the first time that corporal punishment (in this case, whipping a prisoner) constituted cruel and unusual punishment and violated the Eighth Amendment. In the years since this decision, professional organizations such as the American Correctional Association and the American Bar Association have come to support the prohibition of corporal punishment (McLaren, 1997).

State prisoners also seek protection under the due process clause of the Fourteenth Amendment, which reads as follows:

> All persons born or naturalized in the United States, and subject to the jurisdiction thereof, are citizens of the United States and of the State wherein they reside. No State shall make or enforce any law which shall abridge the privileges or immunities of citizens of the United States; nor shall any State deprive any person of life, liberty, or property, without due process of law; nor deny to any person within its jurisdiction the equal protection of the laws.

In *Johnson v. Glick* (1973), an indicted prisoner claimed that guards had beaten him without provocation when he was awaiting trial. The court ruled that the guards had deprived the inmate of his liberty without due process of law. However, in *Washington v. Harper* (1990), the U.S. Supreme Court ruled that due process was not violated when correctional personnel forcibly administered antipsychotic drugs to an inmate who had previously been diagnosed as mentally ill. It appears that a claim of substantive due process is usurped when a mentally ill prisoner poses a danger to himself and others.

Despite the decision in *Washington,* prisoners' rights of due process have consistently been reaffirmed by the court system. Both the Fourteenth and Fifth Amendments are relevant for cases arising from alleged violations of due process. The Fifth Amendment stipulates the following:

> No person shall be held to answer for a capital, or otherwise infamous crime, unless on a presentment or indictment of a grand jury, except in cases arising in the land or naval forces, or in the militia, when in actual service in time of war or public danger; nor shall any person be subject for the same offense to be twice put in jeopardy of life or limb; nor shall be compelled in any criminal case to be a witness against himself; nor be deprived of life, liberty, or property, without due process of law; nor shall private property be taken for public use, without just compensation.

Due process suits have been used to prevent prison officials from examining and censoring correspondence between a prisoner and his or her attorney. The courts have also interpreted due process to mean that inmates must have either an adequate law library or legal services available to them during their imprisonment. Furthermore, the right of due process protects jailhouse lawyers, or prisoners who help other inmates with legal issues and suits.

Much legal action has centered on the issues of due process and cruel and unusual punishment. However, the gamut of prisoners' rights extends well beyond these and includes many of the substantive issues raised by the UN's *Standard Minimum Rules for the Treatment of Prisoners*. For example, some prisoners have filed lawsuits about First Amendment issues such as access to media, censorship, and religion. The First Amendment reads as follows:

> Congress shall make no law respecting an establishment of religion, or prohibiting the free exercise thereof; or abridging the freedom of speech, or of the press; or the right of the people peaceably to assemble, and to petition the government for a redress of grievances.

However, court decisions have attenuated First Amendment rights concerning freedom of speech for inmates.

In general, prisoners have First Amendment rights, but in a rather limited capacity. Prison officials are, by and large, relatively free to censor communiqués and media. The decision handed down in *Thornburgh v. Abbot* (1989) exemplifies this point. The court ruled that publications that are detrimental to security, order, or discipline along with those that might facilitate criminal activity are subject to censure. McLaren (1997) summarized the court's ruling as follows:

> Publications which may be rejected by a Warden include but are not limited to publications which meet one of the following criteria: (1) It depicts or describes procedures for the construction or use of weapons, ammunition, bombs, or incendiary devices; (2) It depicts, encourages, or describes methods of escape from correctional facilities, or contains the blueprints, drawings, or similar descriptions of Bureau of Prisons institutions; (3) It depicts or describes procedures for the brewing of alcoholic beverages, or the manufacture of drugs; (4) It is written in code; (5) It depicts, describes, or encourages activities which may lead to the use of physical violence or group disruption; (6) It encourages or instructs in the commission of criminal activities; (7) It is sexually explicit material which by its nature or content poses a threat to the security, good order, or discipline of the institution, or facilitates criminal activity. (p. 357)

The verdict in the *Thornburgh* case gave considerable power to the prison administration and may, as McLaren noted, indicate a renewed hands-off jurisprudential policy.

The courts have levied similar restrictions on the First Amendment right of religion. Specifically, the courts have limited the inmates' rights to act in accordance with religious beliefs inside prison. Although prisoners are free to believe whatever they wish, the rules of the institution are typically not suspended for religious observances. For example, Muslim inmates are required to work their full schedules, making "it impossible for them to attend Friday evening religious services [yet] a Black Muslim cannot be punished with administrative segregation for his refusal to handle pork" (McLaren, 1997, p. 363). Thus, the gains obtained in the realm of religious rights have been marginal.

In summary, state prisoners often bring lawsuits based on alleged constitutional violations. However, inmates also file suits based on other legal factors. For example, prisoners retain the ability to sue under state tort law (Dick, 1978). State inmates may also bring habeas corpus actions in federal court after remedies have been exhausted in state courts. Although habeas corpus claims focus on the legality of confinement, Dick suggested that such petitions sometimes provide a useful avenue for inmates to get a hearing on their living conditions.

Unlike state prisoners, inmates under federal jurisdiction cannot make use of Section 1983. This portion of the Civil Rights Act has been applied only to official acts of state law. However, federal prisoners can submit writs of habeas corpus and actions for declaratory judgments (Dick, 1978). Finally, inmates in the federal system may file lawsuits based on the Federal Tort Claims Act.

PRISONERS' RIGHTS AND THE AMERICAN CIVIL LIBERTIES UNION

The American Civil Liberties Union (ACLU) has worked to advance constitutional conditions of confinement and strengthen prisoners' rights. It was founded in 1920 to promote civil liberties by providing legal representation to clients who alleged violations of constitutional rights such as free speech, association and assembly, freedom of the press, freedom of religion, equal protection, due process, and privacy. The ACLU operates the nation's largest public interest law firm, with offices in all fifty states.

In 1972, the ACLU initiated the National Prison Project (NPP). The NPP combines class action litigation with public education to reduce prison crowding, improve prisoner medical care, eliminate violence and maltreatment in prisons and jails, and minimize the reliance on incarceration as a criminal justice sanction. The NPP has represented prisoners in at least twenty-five states. In 1990, the NPP brought five cases involving prisoners' rights before the U.S. Supreme Court.

Yet, since the early 1990s, the NPP and the ACLU have experienced major setbacks in the realm of prisoners' rights. In 1995, the Prison Litigation Reform Act passed the U.S. Congress and became effective a year later. The act diminished the power of the federal courts to correct even the most inhumane prison conditions (ACLU, 2001a). Furthermore, in *Miller v. French* (2000), the U.S. Supreme Court ruled that federal judges could impose an automatic stay on extant court orders in correctional lawsuits. This ruling might relieve prison officials of any obligation to obey injunctions against unconstitutional and inhumane prison conditions (ACLU, 2001b).

PRISONERS AS RESEARCH SUBJECTS

Research involving prisoners is also relevant to prisoners' rights. Throughout history, prisoners of war often have been used in scientific research to test the effects of different substances and stimuli on the human body and mind. The Nazis experimented on prisoners in concentration camps during World War II. These tests were cruel and inhumane, constituting torture and often resulting in death. Many of the physicians and researchers engaged in the experimentation were later tried for war crimes. The Nuremberg Code of 1947 was a consequence of these tribunals. The code defined the standards for the use of human subjects in scientific research. In particular, the following ten principles compose the main points of the Nuremberg Code:

1. voluntary consent,
2. necessity of experiment for the good of humanity,
3. prior animal testing or other research to indicate the anticipated result would justify the performance of the experiment,
4. avoidance of all unnecessary physical and mental suffering and injury,
5. ban of experiments expected to result in death or disablement of subjects unless the experimental physicians also serve as subjects,
6. involvement of no greater risk than benefit,
7. adequate care and treatment of subjects,
8. conduct of research by only highly skilled and qualified investigators,
9. discontinuation of experiments at subjects' will, and
10. discontinuation of experiments which result in injury, disability or death to the experimental subject. (Mitscherlich & Mielke, 1949, p. xxiii–xxv)

Despite these international provisions, misconduct involving prisoners persisted in the United States throughout the 1950s and 1960s. Mentally challenged inmates were infected with communicable diseases at two facilities in New York State. These inmates had no understanding of what was being done to them, nor did their guardians consent to the experiments.

Related reports of misconduct coupled with increased public attention prompted the U.S. federal government to commission the *Belmont Report*, in which three ethical principles for the protection of human research subjects were outlined (U.S. Department of Health and Human Services, 2000). These included respect for persons, beneficence, and justice. In order to ensure respect for persons, researchers must acknowledge the dignity and autonomy of individuals. Moreover, persons with diminished autonomy, such as prisoners and mental patients, must be afforded special protections. Beneficence requires researchers to do no harm by maximizing benefit and minimizing harm so that the benefits of the research outweigh potential risks. The principle of justice compels researchers to treat all persons fairly. As such, prisoners should not be systematically selected or excluded unless there are scientifically or ethically valid reasons for doing so.

While the Nuremberg Code and the *Belmont Report* guide research involving human subjects in principle, Title 45, Part 46, of the Code of Federal Regulations is perhaps the most direct policy governing research with inmate subjects. The Department of Health and Human Services Office for Protection from Research Risks put forward additional protections pertaining to biomedical and behavioral research involving prisoners as subjects (also known as Subpart C) in 1978. These guidelines were revised in November 2001 and set limits on the type of research in which prisoners may participate.

According to the guidelines, prisoners are considered a vulnerable population, meaning that they have diminished ability to decide for themselves whether or not to engage in research. As such, research is limited to the following four primary fields:

1. study of the possible causes, effects, and processes of incarceration, and of criminal behavior, provided that the study presents no more than minimal risk and no more than inconvenience to the subjects;
2. study of prisons as institutional structures or of prisoners as incarcerated persons, provided that the study represents no more than minimal risk and no more than inconvenience to the subjects;
3. research on conditions particularly affecting prisoners as a class (for example, vaccine trials and other research on hepatitis, which is much more prevalent in prisons than elsewhere; and research on social and psychological problems such as alcoholism, drug addiction, and sexual assaults) provided that the study may proceed only after the Secretary has consulted with appropriate experts including experts in penology, medicine, and ethics, and published notice, in the Federal Register, of his intent to approve such research; or
4. research on practices, both innovative and accepted, which have the intent and reasonable probability of improving the health or well-being of the subject. In cases in which those studies require the assignment of prisoners in a manner consistent with protocols approved by the IRB [Institutional Review Board] to control groups which may not benefit from the research, the study may proceed only after the Secretary has consulted with appropriate experts, including experts in penology, medicine, and ethics, and published notice in the Federal Register, of the intent to approve such research. (Department of Health and Human Services, 2001)

The Office for Protection from Research Risks requires colleges and universities to have an IRB in place to oversee all biomedical and behavioral research. This panel of administrators and faculty works to ensure the rights of subjects during research and upholds the provisions set forth in the Nuremberg Code, *Belmont Report,* and Title 45, Part 46.

PRISON CORRUPTION

Many persons are incarcerated each year for theft, embezzlement, and trafficking. Ironically, offenders sentenced for these crimes may discover that their guardians inside prison are caught up in these same behaviors. Prison corruption involves three specific conditions. First, employees of the prison must be implicated. Second, they must be acting in violation of the official rules and regulations of the prison. Third, the action must produce personal material gain as a consequence of the employees' misuse of their position (McCarthy, 2002). A recent example of prison misconduct involved a female officer in North Carolina who was providing personal sexual services to incarcerated men in exchange for money; the North Carolina prison system still allows paper currency in some of its institutions (R. Elingburg, personal communication, May 22, 2003). The officer was discharged after the incident was aired by an unsatisfied inmate patron. Indeed, prison corruption constitutes a general adulteration of the correctional process.

Forms of prison corruption include misfeasance, malfeasance, and nonfeasance. When officers improperly perform a duty in which they may lawfully engage, this constitutes misfeasance. Examples of misfeasance involve accepting gratuities for preferential treatment, giving special privileges to an inmate for money, and the misappropriation of state monies for personal use. Malfeasance occurs when an official engages in misconduct, which includes theft, embezzlement, trafficking in contraband, extortion, exploitation of inmates or their families for money or services, and entering into criminal conspiracies with inmates for drug sales, forgery, or counterfeiting. Nonfeasance is the failure to act in accordance with official responsibilities. Examples include ignoring inmate violations of the institution's rules and failing to stop other employees from misconduct (McCarthy, 2002).

There are several ways to address prison corruption. According to McCarthy (2002), the correctional department should develop and enforce an anticorruption policy that defines the problem and specifies the penalties for corruption. Prison management should also proactively detect and investigate allegations of corruption; an internal affairs unit is ideal. Correctional administrators need to improve prison management. For example, when hiring staff, a review policy should be followed. During recruitment, the institution's commitment to anticorruption should be emphasized, and job candidates should be subjected to background checks and drug testing. Finally, initiating a merit system for employee promotion and advancement will curb the political incentives for prison corruption.

CONCLUSION

Evolving standards of decency in the modern world require that today's prisoners be incarcerated in a manner that does not violate their basic human rights. After World War II, the UN outlined a number of suggestions aimed at ensuring prisoners' rights. These rules cover everything from personal hygiene to discipline and punishment. This evolution of decency may also be seen in the issues raised by correctional lawsuits. Once considered slaves of the state, inmates may now contest the constitutionality of their conditions of confinement. In addition, safeguards against unethical research also protect inmates.

The fact that prisoners retain certain rights and liberties during incarceration may seem contradictory. After all, the *lex talionis* (law of retaliation) dictum requires the violation of prisoners' rights since prisoners infringed upon the rights of others. Yet how much constraint of these rights is appropriate? This question reveals a fundamental flaw in the eye-for-an-eye perspective in criminal justice. Is it possible to punish in a fashion that is in exact proportion to the amount of harm caused by the original lawbreaking behavior? Perhaps a grater challenge concerns the ability to incarcerate lawbreakers in a manner that is fair *and* humane. Treating lawbreakers who are imprisoned humanely is a reflection of society's development and civility.

REFERENCES

American Civil Liberties Union. (2001a). *ACLU national prison project* [On-line]. Available: http://www.aclu.org/issues/prisons/npp_mission.html

American Civil Liberties Union. (2001b). *Senate vote on prisoners rights, H.R. 3019* [On-line]. Available: http://www.aclu.org/vote-guide/Senate_HR3019. html

Anderson, Lloyd C. (2000). *Voices from a southern prison.* Athens: University of Georgia Press.

Beccaria, C. (1963). *On crimes and punishments.* Indianapolis: Bobbs-Merrill.

Dick, R. P. (1978). Prison reform in the federal courts. *Buffalo Law Review, 27,* 99–138.

Durkheim, E. (1933). *The division of labor in society.* New York: Free Press.

Foucault, M. (1995). *Discipline and punish: The birth of the prison.* New York: Vintage Books.

International Committee of the Red Cross. (1949/2001). *Convention (III) relative to the treatment of prisoners of war* [On-line]. Available: http:// www.icrc.org/IHL.nsf

Johnson, Robert. (1996). *Hard time: Understanding and reforming the prison* (2nd ed.). Belmont, CA: Wadsworth.

Kentucky Department of Corrections. (2001). KY Corrections. [On-line]. Available: http://www.cor.state.ky.us

Legal Information Institute. (2001). *United States Code* [On-line]. Available: http: //www4.law.cornell.edu/uscode

McCarthy, B. J. (2002). Keeping an eye on the keeper: Prison corruption and its control. In M. C. Braswell, B. R. McCarthy, & B. J. McCarthy (Eds.), *Justice, crime and ethics* (4th ed., pp. 253–265). Cincinnati, OH: Anderson.

McLaren, J. (1997). Prisoners' rights: The pendulum swings. In J. M. Pollock (Ed.), *Prisons: Today and tomorrow* (pp. 338–380). Gaithersburg, MD: Aspen.

Mitscherlich, A., & Mielke, F. (1949). *Doctors of infamy: The story of the Nazi medical crimes.* New York: Schuman.

Office of the United Nations High Commissioner for Human Rights. (1957/2001). *Standard minimum rules for the treatment of prisoners* [On-line]. Available: http://www.unhchr.ch/html/menu3/b/h_comp34.html

Sheleff, L. S. (1997). *Social cohesion and legal coercion: A critique of Weber, Durkheim, and Marx.* Atlanta, GA: Rodopi.

Sykes, G. M. (1958). *The society of captives.* Princeton, NJ: Princeton University Press.

U.S. Department of Health and Human Services. (2000). *The Belmont Report* [On-line]. Available: http://ohrp.osophs.dhhs.gov/humansubjects/guidance/belmont.htm

U.S. Department of Health and Human Services. (2001). *Protection of human subjects (Code of Federal Regulations, Title 45, Part 46)* [On-line]. Available: http://www.ohrp.osophy.dhhs.gov/humansubjects/guidance/45cfr46.html

Part III

LIVING IN PRISON: ONE MAN'S JOURNEY

7

A PRISONER'S NARRATIVE

Stephen Stanko

INTRODUCTION

A narrative is a story. This is my story. It tells how I came to be incarcerated and what life is like in prison. I discuss pretrial detention, plea bargaining, and different correctional institutions. Keep in mind that I am telling this story. It is my perception of life on the inside, though it is an informed one, since I have lived inside maximum-, medium-, and minimum-security facilities. Other inmates may have slightly different perceptions of what it is like to live inside prison. It is certainly true that not all inmates are identical; prisons are also quite different. The context of imprisonment involves interplay between the convict and the prison environment. The generalizations I make about the prison contexts are based on years of time served. I do not speak for all inmates, but I feel that I speak for most.

THE CAUSE OF MY INCARCERATION

I was completely lost. Although I had been a model student and an above-average athlete during school, in the years that followed, I did not accomplish my dreams and goals. In my mind, I was a failure, and I had reduced myself to cheating my way to fortune and fame. I lost sight of the distinction between right and wrong somewhere along the way. However, I never planned to commit a crime, and I never expected that I would ever become a criminal. But, in the end, my actions were labeled "Breach of Trust" and "Obtaining Property by False Pretenses."

Before any warrant had been issued for my arrest, my spouse sensed that I had been up to no good. She knew I was hiding something, and my actions were not normal. She tried to talk with me, but talking was useless. I denied everything. So we inevitably argued. Some couples work through their problems by arguing, but I have a temper. I was unable to remain rational or calm during our arguments. One morning, I woke up and realized that I needed to simply remove myself to some safe place long enough to gather my thoughts and get some wits about myself. I was worried about the looming property-related crimes, and I did not want my wife to be charged as a codefendant or conspirator. I began to pack my belongings.

However, when my spouse saw what I was doing, her anger and frustrations peaked. She was intent upon making me face things right then and there. As I attempted to leave our home, she tried to restrain me physically, but I am a foot taller than she is and twice her size. I easily overpowered her. After the fight that morning, I kissed her at the garage door and drove away. As a result of that altercation, the sheriff added "Kidnapping" and "Assault and Battery with Intent to Kill" to my previous charges. In my opinion, overzealous law enforcement distorted my wife's statements and made them far more colorful than they actually were.

I fled upstate about 200 miles away and spent a day trying to figure out what to do. The reality of my crimes was burning through me. Since I had never done anything like this before, I still had no idea of which way to turn. A night without sleep in a hotel without comfort offered no help, and my life was rapidly spiraling into thoughts of suicide. That was no answer and I knew it. I spent the next day building up the strength to return home to face my responsibility. That morning I had called my wife to make sure she was OK. Due to my ignorance of police investigation, I was unaware that the call was being traced. When I finally had made the decision to return to the hotel and pack for home, a team of officers quickly descended on me for capture.

PRETRIAL DETENTION

By midnight that evening, I was in an orange jumpsuit at the county detention center lying on a half-inch plastic mattress barely cushioning a steel rack. The cell was cold and empty, which was a perfect fit to the emotions going through my head. The fears of my arrest were replaced by the fears of isolation and confinement. I was kept isolated away from other inmates and was given no phone call, no conversation, no toilet paper, and nothing else that resembled a natural existence.

The officers barked commands as if I were a scolded child and opened and closed the food slot with as much force as could be used with steel construction. Finally, I was told to clean up because someone wanted to talk to me. It turned out to be the same deputy sheriff who would later place charges against me. "I need to know what all happened, and I will do everything that I can to help," were his famous last words. My thoughts were eased momentarily with the fact that I might get a little help from someone who knew me, knew my family, knew my background, and knew that I was not an evil person. I was given coffee and calm conversation and countless promises of fairness in the face of everything else. After a couple of hours, I was returned to my cell again, somewhat relieved, but still in total isolation.

I was finally placed in the detention center's general population with all of the other "pretrial detainees." For the first time, I was in the company of murderers, rapists, thieves, drug dealers, and other seedy characters. My fears had, once again, changed and increased in intensity. I was no slouch at six feet four inches in height and 250 pounds in weight, but I did not have the "heart" of the men that now accompanied me. Many of them were without fear. Most were multiple offenders facing more years than I had lived at the time, and the anger in them was neither hidden nor reserved. Eye contact was a bad decision and had grave consequences. In the next six months, it became a challenge just to separate the threats inside the "pod" of the detention center from those of the justice system.

PLEA BARGAINING

I distinctly remember the first meeting with my court-appointed attorney. After a quick handshake, the first words out of her mouth were, "It doesn't look good, you gave a complete statement and there's not much that I can do!" Our first meeting was as short as the rest would be. She had already read the copy of the statement, which was provided to her by the solicitor's office. She asked me only a few questions that she already knew the answers to and said that she would see me again in the next week. Then, I was escorted back to the loneliness of my cell.

During our second meeting, my attorney told me, "Well, you're facing eighty-five years on all charges. The good news is that they are dropping the assault to 'High and Aggravated Nature' instead of 'Intent to Kill.'" I thought to myself, "That's the good news?" Within a week of the arrest, my spouse was supporting me diligently and working as hard, if not harder, than my attorney by obtaining a measure of leniency for me. The solicitor wanted a conviction, and with a fifteen-page statement, it would not be difficult to get one if I were to go to trial. I could have been convicted on any one of numerous charges that faced me. My counsel seemed uninterested in arguing how the statement was obtained, and instead of using the law to provide some measure of justice for me, she decided to use my past and my spouse to build some foundation around the fact that I was a "first-time" offender. In her opinion, the conviction was already cast in stone; now it was time to work on a lesser sentence.

My lawyer visited about once every week, but it would never last for more than fifteen minutes. The discussion involved only updates of the conversations she had had with my spouse, the other victims, and the solicitor. Only on one occasion did she ever ask me for any information that might provide some defense to the excessive charges I faced. When possible sentences and pleas were discussed, the conversation always began with "If you decide to go to trial, you could get more," and then she would take the rest of the conversation to explain my chances of getting a thirty-, twenty-, fifteen-, or ten-year sentence.

For those detainees who have "public defenders," it is almost never a question of fighting the case. It doesn't matter whether the accused are innocent or not. These attorneys handle more cases than their hours could ever allow, and plea bargains are the standard that is now employed. Public defenders show up weekly and call out fifteen to thirty people at a time, giving each one only minutes to update the status of their case. The last question is usually, "Do you want to go ahead and take what the state offered?" A negative response elicits the catchall return of "Now, remember what you are facing if we go to trial."

My attorney attempted some mitigation by getting a psychological evaluation for me. So I was taken to the state's mental hospital and examined by two doctors. A day after the examination, a report was written, and a "borderline narcissistic" diagnosis was made. However, in violation of state statute and law, no hearing on competency was ever convened. Instead, the Friday before court was to be held, my attorney came and explained that if I chose not to plea, the solicitor was ready to go to trial. My choices seemed simple, take the ten or face the eighty-five.

However, during all of the meetings, it was never explained to me that I could take each charge to trial. The charges could stand alone, and I could be found guilty of and sentenced for each separate offense. With the kidnapping and assault, my spouse was willing and ready to take the stand and explain exactly and truthfully what had occurred that day. My counsel never detailed my rights to me, but rather she explained that the state was offering a deal of ten years. I would receive ten years for the "nonviolent" charges of "Breach of Trust" and "Obtaining Property" in addition to three to five years, running concurrent, for the "violent" charges of "Kidnapping" and "Assault." On nonviolent offenses, I would have to serve a little more than half of the sentence, but I would be eligible for parole. On the violent, I would serve 85 percent, as these were newly legislated under the "Truth in Sentencing" laws. A five-year sentence meant serving four years and three months before being given the parole eligibility on the nonviolent sentence. So I understood that I would actually serve between four years, three months and five years, three months in the Department of Corrections. Believing that the alternative could cost me eighty-five years, I agreed to the plea bargain.

I was taken into the courtroom that Monday with all the other "guilty pleas." The solicitor presented his version of the events to the judge after I was arraigned and explained my rights of presenting witnesses, a jury trial, and other matters that were muffled by the thoughts racing through my head. By the time the solicitor was done, I felt guilty, ashamed, and as though my punishment was warranted.

My counsel then rose and spoke on my behalf, emphasizing my education and work history and attempting to downplay the horrible picture painted by the state. Each of three victims, including my spouse, spoke. None asked for a sentence of greater than eight years. Finally, I was given a chance to plea for mercy. There was no blood or broken bones, no weapons or violence in any of my offenses. Deception made up the bulk of my actions. Moreover, no victims lost anything, as all money was returned. Scared like never before, I spoke as honestly and calmly as possible.

Apparently, my words fell on deaf ears, as the court flip-flopped the sentence, giving me ten years for kidnapping, eight for assault, and five on all of the remaining charges. Due to truth-in-sentencing laws, I was required to serve eight years in prison without parole eligibility or any other possibility of early release. The court had essentially decided how I would spend the next ten years of my life.

FROM JAIL TO PRISON

It was a four-day wait until the guard opened my door at 4:30 A.M. and yelled, "Pack it up, you're out of here." In all, eight of us were cuffed to waist-chains and shackled at our feet by two-foot-long chains and slowly guided into a caged van. Once again, the unknown confronted me. The van was silent, as only one of us had ever been in such a position before. During the hour-long ride, I simply stared outward at the last glimpses of the free world, one we would not see for some time.

RECEPTION AND EVALUATION: INTAKE

The beginning of my prison life started at Reception and Evaluation (R&E), where more yelling began as soon as the van doors were opened. We were guided by pushes and shouting into a narrow corridor which was one metal gate after another. I was stripped, shaved, showered, and deloused in less than one-half hour and in full view of any passersby. Pride was the first thing to lose in the prison system, and the man who seeks privacy or any semblance of peace will never make it out.

Incarceration generally begins for most individuals by entering a centralized institution responsible for the reception and evaluation of every inmate that enters the state Department of Corrections. Upon entrance, the new inmates are immediately stripped of all personal possessions, including clothes and jewelry. The only possessions generally allowed to remain with the inmates are watches whose value does not exceed $35 and wedding bands that display no jewels. All other personal items are taken, logged in as confiscated, and either mailed out by the inmate to his family or donated to a local shelter.

After disrobing, every newly arriving inmate is shaved of all head and facial hair. They are taken into a row of shower stalls and given between five and ten minutes to clean themselves from head to toe. These showers are quite often "open-air" areas in full view of anyone who may pass by. Male and female correctional officers and administrative staff as well as new arrivals witness what can only be described as a truly humiliating experience. For me, it was at this point that I realized that rights like freedom and privacy are lost in prison. The officers' commands come fast and continuously, and any disobedience is met with swift and immediate discipline. Orders range from the appropriate way to walk or to stand, to requests that increase the amount of humiliation the new inmate must endure. Most correctional officers claim that their orders clarify exactly who is in charge and who is not.

After this degradation ceremony, our group was escorted to a "holding cell." There we waited until, one by one, we were called out by our newly assigned identification numbers (e.g., #235278). Once called, I remember being escorted into a medical area where I was squeezed, pinched, scoped, scratched, and rubbed on what felt like every square inch of my body. Every birthmark was listed on a standard form, and an immediate assessment and medical history were completed.

New arrivals are then most often processed through a series of medical areas for blood tests, questions of past and present medical problems, and simple examinations. In most states, R&E will customarily last from sixty to ninety days, so any conditions and problems, which may require any further medical attention, can be handled in the weeks following the initial entrance. However, for most inmates the first twenty-four hours of incarceration are made up of a series of poking and prodding of every single square inch of the body. After ten hours of medical tests, questions, and other miscellaneous entry procedures, my group was moved to cells.

For the next couple of weeks, life was a six-foot-by-nine-foot cell with a set of bunk beds, an army cot, a stainless steel sink/toilet combination, and two cell mates. Showers were allowed once every three to five days, recreation was one hour a day (if weather permitted, Monday through Friday), a fifteen-minute phone call was permitted once per week, and the rest of the time was spent either sleeping or waiting to be called for miscellaneous tests. Examinations were given to provide levels of intelligence, mental aptitude, volatility, reasoning, and vocational skills. Department officials would then use the conviction documents and the results of all these tests to determine where each new inmate would be first placed in the system. Unfortunately, for me, a violent kidnapping offense would automatically place me in a high-level, maximum-security prison.

RECEPTION AND EVALUATION: CLASSIFICATION

The internal classification system is the main focus of both inmates and staff regarding inmate placement, programs, privileges, and custody. Inmates are categorized on a number of criteria and given a classification-level assignment. Based on behavior, service time, program completions, and other factors, inmates have the ability to advance to a "lower" custody with additional privileges and fewer restrictions or decrease to a "higher" custody with few privileges and increased restriction.

For purposes of understanding and reference throughout the remainder of this chapter, below is a mock classification system, which is alphabetical, and ranges from an "A+," which is an inmate at a "release" type facility who is allowed to exit prison grounds without supervision, to an "F," which is maximum security. Other listings are included and the chart (classification) will be as follows:

A+	Least Restrictive (without supervision)
A	Least Restrictive (with supervision)
B+	Work Program
B	Minimum (second stage)
B-	Minimum (first stage)
C	Medium Custody (second stage)
D	Medium Custody (first stage)
F	Maximum Security
LDR	Living on Death Row
PDA	Pre-Disciplinary Action
PC	Protective Custody
ST	Security Threat

The system itself is designed and implemented for a variety of reasons. Not all inmates are violent offenders, and most are not multiple offenders. In short, no two inmates are identical in crimes, behaviors, and education level or otherwise, but the intent is to place the populations in groups that are as closely related as possible. Every state correctional department has multiple correctional facilities, and prisons differ based on the custodies of those offenders housed.

Maximum-security prisons will automatically have a high number of perimeter fences, guards, secured areas, and restrictive measures. These institutions will house violent and repeat offenders as well as those who have extensive disciplinary records in the department. On the opposite end, minimum-security prisons have few fences. Minimum-security inmates operate on an honor system, with each understanding that even the absolute slightest of mistakes can cause an immediate custody reduction. The state is able to control the populations by keeping inmates at assigned institutions during their sentences and by decreasing inmate movement (i.e., transfers) outside the fences.

There are a number of factors involved in deciding an inmate's custody level. The first and most obvious deals with the offense committed. Violent crimes, specifically those involving severe bodily harm, rape, or death, automatically place an individual in a high-level custody category. Violent offenses also result in a long sentence, and correctional workers must consider obvious security concerns such as escape, threat, propensity to misbehave, and even possible suicide threats.

The sentence length and, more important, the remaining incarceration length based on date of sentence completion (not parole eligibility), become major factors. An individual with a great amount of time to serve on his sentence is more likely to act out, receive disciplinary reports, and misbehave because there is less to lose. On the other hand, an inmate who has served a large portion of his sentence and is approaching an effective "max-out" date (i.e., sentence-completion date) is far less likely to act in any way that would jeopardize his release.

However, there are occasional instances where these factors do not make a difference in how an individual acts. This is especially so when the adjudicated sentence is three years or less. Custody and classification are designed to affect the greater portion of the department's population. Another factor is prior commitments. Upon entering the department, a history of prior criminal arrests, charges, and convictions is obtained on every inmate. This allows the department to make a more educated and realistic observation of recidivist potential. Those individuals with numerous arrests and convictions are often placed in high custody. Violent priors will also place them further toward a medium (C) or even maximum (D) custody, even though their current offense may only be of a lower, nonviolent nature.

Patterns of criminal behavior do not cease or even slow down just because an individual is incarcerated. Using the same ideology, many first-time offenders will be afforded a medium (C) to lower custody classification because there is no immediate record that would show them as a threat. Prior commitment records are also immediately retrieved and used to see if the inmate acted in accordance with and advanced through rehabilitative processes in previous incarcerations. By policy, any and all acts and behaviors within the prior ten years can be used during evaluations to either allow or deny inmate advancement in custody procedures.

Of these factors, assaultive disciplinary convictions and escape history are of main concern. An individual with a pattern of acting out physically will likely advance at a slow pace. For security purposes, correctional workers must determine that an inmate will not be a threat to himself, the staff, or the population when he moves to institutions with less restrictive security measures and decreased staff to handle such misbehavior. Assaultive disciplinary convictions will often require inmates to remain for one to three years in high custody before even becoming eligible for advancement.

Equal to assaults, escapes can cause great loss to an inmate's ability to advance in custody throughout his incarceration. If for public relations reasons only, an "escaped convict" can represent the single greatest fear for the department and the responsible warden's life. If he chooses to escape, the media can portray a first-time offender incarcerated for failure to pay parking tickets as a serial killer. The concept that the corrections department is not able to contain the criminals incarcerated places mass fear in the public's mind, and the escapee can see a future which involves the highest security measures possible. Many inmates with escape records are hampered even long after the ten-year statute of limitations is over. Once an inmate has "rabbit" in him, in the eyes of the department, it never leaves.

Pending prosecutions, such as warrants, parole and/or probation revocations, indictments, and magistrate/family court cases, are also considered in the classification processes. Any of these legal conditions that result in additional sentencing of the inmate are considered most costly. They represent a number of variables that can cause individuals to encounter incarceration for lengthier periods. Furthermore, known as "detainers," pending prosecutions notify administrative staff in the automated system of undisposed legal actions against each inmate.

Institutional caseworkers provide inmates with information on these detainers that includes the count, warrant/indictment numbers, the charge itself, and any supplied dates. Once informed, the inmates or their counsel can file the proper documents for disposition and proceed into court for final adjudication. Upon disposition, the respective clerk of court must file certified true copies of the disposition reports to a division of classification known as "inmate records" at the department headquarters, and the detainers will either be removed or properly changed to an adjudicated sentence, thus allowing the inmate a proper classification. Consequently, departmental officials will accept only documents forwarded by the proper legal officials. This ensures inmates are not released or cleared of pending litigations by way of fraudulent documents created by friends or family members of the incarcerated.

Other factors taken into consideration in inmate classifications include, but are not limited to: special needs (court-ordered alcohol and drug treatments); security threats (gang affiliations, suicide intentions, etc.); separation requirements such as two inmates involved in violent activities who must remain at separate facilities (this is often referred to as a "red flag"); resident stability (immigration); mental analysis, which includes retardation, sedative requirements, and other personality disorders which are of a serious nature; sex offenders, who in most cases are required to attend sex-offender counseling; and medical needs from disabilities, diabetes, and prosthetics to other major physical restrictions such as heart conditions and AIDS.

The longer an inmate is incarcerated, remains employed, and stays disciplinary free, the more points he has subtracted. If the inmate is fired from his prison job, found guilty of a disciplinary, or violates any departmental policy or procedure, points are added to his total score, and in turn, he must work his way back down to the advancement eligibility. By keeping track of point tables, inmates are aware of how near or far they are from proceeding to the next level and possible transfer to less restrictive institutions.

Other classification systems use criteria such as remaining sentence, severity of current offense, disciplinary history, and other factors, but do not necessarily utilize a point system. Instead, the inmates are given set standards, and once met, the board reviews them and determinations are made through a close examination of the inmate's institutional record.

The classification system is quite advanced and complicated in nature. Any one factor can cause an inmate to be continuously denied any opportunity to advance from one level to the next less restrictive one. Some systems use numbered point scales in which an inmate is given a number of points upon entering the system based on all of the aforementioned criteria. The higher the number, the greater the custody level, and inmates work toward decreasing their total point score. As their number decreases, their eligibility to advance increases.

I spent four years at two maximum-security facilities. It was a series of emotional, mental, and physical roller-coaster rides. It was simultaneously a world of loneliness and a source of strength. For most, there are no friends or family in prison.

RECEPTION AND EVALUATION: IDENTIFICATION

Every individual is then assigned a new identity—a number. From that moment on, first, middle, and last names become secondary in nature to the number. It is the number that represents who the individual has now become. A six- or seven-digit number is then the only thing that signifies one's existence. An inmate's access to mail, phone calls, housing, programs, institutional assignments, clothes, hygiene, visitation, credits, and everything of significance is now governed and directed by and through that number.

The number given will be with each inmate from his original date of incarceration until the date he is released or maxes-out. It will never change nor will it ever be given to another individual. The significance of the number is such that upon release, ex-convicts can never forget that it represented a part of their life. Social security numbers, birth dates, phone numbers, addresses, and every other number may leave one's memory, but this number is one that can never be forgotten.

I was issued an identification card (ID card) that displays my picture, my full name, and my assigned number. The back of this card is encoded with a metal strip like that of a credit card. All purchases at institutional canteens and mailrooms are made by using this card because most inmates are strictly forbidden to have money in their possession at any time. Money instead is forwarded by family and friends to an account administered by the Department of Corrections. U.S. postal money orders are the only form of currency that prisoners are allowed to receive and deposit into their accounts.

The ID card is also used when an inmate is supplied with clothes, sheets, and other supplies by institutional commissaries. Where I was imprisoned, it was policy that a card last two years before it could be replaced without charge. Lost or stolen cards will be charged to the inmate's account. Every inmate is supplied with a plastic ID carrier (with attached clip) so that the card may be displayed by the inmate whenever he is not in his cell.

The number, the card, the rules eroded at my individuality. I was no longer an individual, but instead, I was a number on a tan uniform. I was ordered around by people in blue uniforms, many of whom had one-third my education and even less experience in life. Noncompliance with any of their demands would result in disciplinary procedures and possibly more time. This is a life where no emotions, save anger and control, can be shown unless you wish to become a target of the predators around you.

RECEPTION AND EVALUATION: HOUSING

Once all initial processing is completed, new inmates are taken to their housing units. When being moved and transferred in and out of most institutions, inmates are generally bound by steel "leg-chains" and "belly-chains," otherwise known as "shackles." A large handcuff-style fastener is placed around each ankle and connected by a chain no longer than two feet. The belly-chain consists of a chain, which wraps around the inmate's waist in the form of a belt. Handcuffs then fasten the arms to each side of the waist.

A square cell block characterized by cement and steel with electronic doors is opened, and each inmate is told the number of the cell that will house him for the next two to three months. In most institutions, cells are approximately six and one-half feet wide and eleven feet long. A set of steel bunk beds and an additional mattress either on the floor or an antiquated "army-cot" style foldout bed generally make up the sleeping arrangements. A stainless steel toilet/sink combination is the only other fixture in the cell. Most cells house three new arrivals, and all business, private and personal, is conducted with everyone in the cell at all times. There are neither partitions nor any opportunity to request that cell mates be allowed to exit for any period of time for any reason.

During my R&E, inmates were in lockdown Monday through Friday for twenty-three hours a day. For an hour a day, when security and weather permitted, the inmates were granted the opportunity to walk out to a forty-by-forty-foot area surrounded by a series of fifteen-foot fences and allowed to walk in the open air. On Saturdays and Sundays, the inmates were given no opportunity to leave their cells and, instead, had to remain celled for the entire two days.

Cell assignments in R&E most often place individuals in small, confined quarters with two other individuals they have never seen or met before. While most Department of Corrections officials may attempt to house together inmates with similar characteristics, it is a match dictated mostly by the physical sizes of the individuals and by the crimes they committed. It is no surprise that aggression and anger can spark volatile confrontations when men with no similarities are placed in these tight and confined conditions. These men have each been recently convicted and sentenced to prison terms for various periods of time. The only release from the mental stress and psychological punishment of prison life is communication with fellow inmates. If this relationship becomes one of decency and mutual respect, the cell mates can be of great help in beginning a sentence. On the other hand, constant contact and early anxiety can turn a small cell into a battleground if any two of the three develop a situation of ongoing confrontation.

In the early weeks of R&E, each inmate is routinely taken out of the cell for further evaluations. These tests generally include basic skills assessments, intelligence tests, mental evaluations, and questionnaires concerning prior alcohol and drug abuse. In theory, these numerous questions and tests are for helping to create a record on the inmates so that productive rehabilitative programs (e.g., Alcoholics/Narcotics Anonymous) can be utilized during their incarceration. They also assist in placing the men in institutions designed to house violent versus nonviolent offenders. The criteria of years of sentence, level of crime, prior criminal history, and age are also taken into consideration. These factors make up each inmate custody or classification level.

Privileges and rights are at an absolute minimum during the R&E process. In most institutions, each inmate is afforded one envelope per week for purposes of writing family, friends, and/or attorneys. Paper or pencils are given at the discretion of the officers. In the event of a broken pencil, the inmate may have to wait three to four days before receiving another. Inmates will write their families, but are actually unable to provide a return address in most cases, as R&E is in no way a permanent housing facility.

ASSIGNMENT

It seemed like déjà vu when the door opened the morning an officer told me, "Pack it up, you're out of here." I was ready for assignment. Incidentally, my attorney had filed an appeal to the State Supreme Court, arguing that my plea was "involuntary" because I didn't understand the legal process and had not agreed to the original plea. So, as I walked out of the administration building and into the yard of the prison where my sentence would truly begin, there was a slight gleam of hope that I would somehow escape this nightmare.

After the six-to-eight-week period of R&E, inmates are assigned to their initial institution. They are transported, in chains, by departmental transportation procedures, and within two days are taken before another classification process. Prior to their arrival, inmates are assigned to a cell with another inmate close to their physical description and closely related in offense (violent with violent, nonviolent with nonviolent).

In their initial institutional assessment, inmates are immediately assigned to a position of employment. While the concept is to place them according to their knowledge and background, most initial arrivals are assigned based on institutional needs such as cafeteria work and yard detail (lawn mowing and trash pickup), rather than a position closely fitting their skills. It must be noted that all inmates who score below set levels are automatically assigned to educational programs. Other assignments at initial assessments include mental and medical program recommendations as well as substance abuse recommendations.

Each dorm has a caseworker for its inmates. These are administrative staff workers employed specifically to assess inmates and assist them with the rehabilitative programs available in the department. Caseworkers are social workers who assist with employment assignments and changes, program assignment and completions, cell assignments and changes, inmate reviews, detainer notifications and dispositions, and advancements in custody level.

Each year of an inmate's incarceration, he is presented before a prison's assessment committee. Six months prior, he is given a biannual review, which is done by the respective dorm caseworker. This review looks at the inmate's custody, cell assignment, and job and treatment programs. The caseworker may make recommendations of any programs and activity, which may help the inmate in his annual assessment.

Other reviews may be done prior to the annual assessment. During these reviews, inmates may receive additional sentencing or an attempt to dispose charges or make additional pleas. Reviews also may result from convictions of major disciplinary charges in the department, program completions such as alcohol and drug abuse treatment, and discharge from medical or psychiatric units.

Annual assessments are done in a more formal, regimented way. These assessments are done before a board consisting of a chairperson (e.g., warden, assistant warden, or the institution's highest-ranking security official) and four or five administrative or security staff members. Nurses, teachers, job supervisors, guidance counselors, and/or prison chaplains are often used to represent the boards. These boards are used for numerous duties with their respective prison population, which include

- job and cell transfers (this includes approval for all job terminations);
- assessing inmates convicted of multiple charges and/or high-level (assaultive/ security risk) charges;
- assessing inmates for placement in special treatment or educational programs;
- assessing inmates for transfers based on hardships, security risks, protective custody, and interprison transfers;
- assessing inmates for advancement/reduction in custody levels and recommending inmates for advancement to the least restrictive custody levels;
- final approval for advancement to least restrictive levels from classification at headquarters (discussed below); and
- other assessments and reviews for
  - disposition of detainers,
  - release from predisciplinary detention.

At the hearing, the panel faces the inmate while the caseworker explains the particulars of why each inmate is present before the board. All annual assessments are recorded for appeal procedures. A brief explanation of the inmate's record is provided, including charges, effective max-out dates, parole eligibility dates, violent/nonviolent status, current employment position, program participation, custody level, and disciplinary conviction record. Once the caseworker completes the explanation, the inmate is provided an opportunity to give any information on his behalf and ask any questions dealing with the matters at hand. The information contained in the inmate's file is made available to him as well as the board for review, information gathering, and applicable questions.

Each panel member has one vote, with the chairperson making the last. In order for an inmate to receive the advance in question, a majority is required, and without the majority the request is denied. No matter what the decision, the panel is required to document their reasons for the decision made. These reasons must be recorded in both the paper file and the automated system. Inmates can appeal the board's decision at both their respective prison and at headquarters level. The prison case manager can review the circumstances and, along with the warden's approval and consent, can either affirm the board's decision or let it stand.

In some instances where inmates have either acted to a point where disciplinaries place them as security concerns, or in rare instances when inmates may be recommended for an advancement without meeting all required criteria, the board can override the set parameters and recommend either reduction or advancement in custody. Such recommendations require extensive documentation and information that explains, in detail, why the board would do such. They cannot be made without some significant circumstance connected to classification and/or security policies.

The larger percentages of institutional review boards' decisions are final upon the vote. However, there remain some decisions that must be approved by classification at headquarters. The Headquarters Classification Committee (HQCC) is designed to effectuate all inmate transfers through state facilities. It consists of a larger number of members, which includes a chairperson, vice-chairperson, and up to ten members. Along with bed management and transfers, the HQCC has final approval for all inmates advancing to the least restrictive custodies (A+, A-), as these custodies will often deal with inmates receiving employment outside of the department and/or constant interaction with society.

Such delicate positions require approval of both the respective institution's board and Department of Corrections headquarters. Other final decisions required by the HQCC are inmates placed on security-threat status; protective custody; separations for security purposes; transfer to counties (where state inmates can hold "trustee" positions); Interstate Corrections Compact Agreement (mutual agreements between two State Corrections Departments, which allow an inmate to transfer to another state to complete his sentence there); and immigration coordination. All of these decisions are made by the HQCC, as they also often utilize the departmental legal division to insure that all legal considerations, rules, and guidelines are appropriately followed.

The concept of advancing in classification processes is equivalent to a programmed learning. By consistently obeying the rules, guidelines, and procedures, inmates can move toward less restrictive custodies and receive added liberties. Work programs in the department actually allow some inmates to work jobs in society earning minimum wages and then return to incarceration at the end of the workday. Others allow inmates to do construction and maintenance work at different institutions around the state. In essence, inmates become a form of Pavlov's dogs. Yet no matter how far an inmate advances, it can sometimes take only one disciplinary to send him all the way back to the most restrictive and high-security classifications.

THE APPEAL PROCESS

My direct appeal lasted almost two years. During this time, I was then transferred to a prison some 150 miles away from home. It was a newly built facility, but the only difference in my eyes was the cost of phone bills for my loved ones. Otherwise, I was no closer to freedom than before. The new settings initially made the year pass by quickly, and the second year there began to pass slowly. As with any institution, the days became routine and mundane, making boredom a dominant factor of existence. After the appeal, however, I had filed a "post-conviction relief application" in the courts that presented issues and allegations against my original attorney, the solicitors that prosecuted the case, and the court. Arguing issues of "ineffective assistance of counsel, involuntary guilty plea . . . and . . . violation of due process," a hearing was convened where testimony and evidence were presented in a civil court that challenged the constitutionality of the criminal conviction.

Once all evidence and testimony were given, the court addressed counsel, and he said, "I don't believe I can let this conviction stand." My friends and family in the courtroom were ecstatic, as was I. Now it was only a matter of waiting for the written order.

It came some four months later and was not what I had expected. The court allowed the conviction to stand and wrote an order that in no way resembled the discussions that were had that day. Once again, the depression and gloom of prison life encompassed my thoughts and emotions. I felt as though I was at the very beginning of the appeal process. The order was appealed to the State Supreme Court.

In the meantime, it was the middle of my sentence, and it became difficult to remain positive. Over the years, I had seen men beaten, almost to death, over a piece of chicken or a pack of cigarettes. I had seen what many would not see in a lifetime. Men who had committed truly violent offenses against others had come and gone and even come back again while I was still fighting to reach the end of my first and only sentence. I had seen men abuse their families and friends for money and support. In all that I had seen and done, there was still much more ahead. What would come next?

TRANSFERS

Busy at work, I was called up to the administration building. One afternoon, I entered the "operations" office and was handed a multiple-sheet document. The department had decided I would be transferred to a medium-security prison. By 6:00 the next morning, I was headed to a prison for youthful offenders. The facility had a fractional amount of "straight time" offenders like me who were used to maintain the daily operations of the institution.

With my educational background, I was assigned in the education department. It was here that my life would begin changing more drastically than ever before. My position was as a teacher's aide, but I was later given the ability to teach class entirely on my own. My students were preparing for GED, or high school equivalency, exams, and because I wore the same uniform and empathized with their position, it was easier for me to communicate with them. They were more open to explain their weaknesses and strengths with me than they would be with someone who was "part of the system." It showed in the over 95 percent passing rate of my students.

It was also here that I joined the Inmate Representative Committee (IRC), an inmate organization that communicates the concerns of the population with the administrative staff. I became the chairperson over the entire population and was given the ability to act directly with administration, security, and support staff to deal with daily institutional concerns and problems. It gave me insight into the views of everyone concerned and endless knowledge of both sides of the system. My eyes were opened to the need for staff to make sure that inmates were kept "inside the box."

For three years, I did everything in my power to make a difference at the institution. It was my goal to provide some comfort and humanity to the population, while not overstepping the parameters of security. In doing this, I was able to befriend a warden, an associate warden, and other staff members. But I'm sure that I alienated myself with others. There are those correctional workers who simply believe that it is their purpose is to create excess and continual hardship on inmates, a harsh reality that will never be changed.

After those years, I was finally transferred to a minimum-security prison. It is here that I now continue my writing, my research, and my preparation for returning to life in society. As I look back, it is of some 2,600-plus days of being told when to get up, when to eat, when to go to work, when to quit, when to shower, how to walk, where to go, what to do, and how to live. It is being told how fast to eat, what I could watch on TV, and when I could relax. It is a life of avoiding contact with almost everyone around me and having to follow every command barked at me by people who just want to make my existence difficult.

CONCLUSION

Over the years, I have lost family and friends, and my ability to comfort loved ones during those times has been stripped away. I have missed birthdays, anniversaries, holidays, weekends, trips, births, and every other day that might have provided a smile, laugh, tear, or memory of some sort. They are all gone and can never be brought back. I have missed years of starting and building a family, and upon release, I will be many years older and face the hardships of being labeled as a "convicted felon."

These are the things that I have faced, deal with daily, and will soon face. For now, however, these times continue, and every day gone is one less to do. My appellate matters are now in the federal venue, where the Constitution of the United States is respected and upheld. The worst-case scenario is release in less than six months. In many ways, prison may have saved my life, while in others, it has undoubtedly taken life. What I fear most now is that I may carry some of this total institution back into society with me.

8

THE PRISON ENVIRONMENT

Stephen Stanko

INTRODUCTION

The majority of the public has no idea what goes on inside the typical state prison. They read the newspaper headlines about a crime or watch a news report about the sentencing of an individual. Most do not care to think any further than to hear the sentence given in relation to a crime committed. No matter what sentence is given, most in the American public will not believe it is "enough."

I wrote this chapter to explain what it is like to "serve time." The purpose of this chapter is to give an insight into the daily operations of a prison and the impact that it has upon those inmates living inside the walls day in and day out. Care has been taken to report each and every step that an inmate has to take inside prison.

INSTITUTIONAL CUSTODY LEVELS

Most state correctional institutions are divided into levels (e.g., I, II, III, IV) that are designed in accordance with the classification level of the criminals they house. Starting with Level I institutions, which house "nonviolent" prisoners with sentences shorter in length, all the way to Level V institutions for Death Row, the rules and regulations remain the same, while the restrictions may vary. Inmates are afforded the ability during their sentence to advance to less restrictive institutions by advancing in their custody and security classifications, but it is important to realize and understand that no matter what institution an inmate resides in, he is still incarcerated. As long as the number mentioned earlier is active, there is no freedom.

The immediate visual identity of institutional levels is the number of perimeter fences that surround it. A Level I institution may have no fence or one that is not capped by razor wire. Level III institutions customarily house inmates by surrounding them with three perimeter fences. Each fence is twelve to sixteen feet in height, with razor wire surrounding the tops of each fence. The fences are approximately eight feet apart, and the second-to-last and outermost fence are also divided by razor wire, making escape by climbing virtually impossible. A fourth fence also secures the outer perimeter of every building inside the institution. This fence, too, is topped by razor wire and is locked at every possible gate and secured by either cement or steel at its base.

For example, the Level V institution in South Carolina, which houses Death Row prisoners, is accented by covering all walkways with fence. A roof made up of fence and razor wire contains every inch of space in which a Death Row prisoner may make any type of passage, thereby imposing immediate threat to any attempt at absconding or escaping.

CELLS AND DORMS

No matter what level, no matter which state, every institution represents a community in and of itself. After R&E, inmates are transported via caged buses and vans and armed officers to the institution to which they have been assigned. Upon arrival, every inmate is received in a "holding cell." The cells are nothing more than rectangular rooms designed of cement and steel, with either benches or steel pipes which line the walls for sitting on or leaning against. One toilet and sink are placed behind a four-foot privacy wall for use by awaiting inmates. Each inmate is then inventoried of his possessions. An officer carefully documents each item of clothing in his possession, any hygiene items, and jewelry. Inmates then proceed to medical for a short consult on existing problems and concerns.

A cell is then assigned, and each individual is directed to his dorm. In most institutions, all inmate cells are designed and built identically, with the single exception of certain cells modified for handicapped inmates. My cell was approximately six and one-half feet wide and eleven feet long. A set of steel bunk beds was mounted to the floor for my roommate and myself; the beds take up some twenty-one square feet of the available space. A stainless steel toilet/sink combination is in each cell for inmate use. The toilet sits at the base of the unit with the sink at the top. The sink has a push button that allows a set amount of cold water (no hot water in cells) to flow from a fountain-style nozzle. There is very little pressure and the release valves will often stick, allowing the water to continuously flow. The only access to the plumbing is through a chase door found between every two consecutive cells.

Also located in every cell are two wall-mounted lockers that are approximately four feet tall, three feet long, and two feet deep. Barnyard-style doors open on each locker to expose two sides. One side has a closet bar for hanging uniforms by plastic hangers sold in institutional canteens, while the other side has two shelves that comprise three compartments for all other belongings. An inmate just entering the state Department of Corrections has very few possessions, and these lockers will certainly accommodate these small amounts. However, after serving a number of years, inmates will gather numerous items of clothing as well as legal work, books, hygiene supplies, and other miscellaneous items. The only other storage allowed by most policies is one legal box for documents involving appeals and postconviction procedures. Storage becomes minimal, and thus, inmates must prioritize those things that are most important and are kept.

In some cells there is also a desk-and-chair combination. The desk itself is approximately two feet long by one and a half feet wide. With attached seat and no drawer of any kind, the combination provides nominal workspace and is usable for little more than writing and/or reading. Two adjustable steel hooks extend from wall mounts for hanging coats, towels, and dirty clothes bags. With the exception of a stainless steel mirror above the sinks, inmates are strictly forbidden to hang, paste, glue, or affix any other items of any kind on cell walls. The only items allowed on top of lockers are televisions and/or "boom box"–style radios belonging to inmates under a grandfather clause (see below). Coolers must be placed neatly under locker areas, and shoes must be kept in orderly fashion under the bunk beds.

The institutions where I served my sentence had four to eight dorms that were made up of two wings. Each wing consists of sixty-four rooms housing two inmates each; so, each dorm may house 256 inmates (i.e., 64 cells × 2 inmates = 128 per wing × 2 wings = 256 total inmates). Wings are designed as square, rectangular, or triangular so that an officer station can be centralized for view of the entire wing and all cell doors. For reasons of security, an officer must be able to visualize any physical confrontations that may be occurring in the unit at any time. Wings are set up on two tiers, an upstairs and downstairs, with thirty cells downstairs and thirty-four upstairs. The cement area and flooring downstairs makes up the public area and is known as "the rock." This is the area in which inmates are allowed to intermingle and have open conversation.

Also downstairs are the showers. Community showers are entered through barnyard-style doors and have six to eight showerheads where inmates can conduct hygiene when not locked down in their cells. As is often portrayed by the media, showers can often become an area in the dorm where homosexual or violent activity occurs. A decoy inmate may request the officer to unlock his cell door at an opposite end of the wing while one or more other inmates enter the shower to threaten to beat, bludgeon, and/or rape an unsuspecting victim. A lookout is posted to warn the attackers of the officer's return.

These incidents take only moments to occur, and in most cases, the only chance at disciplining the attackers is if the victim is in some way willing to identify his assailants. Victims are usually returned to the same wing from medical or a hospital. However, they will most often not identify their attackers for fear of being labeled a rat or snitch. They are forced to live with the horror of their memories or seek vengeance by their own hands. This is an unwritten code that every inmate must live by if he is to survive his sentence.

Most dorms have one or two community toilets upstairs and downstairs. Again, separated from view by only a four-foot privacy wall, these toilets are open-air and are used when cell mates do not wish to burden each other by the use of the cell's toilet.

Because these toilets are often in view of officers' stations, some inmates will use them as a form of barrier for masturbating while looking at female officers. The vast majority of most inmate populations find such acts to be disgusting, but again, to point the responsible culprit out would immediately label the pointer as a snitch and lead to future repercussions. Thus, the act becomes a matter of silence unless the officer catches the inmate in the act.

Naturally, an act of this nature results in a discharge of bodily fluids. When these fluids end up on walls and/or floors of community areas, inmates can take matters into their own hands to insure that it does not happen again. This is when the showers are often used for "training" and/or "teaching" inmates that there is a consequence to every act.

Bathroom areas also consist of small porcelain sinks with buttons for hot and cold water. Each button will release water for small intervals of time, making shaving and washing hands possible. Above each sink is a small stainless steel mirror affixed to the wall. These mirrors can neither be broken nor removed, but are instead permanent fixtures.

Bathroom and shower areas are cleaned by inmates assigned as "dorm workers," but the large number of inmates that must utilize a small number of sinks inevitably gives way to a more disgusting than clean area. Sinks are often used to clean food bowls, individuals rarely clean toilet seats after urinating, and showers regularly become trash deposits, not to mention those who urinate and, in some cases, defecate in the showers. Dorm lieutenants are responsible for their dorms and wings and will often delegate that workers clean their respective areas. Strangely enough, dorm wings which house inmates with greater sentences are often cleaner and easier to manage. These inmates are of an understanding that these wings are their homes and as such, must stay clean. The last thing an inmate wants is medical treatment for diseases and infections brought about by a dirtied living area.

The small confines of cells always made me feel a constant sense of enclosure and confinement. These confines are never so apparent as when inmates are under a "lockdown" status (i.e., locked in their cells). Every night from 11:30 P.M. to 5:00 A.M., inmates are locked in their cells, but because these hours are mostly sleep, lockdown is not as apparent. Large fights, riots, attempted escapes, and numerous other security-related instances can result in wing, dorm, or institutional lockdowns, which can lead from hours to days to weeks and even months of being confined to cells. Cell mates can quickly begin to hate each other when placed together for extended periods of time. In lockdowns, every little noise and movement can become ten times more annoying. The inmates are already mentally stressed by the fact that they are locked up, and things are simply compounded with additional time.

INSPECTIONS, COUNTS, AND MOVEMENT

In most institutions, cell inspections are performed seven days per week, 365 days per year. Officers will go from room to room insuring that rooms are clean (floors and shelves), that toilets and sinks are clean, and that there are no clothes and shoes thrown haphazardly about the cell. All beds are supposed to be made when each inmate leaves his cell after the morning count. Inmates, by policy, are not allowed to return under their sheets until after the third count of the day (4:00 P.M.).

At 7:30 A.M., the institutional intercom announces "ten minutes to count," giving notice of count procedure to all parties. At 7:40 A.M., "count time" is called. Count procedures vary slightly from one institution to the next. Some require inmates to stand in their respective cells, while others demand each inmate to stand outside the door. Two officers in each wing and/or work area then go by each cell and count the inmates in that area. Once counted, inmates are allowed to relax in their cells with the door shut. Level III or greater institutions will customarily lock the cell doors during the procedures. As the two officers complete their count and check each other's to insure a consistent and correct number, the total count is then called in to the "control room" in administration.

Here, the institutional count is tabulated to insure that the number matches the exact number assigned to each institution. This number changes daily at every institution as a result of releases, new inmates, transfers, medical transfers, court proceedings, and outside work assignments. Every institution in a department can give an exact count of the number of inmates accountable to their respective yard at any given moment.

In the event that a count does not tabulate exactly, an immediate "recount" is called. Inmates remain in their cells while officers change their posts and again go cell to cell taking a physical count of every inmate at the institution. Reasons for recounts can be attributed to both officers and inmates, and while officers may sometimes simply make mistaken calculations, the inmates may hide under their bunks and even in the lockers in an attempt to create recounts when they fear an upcoming altercation with another inmate. Some are simply trying to avoid work or other scheduling.

In the event that a recount fails to reach the correct number, a "final call" count is then announced. All inmates are ordered to return to their assigned cells, leaving only a skeleton crew in the cafeteria. Inmates stand outside their cells while the officers go door to door with a window roster (printout of cell living assignments). The officers must now match the inmate's face, name, and number to the roster, making the process tedious, but allowing any discrepancies to be instantly found and corrected.

It has been my experience that schedules in prison do not change from day to day. Each dorm is assigned one day per week for access to the mailroom, the commissary, the barbershop, the library, the canteen, and the multipurpose building. For instance, Dorm A may be given every Monday to have access to these administrative units. Dorm B may be given Tuesdays, and so on. Color-coded stickers placed on every inmate's identification card makes easy reference for every officer to know if inmates are "out of place." An inmate assigned to Dorm A is not allowed these privileges on a Tuesday and vice versa. Likewise, inmates are not excused from their job assignments for the purpose of utilizing their privileges, so they must prioritize their needs with the time available.

Libraries, canteens, commissaries, and barbershops are generally scheduled to be open three times daily, between counts. These openings, however, are subject to numerous delays and/or outright denials. Staff reporting late, lack of available officers, recounts, and computer problems can cause any of these privileges to be cut short or entirely stopped on any given day. Likewise, the wrongful acts of a few inmates can cause the staff to deny an entire dorm its privileges for the day. Counts alone can take up to two hours to clear, leaving no time between for access to any of these places, and with an average of 270 people trying to gain access to canteens once per week, problems can quickly arise. Matters are only compounded when a dorm is denied this access for whatever reason for multiple consecutive weeks.

For those instances when an inmate is scheduled for any form of appointment or meeting, an "Order to Report" (OTR) is sent out in advance. These OTRs include the inmate's number, name, and living area and direct him as to where he is to report; the date and time must be signed by the issuing official. The inmate and an officer will then sign the OTR upon receipt, with a carbon copy being returned to the issuer the following day. Failure to report may result in an "Out of Place" charge on the inmate, and as a result, OTRs are one of the only allowable reasons for an inmate to leave his job assignment without fear of disciplinary sanctions.

Dorm recreation is daily, with one wing having access to the dorm recreation field between the morning and midday count and then again after the 4:00 P.M. count until approximately 7:30 P.M. or dark, while the other wing receives it between the midday and 4:00 P.M. count.

This changes the following day, giving a wing two opportunities on every other day (i.e., A wing has two on Monday, Wednesday, and Friday, and B wing has two on Tuesday, Thursday, and Saturday). Sundays are decided by the warden's discretion. Some institutions, for example, let the A wing receive two Sundays per month and the B wing two per month, while others simply give it to one of the wings every Sunday. It is a privilege decided solely by the warden and can be given and taken at any time. Multipurpose building recreation is between 7:00 P.M. and 9:00 P.M. on each dorm's respective day and once on weekends. The Dorm of the Week receives one additional evening in multipurpose.

COMMON PRISON FEATURES

Although I am not an expert on correctional systems in each and every state, it has been my experience that different prisons have similar components. This layout includes structural and organizational features such as recreational facilities, commissary, canteen, chapel, libraries, medical, and communications (e.g., phone and mail). The remainder of this chapter is devoted to each of these institutional structures.

Recreation

On each tier of a wing, there are recreation rooms. These are rooms enclosed with cement and windowed walls where the population can play cards and board games. When not in lockdown or at assigned jobs, inmates are free to play cards and games such as checkers, chess, and backgammon. There are no computers, video games, or other such luxuries for inmates to occupy their time. Poker and other gambling games are plentiful, with varieties of stakes. With games such as spades, the loser may be forced to either do a set number of push-ups or drink a completely filled cup of water without delay or stopping. In poker, however, inmates will vary the ante, ranging from cigarettes and food to money and drugs. Obviously, the latter stakes are already illegal, and resulting losses can lead to increased adverse reactions. Cheating in prison is a big taboo and is often responded to with violence from those cheated. There is little conversation and/or bickering. The winner of the fight generally decides whether or not anyone cheated.

Recreational activity like cards and games is the one way in which an inmate can set himself apart from others. To be the best at anything in prison automatically gives an individual some sense of individuality and/or superiority. Just to be able to say that "I am the best" at anything gives an inmate the same feeling that a child succumbs to by being the best thrower in a dodgeball tournament on a playground. This analogy is true not only in reference to the emotion of the inmates but also in the separation of (or lack of) intellectual measures.

Upstairs dayrooms are for quiet study and reading. Many inmates are unable to find peace in their cells, as cell mates may come in and out with friends and disruption can be plentiful. To cure this problem, the upstairs dayrooms are often structured with the premise of no conversation, no games, and no interaction—unless it is that of study and/or tutoring—

allowed. The attempt is to create a library-type atmosphere. Small groups can often reserve these rooms for religious prayer and/or study.

Also located in most living areas are four televisions that are mounted in steel cages to the base of the second tier. There are two televisions each on opposite sides of the wings. No exterior volume is given by any television. Instead, the televisions are fitted with electronic transmitters that broadcast over FM frequencies. Inmates are allowed to purchase small, handheld AM/FM portable radios through the institutional canteen that can be tuned in to a set frequency, allowing the inmate to view and hear the desired station. Directly in front of the televisions are five benches that can allow approximately thirty inmates to sit and watch the televisions. These benches are mounted to the cement floor and are stainless steel with no padding of any kind. In contrast to what many believe, comfort is not an option in prison.

Chairs from dayrooms usually cannot be moved or placed in cells. So the general population areas can become a mass of men standing in front of televisions. Movies or sporting events can often bring a flood of spectators in a small area. The Super Bowl crowd alone could be compared to a celebration. Such close interaction by a large group of men often cheering opposite teams can create possible problems. Plays lead to words, words lead to sarcasm, and this can all lead to physical confrontations. Thus, a simple recreation becomes a dangerous combination of activities.

Contrary to the media's portrayal of "cablevision prisons," inmates are not given a cornucopia of satellite-dish choices for viewing. The four televisions in each dorm wing are generally preprogrammed and can only be changed by a designated maintenance supervisor. Primary stations of ABC, CBS, and NBC are programmed, and either a FOX-type affiliate or educational channel is placed on the fourth set. Some institutions will set the televisions to allow closed-captioned reading so that the inmates without means to purchase radio headsets can follow the story of shows. This, of course, is only beneficial for those inmates with the ability to read.

In most state-run institutions, televisions can no longer be purchased by inmates or sent in by families. There still remain a limited number of sets (13 inches or smaller) that are owned and kept by inmates who were serving their sentences at a time when such things were allowed. Under a grandfather clause, these inmates were given the ability to keep their sets even after the policies changed. However, when these inmates complete their sentence, by max-out or parole, they are required to take their televisions with them. Because these sets are on inventory, each institution has a standing record of every inmate's belongings and, in many cases, will hold a release to make the inmate make arrangements for his set once he is released.

An inmate approaching his release date will often place the television for sale. A color television in working condition can be worth upwards of a thousand dollars. The price is decided largely by the amount of sentence remaining to be served by the buyer. For instance, Inmate A is going home and has an eight-year-old color television. Inmate B has approximately six years remaining to serve on his sentence and will offer $800 for the set, while Inmate C has just started a twenty-year sentence and is willing to pay a $1,000 for a set that is worth less than $100 but is otherwise impossible for him to get. The deal is completed, in most cases, when the buying inmate's family sends money into the selling inmate's account, or when money is sent from family to family.

These sales are entirely against policy and procedures, and the purchasing inmate clearly understands the threat of losing the TV the first time his cell undergoes a "shakedown." To insure no immediate confiscation, the purchasing inmate will often place the set in a third-party cell unknown to the seller. In some cases, the set will remain with the seller being released, but in almost every case, the set is eventually confiscated.

The bottom floor also houses a laundry room used specifically for receiving and passing out inmates' clothing and linens. Twice a week, each dorm's laundry is gathered together and sent to the institutional commissary for washing and then sent back to the wings for return to each inmate.

Commissary and Laundry

The commissary maintains two separate and distinct purposes. It is the central point of issue for clothing, linens, indigent hygiene supplies (see below), and all janitorial equipment and supplies to inmates and wings. It is from this area that inmates receive their uniforms, shoes, hygiene products, and linens, and likewise where dorms receive their weekly supplies of cleaning products. For example, personal hygiene products are supplied from the commissary if an inmate is too poor to afford items from the canteen.

Where I was imprisoned, inmates arriving at their designated institutions were assigned a set number of uniforms. These uniforms consist of pants and shirt as well as a baseball-style cap. Cafeteria workers receive white uniforms for work and tan uniforms for all other activities. Tan uniforms are issued to all other inmates. A dark brown jacket is issued to all inmates for winter months. Shoes are "job-specific," so an inmate assigned to cafeteria, maintenance, and/or horticulture or yard detail will receive state boots, while those placed in education, commissary, canteen, chapel, or administrative positions will receive the light-duty style tennis shoes, as do inmates who are unassigned. Inmates may purchase certain tennis shoes through the canteen. Most departments offer two styles of sneakers: a canvas type and leather one. Inmates must file proper documents and pay for them through their respective accounts. Once shoes are purchased, an inventory is maintained in each inmate's file, and to purchase another pair, the inmate must turn in his old set. An additional pair of dress (Hush Puppy) shoes may be purchased as well.

Socks, briefs, and T-shirts are also available in institutional canteens. Every inmate also receives two sheets, one pillowcase, and a wool blanket.

Generally, indigent inmates whose account balance does not exceed a set amount (e.g., $10) over a set period of time can receive an indigent package, which consists of a bar of soap, razors, envelopes, a toothbrush, toothpaste, and minimal hygiene needs. Indigent inmates can also be provided socks. All inmates are authorized to receive a set number of boxer-style underwear. All supplies are issued and documented by computer by utilizing the inmates' ID cards. Clothing items have set periods of time in which they cannot be replaced. A policy of the state Department of Corrections guidelines specifies the exact period each item should last and can then be replaced. This includes underwear. Other specialty items, such as jumpsuits and rainwear, are supplied to certain inmates such as maintenance and "outside work detail" inmates. Each dorm has two assigned days on which their clothing is washed. Linens are done on one of those days. Inmates turn in their clothes at the wing laundry room between the hours of 6:00 P.M. and 9:00 P.M. on the evening prior to their assigned days. Linens are turned in before 7:00 A.M. Each inmate gives his "count" of clothing and linens to the dorm laundry worker so that it can be documented. Once all laundry has been turned in, the laundry worker has an individual and total count that must accompany the clothes to the commissary. Clothes are separated into pants, shirts, towels, and whites. They are placed in mesh bags with each inmate's state Department of Corrections number affixed. These items are then placed in two or three large bins and rolled to the commissary where they are washed in industrial washing machines and subsequently dried in gas dryers. Commissary workers fold the clothes and linens and, after being counted to insure no loss or theft, the clothes are returned to the inmates, usually between 6:00 P.M. and 9:00 P.M. Any lost or stolen clothing must be reported to the wing officer, who writes an "Incident Report" explaining the events.

Institutional laundries provide minimal, ineffective cleaning because of their community nature, and as a result, many inmates wash their own clothes. This is done by using the bathroom sinks, mop buckets, and in many cases, toilets. Body soap bought in institutional canteens and hand washing provide for many a makeshift "Chinese" laundry. Inmates will string shoelaces in their rooms to act as clotheslines for drying. Policy specifically states that these lines are forbidden, and inmates know that there is a risk of disciplinary action in the event that officers pass their room. Many inmates also obtain bleach illegally from the cafeteria and commissary and risk charges of "contraband" to maintain clean clothing and linens.

The commissary also supplies janitorial products to every building in the institution. Supplies are limited to an all-purpose cleaner, glass cleaner, deodorizer, and floor cleaner for the wings. Because all cell and general population floors are cement, an all-purpose cleaner meets most needs. Brooms, mops, and toilet-bowl brushes are made available in the wings in limited supplies and are accounted for daily, as they can easily become weapons. Inmate dorm workers are assigned to clean all general population areas from floor to ceiling, including windows, benches, toilets, sinks, and showers. Once weekly, an inspection team enters every dorm, and the dorm scoring highest becomes a "Dorm of the Week," receiving some privileges such as additional library, multipurpose room, and canteen hours. The commissary also supplies certain specialty products to the administration, education, and dorm offices such as wax and buffing pads to insure that these areas are kept at a higher standard than others. Trash bags and receptacles are also supplied via commissary issue.

The Inmate Canteen

Prisons also house an institutional "canteen" where inmates may purchase certain items. Each dorm is assigned one day per week for inmates to go to the canteen. Items sold in institutional canteens include hygiene products such as soaps, shampoos, baby oil, lotions, razors, shaving cream, toothpaste, nail clippers, combs, Q-Tips, hair grease, and selected antibacterial products. Pens, paper, and envelopes are provided, as are small plastic lamps and bulbs. The bulk of items sold in the canteen are food items. Coffee, sodas, candy bars, cookies, snack cakes, small bags of chips, wafers, individual pastries (honey buns), crackers, and ice cream are available as snacks. Inmates may also purchase canned meats such as tuna, chicken, sardines, salmon, corned beef, and roast beef. Canned vegetables such as corn, potatoes, tomatoes, tomatoes and okra, and pork-n-beans are sold, as is instant rice in individual serving packs. Inmates may purchase canned chicken soup or dried oriental noodles. Condiments of mustard, mayonnaise, ketchup, hot sauce, and jalapeno pepper slices in small containers are available.

Inmates will often make "set-ups," or casserole-style meals, by combining items together and mixing them in one bowl. Roast beef, corn, potatoes, rice, and a couple soups make a feast as compared to state stewed beef liver. Flavor can be added by salt, pepper, and butter, also sold in the canteen. Varieties of packaged sandwiches are also available (e.g., fish, cheeseburgers). The number of food products is quite limited, and there are no choices of brands. For example, there is one brand of tuna, one type of rice, and so forth.

Other miscellaneous items which can be bought include vitamins, over-the-counter medications in small dosages, sewing thread, T-shirts, underwear and socks, extension cords, batteries, plastic cups and bowls, wind-up alarm clocks, electric shavers, and portable typewriters (nonmemory, noncomputer).

As I have observed on many occasions, the choice is not which products to buy but rather whether to purchase the products that are available. Weekly spending amounts are limited to $75.00 per inmate and only one trip to the canteen is allowed per week, unless the dorm is the Dorm of the Week. Canteen items are the number-one form of currency in institutional yards. Drug purchases, legal fees for work performed by inmates, and other debts are billed by canteen lists and collected in bags. Here again, inmates place themselves at risk with possible charges of gambling/loan sharking.

Prison Library

Institutional libraries can also be found in every educational department. These are libraries that may consist of only a couple thousand books. Reference and nonfiction make up the greater number of books, while fiction and romance and/or novels are fewer in number. Each dorm is given one day per week for library visits and each inmate can check out two books at a time to be returned the following week. Reading is one of the best and safest ways for an inmate to pass time. Many increase their knowledge and intellect by spending countless hours in books.

Newspapers from the main regions of the state can also be found in institutional libraries. The weekday papers are purchased by subscription through the library fund. Magazines of various subject and nature are also allowed through approval of the librarian. These may include such magazines as *Time, Popular Science, Popular Mechanics, Newsweek, U.S. News & World Report, National Geographic, Discover, People, Jet, Car and Driver, Auto Week, Muscle and Fitness,* and other miscellaneous titles. Magazines cannot include any sexually related topics and are censored upon arrival. Inmates may also subscribe to and purchase magazines through their inmate accounts. Personal magazine subscriptions can include those that contain sexual content, but they must show no physical penetration or any kind of child-related pornography.

All books entering the institution must be mailed by bookstores and publishers and are brought in through a department known as "property control," where they are inspected upon opening to insure that no drugs and/or contraband are entering the institution. Family and friends are not allowed to send in any such items, although they may donate used books to the institution library.

Multipurpose Areas

Most institutions are equipped with gyms or multiple purpose buildings for recreational activities. Contrary to public belief, weights are no longer allowed in most prisons. There are no massive weight piles with "Adonis-like" men lifting the equivalent of small automobiles. The multipurpose building provides a standard basketball court (with cement floors in most cases), handball courts mapped out on certain walls, Ping-Pong tables, and jump ropes.

Physical fitness is by choice in prison, not by design. Inmates maintain their health and physique through jogging on the recreation fields, walking the inside perimeter of the dorm (including stairs), push-ups, sit-ups, and makeshift weights of filling laundry bags with books or milk bags from the cafeteria with either sand or water. However, these items are contraband. Inmates run the risk of additional charges if they are discovered with these things.

Chapels and Chapel Services

Generally, institutional chapels are small in size, with one or two chaplains employed to oversee all services for the faiths of the population. Christian services are held on a weekly basis both Saturday and Sunday. Many outside programs are often brought in on Friday evenings that include singing groups, speakers, and choirs.

Prison faiths are many in number, ranging from Protestantism to Catholicism and on to Rastafarian communities as well as Muslim. Most Departments of Corrections also recognize the Wicca and Pagan faiths. All religious materials are received through property control and are then received in the chaplain's office. Before they can be distributed to the inmates, a warden's approval is also required. Religious groups are also placed under a certain amount of scrutiny and are closely monitored.

Occasionally, religious groups clash due to one group's lack of knowledge and understanding of the next. This often leads to problems. For instance, many believe that the Muslim community directs its attention only toward the black population, and others believe that the Wicca population is nothing more than a satanic cult. However, both of these beliefs are entirely inaccurate. Ignorance of other religions leads to rumors, and rumors cause problems in prison.

To keep control of such things, religious groups are made to meet in designated chapel areas and not in wings or any other administrative building. While officers, by policy, cannot actually be included as part of the group, they can maintain set distances and monitor its activity. There do not exist as many confrontations between security and religious groups as the media would like to portray. These groups are rarely rebellious and are, at most, outspoken.

Outside song groups and motivational speakers are given the ability to enter institutions on Friday and Saturday evenings to perform. These are one- or two-person guitar groups promoting their faith. Many are ex-convicts who tell their stories in ways that appeal to those currently incarcerated.

Because these occasions are available to the entire population, it becomes a meeting place for friends, enemies, business associates, and even homosexual partners. All Departments of Corrections are greatly outnumbered in the ratio of inmates to officers. It is common for over 200 inmates to be guarded by only one or two officers. Without any possible way of monitoring that many inmates with accuracy, there are opportunities for drug transactions, deal making, and sexual escapades. If an inmate is not assigned to and living in the same dorm wing as whomever he needs to make contact with, this is an opportunity to rendezvous.

Prison Medical Facilities

Institutional medical departments are generally governed not by any appointment but rather by the emergency at hand. A life-threatening problem or flowing blood are the only two immediate opportunities to see a doctor in prison. All other requests are done in a written form to medical. For example, with some 1,400 inmates at any given institution and one doctor, there is little time for routine procedures and minor problems.

Not every institution has a twenty-four-hour medical department. All of the maximum-security (Level III–V) institutions are equipped, as are most of the medium- and minimum-security institutions (Level II). However, since minimum-security institutions are designed as prerelease or work-release, they typically do not provide on-site medical care. These institutions will transport their inmates to either a nearby prison or a local facility, depending on the work required.

Each medical unit contains a waiting area, a records department, a minimal number of examination rooms, an X-ray lab (in some cases), an emergency medical room, a dentist's room, and an infirmary designed slightly larger than the institutional cells and equipped with full security measures. Medical areas are not equipped with any pleasantries and utilize equal if not more security supervision. A pharmaceutical area also allows dispensing of any required prescriptions that are ordered and sent to and from the state department headquarters.

Inmates suffering from AIDS are now generally housed in a centralized institution equipped with larger medical facilities for better handling and treatment. Hospice programs are designed to use inmate workers to assist in the care of those infected. Treatment of inmates with AIDS can be extremely dangerous, and security staff must take the greatest caution in performing every possible duty and task. An inmate with a life sentence that offers no parole eligibility (eventual death in prison) can and usually will reach a point in which nothing matters and strike out at every available opportunity, giving no concern to infecting others. Many even strike with the intent to infect. There is no concern of a death sentence when one is already sentenced to a prolonged and miserable existence. Death is seen as a faster and less painful form of relief.

Dental treatment is also prioritized by pain and threat, and there is no cosmetic work done within the prison. Teeth are routinely pulled, as it is cheaper and easier than fixing them. Once an inmate loses approximately 85 percent of his teeth, dentures can be ordered and made if the individual has a set number of years remaining to serve. The thought of utilizing the system, while incarcerated, to have the department provide otherwise expensive work done is not possible. Policies and procedures are set which specifically detail the amount of work allowed for treatment of almost any ailment, and questions are more likely to be answered by costs and expenditures rather than quality care. Understandably, society balks at the concept of providing the incarcerated with any benefit that may be seen as a "luxury." However, it must always be remembered that most of these individuals will one day return to society. The question is, what type of individuals do people want returning to them?

Prison Cafeterias

Prison life gets no better in regard to meals provided by the government. National accreditation standards specifically set forth the basic required minimums for daily consumption. Nothing more than the minimum calories needed to survive are provided.

Cafeterias are generally divided into essentially six different areas for the inmate population. For example, a dining area can accommodate approximately 240 inmates. Floor-mounted tables with four seats that extend out from a single, center leg are in the open area of the building. This area merits extremely high security because it is one of the few outer-dorm areas where inmates gather in large numbers. The possibility of a major disturbance resulting from the slightest altercations is high; as a result, the need for added security during feeding or "chow" time becomes paramount.

Directly between the dining and kitchen areas are the serving lines. Entrances at opposite ends of the cafeteria allow the inmates to enter two serving lines where they receive prepared trays of the day's meals. This is not a buffet-style meal. Each tray is required to have set portions of the food items to meet national accreditation standards, and inmates are not given a choice of either selection or amount. Cups are passed out to inmates with their trays, and drinks are in large cylindrical containers on nearby drink lines.

Serving lines in most institutions were previously visible, allowing inmates the ability to view the food and speak to other inmate servers, thereby providing opportunity to request extra portions and, in most cases, deletions from the day's selections. Current construction and renovations across the country, however, are placing "blind" serving lines which place stainless steel walls twelve feet high between servers and the population. The concept is to stop waste of both food and time. Inmates can no longer pass food by hand across the line, such as chicken and hamburger patties. At the same time, conversation between inmates is now minimal. At the end of the serving lines, two small sections are cut out of the wall where trays and cups are passed out. There are no stainless steel cutleries in the prison system because inmates can fashion them into "shanks," or homemade knives. "Sporks," a plastic spoon/fork combination, are now provided to each inmate with each meal.

Food reaches the serving lines from the kitchen area through double-sided hot and cold storage units. As the kitchen workers finish preparing the food in large containers, it is then transferred to serving pans and placed in the storage units. Serving-line workers fill trays and as the pans empty, they simply pull another and continue the process.

Institutional kitchens are generally not large, open work areas. In most cases, they are no greater than that of a small restaurant. Inmate workers supervised by an average of two state-employed food service supervisors prepare three meals a day for the total inmate population. A "bake" section with large ovens prepares biscuits, buns, cakes, and cookies for daily meals, while the central area is designed for the preparation and cooking of meats, vegetables, and starches. Vegetable preparation, pot and pan, and drink preparation areas are directly connected to the main area of the kitchen; anywhere from forty to eighty inmates may be in the area at any given time. Toward the rear of the kitchen are the storage areas that consist of both hot and cold storage. Trucks from state headquarter warehouses deliver supplies weekly to each institution.

Types of Food

Meals provided through institutional cafeterias are neither varied nor select. A six-week rotating menu maintains the schedule for inmate meals. Breakfast is the least varied, consisting of a portion of scrambled eggs, grits, two biscuits, and a spoonful of butter. Once weekly, the population is served two pancakes per inmate with a covering of diluted syrup, usually on Sundays. The only other variations to breakfast meals are sweetened cornflakes and jelly, also served only once weekly on separate days. Orange, grapefruit, and apple or other fruit juices are served along with milk and coffee at each breakfast.

Lunch entrees consist of cold-cut (e.g., bologna, processed turkey or ham, or pepper loaf) sandwiches, tuna salad, chicken salad, hot dogs, grilled-cheese sandwiches, and occasionally stir-fry items. Stir-fries are a combination of rice, vegetables, and usually the leftover meat of the meal from the evening prior. With these entrees, a noodle casserole of some form, coleslaw, or beans are served, and rounding off the meal is a vegetable, rolls, and either two cookies or a piece of cake. Tea or Kool-Aid is provided for drinks.

Dinners provide no greater variety. Liver (beef and chicken) is served weekly, taking up two meals. Sausage and beef patties usually take up two more evenings on the schedule, and the remaining three nights provide the only change in the week's meals. Spaghetti, roast beef, "turkey-ham," roasted turkey, meat loaf, and pork provide the only other variances in the six-week menu. Rice is served at almost every evening meal and is accompanied by either a gravy or bean side. Vegetables consist of greens (peas, spinach, beans, collards), carrots, cabbage, or squash. Two dinner rolls and a piece of cake complete the tray.

Those inmates on special diets (e.g., low-sodium, diabetic, vegetarian) must receive specific approval through medical before obtaining such trays. A doctor's pass will place them on their respective diet and requires them to eat no less than 75 percent of all meals served. In the event that an inmate on the "diet line" fails to get his tray for 75 percent of scheduled meals, as they are checked by roster, he is automatically removed from diet meal scheduling and must go through medical again for approval.

Food Preparation

Every meal is prepared with a lot of people in mind. As a result, recipes call for pounds and gallons as compared to ounces and teaspoons. Everything is done en masse. Inmate workers mix proportions in large vats that border on cauldrons. Because items such as garlic, sugar, hamburger meat, and chicken are in great demand by inmate populations, these items are often stolen and sold. The resulting shortages can provide problems with the last dorms to enter for that meal.

Taste is of little to no concern for every meal prepared. It need only be edible and properly cooked to insure that no disease and/or food poisoning concerns become prevalent. Priorities of institutional diets are simple: (1) meet the standards required by accreditation, (2) prepare enough food to feed the inmates that enter the cafeteria, (3) insure that the food is safe, and (4) do so in a fashion that meets and exceeds security standards.

A huge concern with kitchens is the fact that inmates are placed in a position, in many cases without supervision, to prepare food. Frustrated inmates often taint meals with their own bodily fluids, waste, or miscellaneous ingredients. This is a constant threat to an entire population.

Food Workers

While policy specifically stipulates that inmates who work in institutional cafeterias must undergo a complete medical examination prior to their employment, the practice rarely meets the parameters of the policy. Though there are rare instances when inmates would purposely taint the food presented to their fellow inmates or willingly place a medical threat in the food, the concept of not verifying these concerns becomes a game of Russian roulette for all involved. A more common concern to the population is the reuse of leftover food in secondary meals. Meat loaves are often referred to as "mystery" meat, as they can be a combination of hamburger, chicken, sausage, and other meat entrees used in the previous week's meals. Likewise, it is not uncommon to find red meats and poultry in stir-fry lunches at the same time, along with cabbage and other leftover vegetables.

Meal Time

Above everything else, it is important to understand that meals do not come as a convenience. For example, a dorm of 136 inmates per wing (272 per dorm) has twenty minutes to exit their respective wings, proceed in a single-file line on the right side of the walk to the cafeteria, get their trays, eat, and return to their wing. Twenty minutes is set for the entire wing and not each individual person. There is no opportunity for calm, quiet consumption, or neighborly chitchat. Like everything else in prison, there is a requirement to abide by the policy and guidelines in order to obtain that which is provided.

Communication with the Outside

Once in prison, communication with the outside world is no longer a matter of simplicity or convenience. Like everything else, it becomes a matter of policy and procedure that requires the proper paperwork and approval before any contact can be made. Even internal communication with departmental employees and officials is to be done by written requests first.

Telephone

Upon entering the department, inmates are given the opportunity to submit, in writing, a privilege (telephones are a privilege in prison which can be denied at any time) request form, which requires each inmate to list the names, addresses, relationships, and phone numbers of those individuals whom he would ask to be allowed to call once incarcerated. This form is forwarded to headquarters and then on to the long-distance carrier contracted with the department, where a personal identification number is then assigned to the inmate. This number usually consists of the inmate's number and an additional four-digit number (e.g., 235278-1234).

Once the inmate receives the form back (usually in four to six weeks), he is able to contact these numbers by placing collect calls. Department phones provided to the inmates can only make collect calls. Rates are notoriously high and vary widely. The charge is based on an amount for the "first minute," which can range from $1.40 to in excess of $3.00, and then an additional charge "for each minute after," which can be from 18 cents to 45 cents, depending upon the area called. These rates often become a heavy burden on families, friends, and attorneys, as a single fifteen-minute phone call can cost upwards of $8.00 per call. An inmate who calls just his family twice a week can quickly establish a high monthly phone bill, causing hardship on them and denying his family continued communication with him.

To accept calls, the receiving party is first greeted with an automated recording which immediately tells them that they are being contacted by a state Department of Corrections institution, and then they are given the inmate's name. The recording next identifies the fact that the call may be recorded and any attempt to use three-way or other specialized calling features may result in the call being immediately disconnected. A breakdown of the rates for that particular call is then announced, giving specific amounts for both the first minute and each additional minute. Finally, the party is instructed to push one number if they wish to receive the call or push another number if they wish to stop any further contact from the caller.

Calls are limited to fifteen minutes, and there are no exceptions. When the call has one minute remaining, the automated voice disrupts the call and announces such, giving the parties an opportunity to make any final comments and salutations before the computerized system automatically disconnects the line. Once the line is disconnected, the inmate is allowed to call the party again, and thus, the billing procedures begin anew.

By policy, inmates are allowed to add or delete a set number of authorized contacts every month. Because the number of authorized parties has a maximum amount, inmates are forced to prioritize those people that they would wish to call. Additions/deletions must be submitted by form before a set day each month, and again, the processing of these numbers can take anywhere from four to six weeks before completion.

Telephone calls with your attorney are free from monitoring or recording if the attorney files written documentation with the department of the relationship and ensures that the calls are of a legal nature. By law, the department is then required to cease any monitoring and/or censorship of these calls.

Mail

Each institution maintains a "mailroom" through which mail enters and exits the institution. Current corrections policy places great limits on the items which inmates are allowed to receive through mailing procedures, and allows only letters, pictures, newspaper and magazine clippings, and postcards. Books and magazines are also allowed but must be from the publisher and/or a bookstore or supplier.

Correctional officials automatically open regular mail that enters the institutions; this procedure is necessary to insure that no unauthorized materials or "contraband" get in through the mail. The department also has the ability to actually read inmates' incoming and outgoing mail when claiming that it is for "security" purposes. Items not allowed to enter institutions include envelopes and blank paper, stamps (these items must be purchased by inmates through institutional canteens), original government documents, money, cigarettes, drugs, weapons of any kind, recognized cult material, and any other written documents which may pose any form of a security threat to the institution. Family and friends are no longer allowed to mail clothing, food, or hygiene products. These items are now supplied by the department or can be purchased at the institutional canteen. In recent years, however, many departments have allowed a "Christmas" package to be sent in from family and friends. In these packages, outside sources were allowed to forward a set number of undergarments (e.g., white T-shirts, underwear, socks, long underwear, etc.) to their inmate family members. The inmates were given specific dates and guidelines with which to have these items forwarded.

Any general mail or items received and deemed as "unauthorized" are immediately taken from the mailroom to a department known as "contraband." An officer will then locate the respective inmate of the items confiscated and determine the nature of their classification and the mode of disposition. Some items will be immediately destroyed, while others can either be mailed back out (at the inmate's expense) or donated to local community organizations. Items recognized as possible security threats can often place the inmate under investigation and subject him to disciplinary procedures.

Legal or privileged mail cannot be opened unless it is in the presence of the inmate. As a result, these types of mailings require the inmate to be called up to the mailroom where the mailroom operator then opens the letter/package, inspects for any contraband, and then immediately gives it to the inmate. Pornographic magazines fall under great censorship now in the department, and very few are allowed. Any that show penetration, child pornography, homosexuality, or animal abuse are immediately denied. Questionable materials are sent to headquarters, where a reviewing committee is given the opportunity to decide whether the material should be allowed to enter the institution. The mailroom immediately informs the inmate of the item in question, and after the committee makes a determination, the inmate receives a letter of disposition.

Mailrooms operate Monday through Friday at all institutions; however, access to mailrooms is limited to one day per week per dorm. The hours of operation are posted on the controlled movement schedule and remain the same every week. All mail, incoming and outgoing, must be properly addressed with the inmate's name and number and the institution's name and correct address. For example:

Stephen C. Stanko #235278
Named Correctional Institution
(Example: Dorm A-124)
P.O. Box 1000
City, State ZIP

Once mail enters an institution, it is considered to be the property of the department. Likewise, it is considered this way until it is delivered to the U.S. Postal Service. The mailroom operator of each institution divides up the incoming mail for respective dorms and bundles it all together for that dorm's lieutenant or sergeant to come and pick up. Once it reaches the dorm, it is then divided into stacks for the wings and is carried out to the wing officers who then call the mail out. Before an officer gives mail to any individual, their name and number must be matched.

Because inmates are not allowed any form of currency in their possession, checks and money orders cannot be received but instead must be forwarded out to the department trust fund to be placed in the inmate's account. The money is deposited in the inmate's fund, and the following day, a computer printout of the deposit and account balance is generated and delivered to the inmate.

Inmates must send all outgoing correspondence of a general nature (i.e., nonlegal, nonprivileged) unsealed. This allows a quick inspection for contraband. Inmates are allowed to mail out as many letters as they choose unless the individual is indigent and provided envelopes by the state.

Contact via mail by inmates in separate institutions is only allowed when: (1) the inmates are direct family members, (2) the inmates are witnesses and/or parties in any pending legal matter, and (3) there was at some point a hospice connection between the two inmates (one terminally ill and the other a volunteer). Inmates must make requests in writing, and the wardens of both institutions must approve any such contact.

Telephone and mail communications are the main links for many inmates in serving sentences. Contact with family and friends keeps memories, hopes, dreams, and focuses intact. Knowing that someone outside of the walls and fences awaits to share more future good times and bad and, more important, hearing from them, can help ease the pain of incarceration. At the same time, not being able to communicate can cause stress and anger to immediately skyrocket, and often results in wrongful actions.

The more prominent concern is that telephone operation in institutions is haphazard at best. It is not uncommon for phone systems at these complexes to be inoperable for days at a time. An inmate may be able to make a call to one of his authorized numbers one day and not the next. For various reasons, technical and otherwise, the system fails to allow many calls. In the same category, calls are often disconnected when called parties receive an incoming call, and the call-waiting feature of their phone gives an audible "click" that is interpreted as a third-party call attempt. The disconnect results in another unnecessary charge for the called party and continued aggravation for the inmate.

There is no easy explanation for the overwhelming comfort an inmate experiences with speaking to family and friends or receiving a simple letter or postcard. It is contact, life, and the never-ending reminder that there is hope and there are dreams on the other side of the fences.

Prisons do not offer Internet access on computers. In fact, access to computers is limited to no more than rare clerical assignments that are done on often antiquated equipment. Simple tasks such as library inventory, inmate rosters, and other tedious tasks make up the bulk of inmates' operation of any technological work. Some facilities do offer an ability to take "typewriter" lessons that are performed on computer systems, and some pre-GED tests are provided on centrally networked systems. Nevertheless, there is no ability for communications with outside sources by way of computer technology.

Along with privileged phone calls to attorneys, inmates may also receive confidential visits from their counsel. By contacting institutions in advance of their visits, attorneys can visit their clients Monday through Friday during normal work hours (8:00 A.M. to 5:00 P.M.) to discuss legal matters. Both parties go through standard shakedown procedures before and after the meeting. Inmates must even be strip-searched before returning to the general population.

CONCLUSION

What should be most clear from this examination of the correctional environment is that it is nothing like the images portrayed on television and in the media. The prison system is often presented as a mass of lazy individuals with televisions and pool tables and in-house stoves where meals are prepared in gourmet fashion. Such is not the case in most prisons across the United States.

Life in prison is routine and rarely changes at all. Saturdays and Sundays are generally no different from weekdays, with the exception of inmates who work for administrative supervisors with weekends off. These are the only exceptions. Most Departments of Correction now utilize a "controlled movement" schedule for every day of the week. There are so many mundane routines that have to be repeated every twenty-four hours in an inmate's life, that it is not surprising that the results can be seen daily in prisons with violent outbreaks and suicides.

9

SURVIVING IN PRISON

Stephen Stanko

INTRODUCTION

The embarrassment and shame that I had brought on my family was evident when I was initially allowed to call them from the county detention center. The conversation was short and responses were quick. All of the apologies in the world would not relieve their pain at that time and have not helped much since then. During my time in the county jail, I was in a pod of some 200-plus men who were all in the same, or worse, position. It is no understatement to say that the anger, frustration, and tension in the air could be cut with a knife. Three men per six-foot-by-nine-foot cell with one stainless steel toilet/sink combination. Four phones for making collect calls were available only in nonlockdown time periods, and one television was available to all those involved. The channel, of course, was decided by the officer in the control room. Fights occurred on a daily basis for any and every reason. It might be over a prior argument in society, a good seat in front of the television, or a piece of corn bread. The only thing certain in all of it was the promise that it would be violent and over just as fast as it had started. The pod was like an incubator for growing fear and intimidation among men.

The isolation of confinement also breeds fear and uncertainty. Family and friends are seemingly out of reach and control. Doubt becomes magnified tenfold as spouses may not be right by the phone to pick it up on the first ring, and suddenly there are questions of loyalty. Mentally, it becomes an absolute struggle just to survive through each day. For those who accept the responsibility of their own actions, that responsibility begins to chisel away at them with every second spent awake.

The initial shock of my sentencing hit family and friends as hard, if not harder, than me. In less than ten minutes, a once permanent fixture in the family structure was now gone. For me, the entire family structure was now gone. Before I could even turn all the way around, handcuffs were on my wrists, and I was being escorted through a concrete tunnel from the courthouse to the detention center. As with most newly convicted felons, I was placed back in isolation for fear of either suicide attempts or outwardly aggressive activity.

Emotionally, every day in prison is a constant series of challenges. I spent each day wondering what I had lost on the outside while my life dragged along inside. With time in prison, friends and family slowly become distant, and an inmate's position as "missing" is gradually replaced by everything else except him. It is unlikely for a spouse to remain true to her beloved inmate partner for periods in excess of seven years, and the "appeal" process only helps for so long with promises of "I might get it overturned soon, just hang in there for me." The simple truth is that life goes on inside and outside the penitentiary, and people will often find new love with someone who can put their arms around them and provide daily comfort.

While inside, I fought insanity almost every breath. Outside, I was losing my family, my friends, my job, my position in life, future memories, and anything else that might ever provide a smile. Inside, I was in a world of murderers, rapists, drug dealers, thieves, and the general scourge of society. Would I be attacked today for bumping into someone at "chow," or would I be robbed of all my belongings while eating?

Aside from these emotions, the mental strains can be equally unbearable. Legal redress to the courts provides not only small measures of hope but also intense pitfalls. Once an inmate has been convicted and sentenced, it does not matter what the truth is or where it lies. It doesn't matter that solicitors threatened him with exaggerated sentences in order to coerce pleas and even convictions of wrongful charges. It doesn't matter that the facts and truths were never presented to the judge, but instead, what matters is that the law now demands that you prove these things to the court in order to just be considered for some minute amount of fairness. Anger and frustration overwhelm your thought processes, making it more difficult to deal with every passing day, every lost day.

The emotional and mental frustrations that come with the incapacitation and isolation of prison cannot be either imagined or understood without the experience of it. It's not being kissed, hugged, or even touched by your wife, your family, and your loved ones. It's missing every birthday, Thanksgiving, Christmas, and holiday that goes by. It's feeling useless and lost with every passing day. Every time a man calls home and something is occurring in the family that he could have otherwise been there to fix or provide comfort or support for, the pain of his life is exponentially magnified.

For the first two years of my sentence, I was at a maximum-security prison only thirteen miles from my family. It may as well have been a million miles away. Incarceration strains the relationships I had on the street. Family and friends felt ashamed, disappointed, afraid, and even guilty. Furthermore, maximum-security institutions are very intimidating. The security measures that family and friends endure during visitation reinforces the negative feelings they already have. During these first several years, I felt isolated and abandoned.

PRISON VIOLENCE

Maximum-security institutions are violent places, and getting caught up in this violence can have harsh consequences. The fear of fighting in prison is much greater than it is on the street for numerous reasons. To begin with, each fight exists as a possible catalyst for a greater disruption. Other inmates may seek to take "sides" of their fellow inmate and create further fights with the opposite inmate and his friends. Gangs often form in an instant, and riots can break out. The situation can also be exponentially increased when security steps in.

Once a fight is recognized by an institution, a group of officers is immediately summoned to the area. If the show of force is directed at an officer, multiple officers use force on minimal inmates. Those inmates observing quite often see this force as excessive. These inmates begin verbally attacking the officers, and if not handled professionally, the verbal arguments can lead to pushing and shoving, and from that, small battles become internal wars. Officers are instructed in using "the minimal amount of force" required to contain these situations, and, in many cases, they do just that. However, it is often the perception that the force is beyond minimal when five or six officers converge on two inmates. I have even seen this many officers subdue a single inmate who was being disruptive. Assaultive disciplinaries are a strong deterrent from fighting because this type of institutional rule violation will decrease the chances of an inmate's advancement in the department from maximum to minimum custody.

I have seen inmates fight over things that people take for granted on the street. For example, "fried chicken nights" in institutional cafeterias present an opportunity for violence. Fried chicken is one of the few meals that can actually provide both taste and nutrition to the population. The result is a larger percentage of inmates who actually go to the cafeteria. Crowded lines of men pushing and shoving can often turn into a melee of violence. At the same time, inmates will often place their trays on a table momentarily to fill their drink cups. I have seen inmates bludgeoned or stabbed because they took a piece of chicken from another convict in the sixty to ninety seconds it may take to get a drink. Such violent and excessive acts come not only as a result of the minimal amounts of food supplied to inmates, but also due to the constant need for inmates to establish the fact that they cannot be, in any way, mocked, stolen from, and/or disrespected.

INSTITUTIONAL MISCONDUCT AND DISCIPLINARY TICKETS

Where I served time, the prison listed about sixty different disciplinary infractions with which inmates could be formally charged for violating the rules of the institution. Charges may include (1) lower-level abuses such as obscene language and being "out of place" (i.e., the act of an inmate being anywhere he is not supposed to be, such as another wing or the administration building), (2) midrange abuses, and, of course, (3) major violations, including assaults with a weapon, illegal use of narcotic and alcoholic substances, and inappropriate conduct with administrative or staff members.

While disciplinary actions are categorically a security-based measure, any administrative or security staff employee has the ability to recognize, report, and charge any inmate when they either see or gain knowledge of the inmate's conduct. A standardized form is used for a written report by the acting employee of his or her knowledge and information surrounding the circumstances. Names of all inmates involved, other employees who may provide information and testimony, a description of the offense, and the charge requested are all to be made part of the written report. This report is then forwarded on to the immediate supervisor, whose job it is to approve or disapprove the action requested and then begin the formal charge proceedings.

State departmental policies differ with regard to attempts at "informal resolutions." Many minor infractions such as cursing, stepping out of lines, smoking in unauthorized areas, and things of this nature can be resolved by simply ordering inmates to perform "extra duties." Duties not normally assigned to these inmates may be to scrub showers, rake recreational fields, mop general population areas, and other tedious tasks which can serve to provide adequate punishment without placing an otherwise harmful charge on the inmate's prison record and thus will not deny the inmate a possible upcoming advancement in classification or programs.

If an informal resolution is deemed inappropriate, the report is forwarded on to the acting supervisor and then on to the administrative hearing official (AHO). Customarily, this is the highest-ranking uniformed security official. This individual assigns the disciplinary as a "major" or "minor" offense. From the point of the incident to the point of the AHO's decision, policy stipulates that certain time frames must be properly met, with an approval/ disapproval by the AHO within four calendar days.

Inmates must be served their disciplinary charges at least one day prior to the actual hearing. The differences between major and minor hearings are many. These differences range from the ability to have counsel present to sanctions imposed. Inmate counsel is not allowed at minor hearings, but rather, the charged inmate is expected to provide any and all evidence on his behalf to prove his innocence of the charge. In the hearing, the inmate is notified of the offense and read the incident report against him. He is then given an opportunity to present all evidence on his behalf. The hearing officer (e.g., in minor disciplinary cases, this officer can be a lieutenant) will then review the evidence and information presented and make a finding of guilt or innocence. However, the inmate, if found guilty, may appeal the finding through the grievance or appeal process. In this case, the warden reviews the case and sanctions imposed, and affirms, modifies, or reverses the decision.

Major disciplinary proceedings are more complicated. Once informed of the charges, the inmate may submit a list of the names of possible witnesses to inmate counsel and the AHO. Inmate counsels are administrative employees who assist the charged inmates with the witness statements, questioning of accusing officials, gathering information, and presenting all material evidence to the AHO. Because these proceedings put inmates at risk for greater loss, more rights are afforded in their defense, and in turn, a higher-ranking security official is placed over them.

In the hearing, the AHO presents the charge and all applicable evidence against the inmate. In many cases, this may include physical evidence such as "shanks" (handmade knives), drugs, "buck" (homemade alcohol), stolen property, and other miscellaneous items. This can be provided with photos of the items that were taken upon confiscation. The inmate, or inmate counsel, can give testimony and present evidence concerning the offense and call witnesses to present same.

Inmate counsel then has the ability to question the accusing official about any circumstances surrounding the events, and once all testimony and evidence is presented, the AHO will make a finding of guilt or innocence. All major disciplinary proceedings are recorded for purposes of appeal processes. And the AHO is required to document in writing on standardized disciplinary reports such things as the inmate's presence at the hearing, names of requested witnesses and their presence, any documentary evidence, guilt or innocence, and the reasons for such decision along with the sanctions imposed in the event of guilt.

Once completed, the warden must automatically review the written record and approve or disapprove the finding. After said approval/disapproval, inmates are still afforded the opportunity to appeal findings. The penalties of major disciplinary proceedings can involve sanctions such as counseling, loss of privileges, cell restrictions, visitation suspension, and even monetary restitution. More extreme penalties include loss of "good time" (time earned by inmates which reduces their actual sentence service time based on good behavior) and custody reductions.

These serious penalties can cause inmates great hardships. Major disciplinaries can, by policy, cause an inmate who has earned A+ custody to go straight from a work program all the way to a maximum-security prison. The same may occur when an inmate acquires a number of minor disciplinaries. A general rule of thumb is "three minors equals one major."

Disciplinary charges represent an integral part of every inmate's progress while incarcerated. With very few privileges during incarceration, advancing at every possible opportunity can make the difference not only during the sentence but also as the inmate prepares and, if eligible, eventually returns to society. Historically, prisons were designed by most state legislatures to be rehabilitative and not simply punitive. That is, imprisonment was supposed to change the convict's motives to offend. Inmates are in a position of constantly controlled environments, and in learning that proper actions and following rules will allow advancement and more freedom and privileges, the individual goes through a programmed learning. Bad judgment and improper actions result in equally severe consequences. These systems, when properly followed, can make or break an inmate and his future.

INMATE AND OFFICER INTERACTIONS

Officers employed in correctional institutions typically handle a difficult task. The job of any correctional officer is particularly challenging when inmates are beginning their incarceration. At this stage, inmates have just been sentenced to a period of time away from family, friends, and life. To most, everything is lost at this point. There are no wives, children, brothers, sisters, mothers, fathers, friends, jobs, money, homes, cars, televisions, pets, and/or anything to provide a form of comfort. Also, it must be remembered that the things in life that give an individual a feeling of responsibility are also gone, such as bills, jobs, home duties, and tasks.

There is also the sudden stress of responsibility that immediately overwhelms an incarcerated individual. It is the responsibility of the pain and loss they caused for those family members, friends, and victims who remain in society. While many inmates will not acknowledge or even speak of the constant pain and turmoil inside, which tears at their heart and soul every minute of every day, it is there. It is not measurable by acts or words and can only be felt in the body and mind of an individual bound by cement and steel. Correctional officers constantly face the threat of these frustrations surfacing and becoming a violent rage.

At the same time that these officers are concerned with such problems, they are also given the responsibility of a sort of "programming" of inmates. Inmates must be cognizant of the fact that the Department of Corrections is a mass of policy, procedure, rules, and regulations. Actions come by orders and must be followed without hesitation. For every action, there is a policy that specifically explains why it occurs, how it is supposed to occur, and when it is to be completed.

For example, correctional officers tell inmates when to walk, where to walk, when to speed up, and when to stop. It has been my experience that most officers prefer to be addressed and spoken to in a concise, direct manner. Inmates must be shown that there are no longer any choices while they are in the custody of the Department of Corrections. It is this constant onslaught of orders and directives that newly incarcerated inmates visualize as abuse and degradation, and these feelings of status degradation can cause inmates to become physically enraged. Any breach of understanding or reason, coupled with the combination of fear and stress, may give way to further problems for inmates and officers.

Additional problems develop if officers or staff members begin to act in a personal manner and not a professional one. I have observed correctional workers giving extra supervision to an inmate due to a personal dislike or prior altercation between that employee and an inmate. Slight embellishments of events and actions can quickly lead to unsubstantiated charges, and a vicious cycle begins, and the inmate is placed in jeopardy. When an inmate's word conflicts with that of the correctional officer's, the prisoner inevitably loses the contest.

SURVIVING IN PRISON

The first realization that a prisoner has, once incarcerated, is that he is "doing time." It comes when the door is first latched behind him. Confinement makes an inmate feel as though he is not living, but rather merely existing. Indeed, it is difficult for a person to flourish inside prison when so much has been taken from him.

Doing Time

Prison cells average six and one-half feet by thirteen feet, but the truth is that they might as well be an inch by an inch. "Time" becomes an existence without the events and actions that compose living. There are no friends, family, or loved ones. Feelings of togetherness, love, tenderness, and care only exist in letters, occasional phone calls, and visitations. But that is only as long as those individuals continue to connect with you. Though the holidays, birthdays, anniversaries, and celebrations can become extremely depressing by the absence of loved ones, that pain only lasts during certain times. The everyday pain caused by the loss of the simple things tears away at the human soul. The drive to work, pumping gas, traffic, deciding what to wear, a loved one's kiss of "hello" and "good-bye," a child's smile, cooking, mowing the lawn—the list is endless. What people in society may see as tasks and chores, a prisoner might very well see as dreams and wishes. The pain and loss in living without these things from day to day cannot be explained. It can only be felt, and that feeling is not one that deserves description.

The punishment of a criminal sentence is "incarceration." While doing time, inmates see the same buildings day in and day out without change. They have walked the same cement path to the cafeteria, to work, to the laundry, to the canteen, to medical, and back. It never changes. Society feels that prisoners are coddled. However, the truth of the matter is that while there are some individuals whose lives are literally saved by incarceration, for many, it is a psychological destruction in many senses.

The immediate argument in this debate is responsibility. After all, convicts deserve what they get because they killed, robbed, stole, and raped. Television shows and media articles make most prisoners out to be horrible ogre-like creatures, and, while it cannot be denied that many are, some are not. Through poor judgment and wrong actions, they committed crimes. They were prosecuted and sentenced; sentenced to "time."

At most prisons, there are no VCRs, no microwaves, no movies, no weights, and few, if any, recreational activities. The daily actions of life include eating, going to a job assignment, and outdoor recreation for no more than a few hours daily. The cells contain no rugs, no comforters, or any such luxury. The floors are concrete, no pictures of any kind can be displayed on walls or lockers, and any form of decorating is strictly forbidden. There are no choices of any kind for meals. Breakfast consists of eggs, grits, and biscuits with occasional cornflakes and jelly. Lunches and dinners involve a seven-day continually rotating schedule of the same meals. Two of the dinner meals consist of chicken and beef livers. Cells consist of two- and sometimes three-man occupation. Steel bunk beds and a small steel desk are mounted to the floor. A toilet, a sink, and two lockers are the remaining additions. Prison is no palace, no hotel, no vacation, and no life. It is concrete, cold steel, and walls. Laughter is not joy, but rather a mask over the face of pain and depression.

There is a saying, "Do your time, don't let it do you." For the mentally strong, a continual pace of just "doing" can make time go by without constantly thinking about what one is missing. Reading, law work, drawing, writing, or anything available will do for many. Unfortunately, many prisoners fall into depression caused by the feeling of loss. That feeling gives way to frustration, then anger, and in many cases, actions that display that frustration.

Inmate Populations and Coping

Prisons populations consist of a veritable melting pot of individuals. Differences in ethnic backgrounds, intelligence levels, careers, and lifestyles abound. However, life before prison means little once one enters the system. In its most simple terms, prison life is "survival of the fittest." The phrase refers more to a combination of abilities and characteristics. It is not just physical prowess but also mental strength, psychological cunning, and the ability to adapt, understand, and overcome the never-ending changes that encompass a prisoner's life.

Whether one is a first-time offender for a nonviolent offense or serving a life sentence for multiple murders, serving time from day to day, year to year, or from beginning to end is done in the same place, dealing with the same people. And the largest part of any population is made up of multiple offenders who have in one way or another lived a life of criminal behavior.

Individual versus Group Choices

When an inmate enters prison, he or she is faced with a choice of how to live in the facility's social environment. There are two choices: doing your own time or getting caught up in the prison culture. Inmates may keep to themselves inside prison and follow their own morals and beliefs. We call this doing your "own time." However, others choose a life that follows the dictates of the majority of the general population. This choice involves nothing more than doing those things that the majority of other inmates desire, such as taking advantage of the administration when opportunities present themselves, reacting without thought to the emotions of others, and generally going with the flow.

Survival with this approach is most often varied. On the one hand, following the larger part of the population allows for group approval. It is a simple and typical "he's one of us" existence. On the other hand, that same group existence comes with hazards. In every prisoner's sentence there comes an event so vile, childish, or ridiculous in nature that he chooses to turn and not be a part of it. That decision can, in an instant, separate the individual from the group. This is often a drastic separation, as that individual had spent his time up to that point in a subservient life. Suddenly, he is no longer openly accepted. To get back in the group, he must take an extremely confrontational stance against the system and jeopardize himself. He may take some other action that the group will view worthy of his return.

The greater problem of living as one of the group is that inmates take these group behaviors, attitudes, and actions with them if they eventually return to society. Adversarial attitudes often go unnoticed in prison, but will stand out in civil society and could very well result in criminal prosecution and a return to prison.

Those who choose a singular existence must first be prepared to find activities and events that utilize greater amounts of time. While group conformity can bring card games, recreational activities, and long conversations that move time by, a reclusive or hermit-like lifestyle requires a busy and more scheduled lifestyle. A job in the institution involving continuous involvement and activity is critical for such a person. Reading, a hobby or craft, and/or continuing-education efforts to fill the voids of after-work hours are required. These types of convicts turn away from group activities that can be seen as useless or unproductive. They are also far less likely to be involved in altercations with either other inmates or staff. Survival is with fewer direct confrontations, and respect is often higher, be it out of a sense of ease or a fear by others that a gentle giant lies within.

Most choose a combination or medium between the two. Most first-time offenders enter a system entirely unknowledgeable about the way things work. Education of this life comes in three forms: hard, fast, and continuous. The thought of conforming with group efforts which could place one in a position of greater loss seems unfathomable to many, yet there are situations in which only through a united front could changes for the better be made. Further, there is often an immediate recognition that trust and respect from the population is a means of comfort and power. When groups band together to correct problems with the administration, most inmates make every effort to stand tall in the crowd. Yet efforts at just creating problems draw most back to their cell.

When another inmate is assaulted or even stabbed for a wrongful act of abusing the convict code, the new inmate's eyes are opened, but his mouth is shut. The same goes for gambling, drugs, and sex. The choice not to talk is simple; the choice not to partake is sometimes impossible. Nevertheless, survival most often depends on those choices.

When the security staff or administration does wrong, paperwork in the form of grievances and letters are plentiful, and battles are formed continuously between a particular Department of Corrections and individual inmates at every stage. Respect from those battles comes sometimes to inmates from certain staff members based on the honesty and resolve of such efforts.

The other side of the scope is dealing with the prisoners. Living, and more importantly "surviving," depend on being a "convict"; that is, placing value in the code, not seeing things in plain view, not knowing the obvious, and not allowing those things to affect you. It becomes a state of mind, the main thought being "never give up." Every day brings a new confrontation or adversity, whether with staff, other prisoners, or family on the outside. To let any one thing tear away at your psychological condition and frame of mind is nothing more than a suicide in itself. Right versus wrong is prison is not morals or values as much as it is life versus death.

Prison Associates

The company one keeps will often determine how a sentence is done. More than ever, the decisions about friends and/or associates will decide both the number and level of confrontations faced during incarceration. If one associates with gang-like groups, one will undoubtedly be prone to problems. Whether one man or many start a problem, the group must follow. Odds are high that the administration will get involved. Many others will gather in close-knit groups such as homosexuals, Christians, Muslims, and so forth. Doing time requires a constant state of busyness with something enjoyable or productive, or it is spent without direction and in chaos.

Relationships with Other Inmates

Surviving requires truth and honesty with the other convicts. Remember that in prison one's word is all one has. Houses, cars, money, and all other material things may be good for conversation, but behind the walls, a man is *only* as good as the word he keeps. When an inmate gives his word to another convict, it is as though he has put his life in the other's hands. The slightest fault in the grip causes doubt beyond the worst lies told in society. That doubt is transferred from man to man until it seems as though an entire institution does not believe a word a particular inmate says. That effort becomes a ripple and then a wave that hurts borrowing, hustling, recreation, friendships, and the inmate's welfare. It takes months and, in some cases, years to build back the reputation that one can be trusted.

Connections

A prisoner's connection to friends and family on the outside is another variable in his survival during incarceration. Every event on the outside, whether good or bad, plays on the emotions and train of thought. Hardships caused by financial difficulties, deaths, sickness, and anything else that is conveyed by loved ones brings unexplainable pain and heartbreak on those incarcerated. Many are overtaken by extreme feelings of guilt with the belief that, had they not acted in a manner that resulted in incarceration, they would be able to solve the problems, console the loved ones, and correct the wrongs. Guilt often turns to anguish and depression, tempers, and physical responses.

During incarceration, there is little, if anything, that a prisoner can do to help on the outside. A man of the house has now become a man of the cage. It is a feeling as if all manhood is suddenly taken away and replaced with inability, and inability carries over to a sense of utter uselessness. Visits from friends and family can have twofold consequences. One is that of happiness in spending time close to those loved and care about and being able to share time discussing the good things that have occurred. However, the end of those visits leads to another separation and the thoughts of, if not incarcerated, what continued events would they be sharing.

The fear of adultery is one that plays most heavily on prisoners. There is a phrase often referred to when discussing spouses on the outside. Don't worry about your wife, "Jody is taking care of her." "Jody" is slang for the mythical god of comfort who takes care of the unending needs of the spouses of those incarcerated. Many spend the initial part of their sentence believing that those spouses will remain faithful and not stray, but depending on the sentence involved, it is a rare chance that faithfulness remains constant. The letter or phone call containing the phrase "I met someone" can tear

down the mightiest of men and turn them into frustrated, careless, and depressed individuals. Individuals with no outlet at all develop very aggressive
displays at either staff or other inmates. Often, that lashing out creates only
more problems, and a domino effect is the result.

Boredom

Another great use of time is the proverbial prison baby-sitter, television.
Along with viewing television comes the sense of brain-dead mentality, and
scheduling becomes a matter of what show can be missed as compared to
the priority of the event to be completed. Soap operas can turn a long, bor-
ing day into what seems minutes, while also placing the prisoner in a state
of constant daydreaming.

Exercise also chips away at sentences, with many benefits. In the mid-
1990s, most state department directors across the United States removed
almost every type of exercise and weight-lifting equipment from their institutions. Some reasons included the threat of prisoners reaching a strength
that easily overpowered the security forces. In fact, those who were involved
with a regimented workout schedule did grow in size and physical ability.
Many men once flabby and out of shape were able to lose weight and gain
strength, but the intent of this exercise was rarely, *if ever*, to overpower security forces. In almost every single case, it was a means to develop a better
self, and with factors of the weapons made by the prisoners, the ratio of prisoners to security, and the increasing number of female officers, the physical
strength of those who maintain a schedule at the weight piles would be of
little consequence to an uprising.

An incident which was to involve a single person would display a greater
number of adversarial officers wielding pepper spray, clubs, and shielding.
Yet the weights were removed. As with any other adversity, convicts find a
way. Walking, jogging, push-ups, chin-ups, water bags (ten- to twenty-gallon
bags filled with water for lifting), and sit-ups (among other exercises) still
allow many to keep an active workout program.

Aside from the activities to keep busy, survival in prison is purely dependent on one factor: self-control. In every day there will be new challenges
and problems. That is a surety. Whether it is an officer who came to work
in a bad mood, a change in policy affecting inmates or staff, or a roommate
who decided today was a day of disrespect, pitfalls and problems are more
certain than death and taxes. It requires self-control to not let anything, no
matter how big or small, overcome one's disposition, and to beat it.

In prison, there is always and will always be pain. Society often forgets
that a prison sentence is punishment. Loss of family, life, and freedom is a
punishment more painful than can simply be explained in words. Aside from
the loss and separation explained, it changes an individual forever. Sometimes
one must do things that are out of character. It means facing one's fears on

a daily basis, choosing physical aggression over good judgment and common sense, turning a blind eye to matters which test one's every moral fiber, and being completely opposed to the people that one once believed were only for one's protection. It is making primitive weapons designed for one's safety in the event of attack, stealing from those who house one just to provide the simple comforts of adequate clothing and linen, and performing illegal hustles to stay ahead of the game.

EDUCATION AND WORK

Whether serving six months or a life sentence, survival depends on an immediate realization of where one is and what one is doing, how much time must be served before release, and how much time will be spent wasted on those things over which one has no control. Involvement with anything that takes a negative approach to surviving only makes matters worse and leads to loss of "good time" credits, lengthening the sentence. Staying busy is the key, and the one thing that incarceration can provide is time for bettering yourself. While the libraries at most institutions are somewhat limited in their inventory, an inmate can be quite sure that there are books he has not read before.

Upon entry to every institution, inmates are immediately tested to obtain an educational level. Tests consist of math, English, and grammar, with some science and reading. If the inmate scores lower than a set grade level, he is automatically assigned to some type of education program. Morning and afternoon classes are set to advance each individual to a point of a high school diploma or GED equivalent. Once the inmate passes, he can then be transferred to an active job assignment and can attend and be part of a graduation ceremony.

Teachers and state-certified civilians often utilize inmate teacher's aides (TAs). TAs are high school or college graduates capable of assisting with absent rolls, grading papers, tutoring, and other general duties required by their supervising teacher. In most cases, the TAs provide a buffer zone between the civilian teacher and the incarcerated inmate, making communications better. Normally less violent and volatile than other inmates, the TAs can take a leadership role with the class, as inmates by nature will lean toward a confrontational relationship with staff members, administrative, or security. The amount of successful teaching accomplished in a classroom is often a direct result of the inmate TA who has the respect of those in his class.

Noncompulsory programs are made available to the inmates on some occasions. Classes such as Victim Impact, which is based on making people more aware of the emotions, stresses, and strains of victims of crime, are given during after-hour periods. Other classes dealing with stress management and anger management, plus Narcotics Anonymous, Alcoholics Anonymous, and various courses, are offered on a volunteer basis. It is important, though, to understand that these courses are not offered in the frequencies of the past, and that nationally inmates are given a very small percentage of programs that will help them in their reintegration with society.

Vocational education, though limited, is another must to both utilize time and increase personal and job skills. Time is only truly lost if there is absolutely nothing positive to show for it. Inmates realize that they must deal with negatives, both inside and out, and decide immediately what they can do about them. Vocational courses offered are limited in both number and class size. Programs such as plumbing, carpentry, brick masonry, and electrical work may be offered at an institution. Classes hold between twenty and thirty people, which allows a possible total of 120 inmates to enroll. With an average of about 1,400 inmates at a prison, less than 10 percent are eligible for enrollment. A mere fraction of the population is addressed.

Whereas vocational programs in the past would offer a journeyman's license that held merit for released inmates when applying for positions in society after release, the state Department of Corrections no longer provides such documents. Instead, a certificate of completion is the only thing offered to inmates who complete vocational courses. The knowledge gained in these classes is certainly helpful; however, employers may tend to place more emphasis on the fact of incarceration rather than that of a possible employee with added learning and training.

In the vast majority of states, no college courses are made available through state-funded programs. While inmates do have the opportunity to pay for their own correspondence courses, most states will no longer assist financially. The inmate and his family must pay for advanced educational courses. Certain correspondence courses, which must be administered by specified instructors, cannot be taken if the institution does not have an instructor certified as such.

One of the greatest problems with educational departments in correctional institutions is attendance. Many inmates already have lower education as a result of not attending school in society. There is less value placed on obtaining education while incarcerated. Unfortunately, most would rather gamble, sleep, and invest their time in any other activity—sad, but true. Along with that, pride can often stop a grown adult from attending a class in which his faults might be exposed. The fear that other inmates would be able to use his intellectual inferiority against him can be overwhelming, and thus nothing changes.

I have noticed much more emphasis placed on work rather than education. Jobs are given to everyone within days of entering an institution and are based more on need than on education or ability. The equivalent of six years of college can put the individual in the cafeteria tray room or on the yard crew (mowing grass, picking up trash and cigarette butts). In most institutions work is mandatory and not optional.

Prisons are primarily self-supportive, with maintenance, horticulture, lawn maintenance, and janitorial crews that maintain the needs of the institutions. With so many inmates making up a general population at any given time, there are only so many jobs and so much work to be performed on a daily basis. The result is a large portion of unscheduled time for inmates; many take on numerous job positions, including extra-educational classes. Others endeavor in pursuing their legal matters, such as challenging their convictions through the appropriate channels. Reading is a typical mainstay for utilizing time. There is a great portion of the population that chooses to either sleep or spend time in the pursuits of gambling, drugs, and other illegal activity. There is a tremendous problem with dead time, as it becomes nothing more than educational for many criminals who simply become better and smarter criminals.

Time also causes many to reflect back on their past and the events that placed them in prison. In my case, it helped me to come to terms with the truths of my life. However, it also brought much anger, denial, acceptance, and finally, even hope. It triggered a change in me that, hopefully, will lead to a greater and more prosperous life on the outside. Unfortunately, in other convicts, anger, frustration, and rebellion grow stronger, creating hatred and disrespect for any and all officials. Incarceration and the daily life that comes with it can be a far greater punishment than individuals in society can ever imagine. It is a physical and emotional battle that tests each individual every moment of every waking hour. A major factor in recidivism is in the fact that there are few rehabilitative processes structurally designed and administered.

Convicted felons are on the average of a lower educational and work-ethic level than the societal mean. The concept of "lock them up and throw away the key" presents absolutely no solution because over 90 percent of incarcerated men and women will one day return to society. Reentry to society in a poor financial position with an education that only further entices criminal activity can only promote further deviation from society's standards. At some point, the motto must conform to "lock them up and give them a key." The concept of continual punishment as a means to deter future crime is antiquated.

CONCLUSION

Unfortunately, living in prison and leading a "morally correct" existence are mutually exclusive. The individual that follows the rules loses out in almost every instance. To report wrongful acts results in the label of a "rat" or "snitch," and these labels come with persecution and attack by the population. To run from confrontation rather than beat or be beaten only brings more assailants, and to follow the rules of the system results in rarely receiving the few items or benefits that policy is designed to provide. Irony is policy in a system that is designed to punish individuals for wrongful deeds but acts as a learning center to advance the criminal arts.

Survival here is being the best con, and prisons actually produce better criminals. The thought of changing the way the system works requires more than thought, and the reality is that it has been forming this way for centuries. Prisoners have never reached their cell and simply decided they suddenly would follow a life of public service.

The fact is that surviving is less about making it to the next goal one has set for oneself and more about making it to the next day, both mentally and physically. It becomes a fight to not wake up in the morning and just lie in bed hiding from the rest of the institution. It is not crying out loud for help and crumbling to one's hands and knees, not ending up in the institutional psychologist's office, not calling home to get support from family and friends, not taking medication that results in a zombie-like existence, and not trying to take one's own life.

Surviving is getting up every morning knowing that yesterday is one less day on one's sentence. It is being prepared to face everything that comes, whether it is from security staff, the administration, other prisoners, or family and friends. It is facing each day and every confrontation knowing that there will one day be an end to these fights. Most of all, surviving comes on the very last day of the sentence when the time comes to leave this hell-like life and return to a society of values and morals. It is truly survival of the fittest— at its best and at its worst.

INDEX

Accommodations, 115, 141–42, 150–53

Administrative hearing officials (AHOs), 174–75

Adultery, 181–82

African Americans, women inmates, 96–97

Aggression, among women inmates, 96

AIDS, 162

Alcoholics Anonymous, 183

Alpert, G. P., 72–73

American Bar Association, 120

American Civil Liberties Union (ACLU), 122

American Correctional Association, 120

American Psychiatric Association, 77

Anger management, 183

Annual assessments, 143–44

Appeals of sentences, 145–46

Arch Street Jail, Philadelphia, Pennsylvania, 45

Arraignment, 13

Arrest, decision factors in, 12

Aryan Brotherhood, 81

Assault, 5

Atchley, R., 71

Atimia (loss of citizenship rights), 28–29

Attorneys. *See* Lawyers

Auburn system, 47–48

Augustus, John, 49–50

Austin, P., 96

Australia, penal colonies in, 37, 39

Bail, 13

Bates, F. L., 95

Beaumont, Gustave de, 45, 48

Beccaria, Cesare, 35, 44

Belmont Report, 123

Bench trials, 13

Bentham, Jeremy, 35–36

Berk, B. B., 73–74

Black Guerrilla Family, 81

Blumstein, A., 8–9

Boards, institutional review, 143–45

Boot camps, for women, 104–5

Boredom, 182–83

Bornstein, R. F., 76–77

Brockway, Zebulon, 50–54

Cafeterias, 163–66, 173

Calvinism, 47–48

Canteens, 157, 159–60

Capital punishment, 6, 105, *106*

Caseworkers, 143–44

Cells. *See* Accommodations

Censorship. *See* Contraband

Chapel, 161
Christianity, justice and corrections under, 33–35. *See also* Calvinism; Quakers
Christmas packages, 168
Cities, crime rates in, 9
Civil law, 3–4
Civil Rights Act (1871), 111, 118
Classical School of Criminology, 35–36
Cleanliness. *See* Hygiene
Cleisthenes, 30
Clemmer, D., 65, 68–71, 74–75, 77
Cohen, A. K., 76
Commissaries, 157–59
Common law, 4–5
Communication, external, 166–70
Computers, 170
Congregate system, 47
Constitution, U.S.: due process rights in, 16; prisoners' rights under, 111; protections from investigation in, 11–12, 102
Contraband, 160, 167–68
Convict code, 66–68
Cooper v. Pate (1964), 118–19
Correctional Institution for Women, Shakopee, Minnesota, 98–99
Corrections, 17–21; in American history, 43–58; community, 17; cost of, 20–21, 48; institutional, 17; lawsuits over, 118–22; reforms of, 37–40; in world history, 25–41. *See also* Punishment
Corrections officers: corruption among, 124–25; interactions with prisoners of, 176–77; sexual assault by, 101
Corrections policies: contemporary, 55–57; great debate over, 47–48; of reformation, 43–47; reform movement for, 50–54; rehabilitation, 54–55. *See also* Parole; Probation
Counts, prisoner, 153–54
Courts, 13–16; first example of, 28
Cox, V. C., 82
Crack-cocaine, 9
Cressey, D. R., 67
Crime: classification of, 4–6; definitions of, 3; trends in violent, 8–10; unreported, 10

Crime Index, 7
Crime statistics, 6–7
Criminal justice policy, 18–19. *See also* Corrections policies
Criminal justice system: case flow through, 10; corrections, 17–21; courts, 13–16; police, 11–12
Criminal law, 3–4
Crofton, Sir Walter, 40, 50
Cruel and unusual punishment, 119–20
Currency, in prison, 157, 169
Custodial prisons, 74

Danner, M. J. E., 103
Deadly force, 12
Death penalty. *See* Capital punishment
Death Row, 150
Dependency, 76–78
Deterrence, corrections policy of, 56–57
Diagnostic and Statistical Manual of Mental Disorders, 77
Disciples, 81
Disciplinary tickets, 174–76
Dixon, J., 13–14
Doing time, 177–78
Donaldson, H., 104
Dorms. *See* Accommodations
Draco's Code, 29–30
Drugs, in prison, 79–80
Drug use, illicit, 5; and female imprisonment, 92–93
Due process of law, 16, 120
Durkheim, Emile, 111

Eastern Penitentiary, Philadelphia, Pennsylvania, 46
Eddy, Thomas, 46
Education, 146, 183–84; vocational, 184; for women inmates, 102
Eighth Amendment, 6, 16, 102, 119–20
Ellis, D. P., 96
Elmira Reformatory, New York, 53
England: corrections in, 37–40; women inmates in, 97
Enlightenment, justice and corrections in Age of, 35–37, 112

Estelle v. Gamble (1976), 119
Exercise, 161, 182

Fagan, J., 9–10
Farkas, M. A., 102
Farr, K. A., 100, 105
Farrington, D. P., 81–82
Federal Bureau of Investigation (FBI), 7
Federal Tort Claims Act, 122
Felonies, 5
Fences, 149–50
Fifth Amendment, 11, 16, 120
First Amendment, 121
Food: in cafeterias, 164–65; from canteens, 159; preparation of, 165
Formal charging, 13
Foucault, Michel, 112–13
Fourteenth Amendment, 16, 120
Fourth Amendment, 11
Freedman, E. B., 96
French, L., 96–97
"Fried chicken nights," 173
Fry, Elizabeth, 38–39, 43, 90
Furman v. Georgia (1972), 6

Gangs, in prison, 80–81
Garner, Edward, 12
Gender, sentencing affected by, 14
Geneva Conventions (1929, 1949), 114
Gilligan, Carol, 93
Glover v. Johnson (1979), 102
Goffman, E., 63–64, 66, 69
Goldman, Ronald, 4
Grand juries, 13
"Great Law" (Pennsylvania, 1682), 44
Greece, justice and corrections in, 28–31
Gregg v. Georgia (1976), 6
Guns, and murder rates, 9, 10

Habeus corpus, 122
Habitual offenders, 18–19
Hague Regulations, 114
Hammurabi's Code, 27–28
Handicapped inmates, cells for, 150
Haney, C., 83
Harlow, C. W., 16

Haynes, F. E., 70
Headquarters Classification Committee (HQCC), 145
Health: rights violations concerning, 119; UN *Rules* on, 116. *See also* Medical facilities
Hearings, misconduct-related, 174–75
Hebrew Law of Moses, 27–28, 32
Hittite Code, 28
Holt v. Sarver (1970), 119
Homant, R. J., 75
Homosexuality: among male inmates, 151–52; among women inmates, 95–96
Housing. *See* Accommodations
Howard, John, 38, 43, 44
Hulks, 37
Hygiene, 115, 136, 151–52

Identification numbers, 140
Illinois, capital punishment in, 6
Incapacitation, corrections policy of, 57
Indiana Reformatory Institution, 90
Initial appearance, in court, 13
Inmate counsels, 175
Inmate Representative Committee (IRC), 146–47
Inmate subculture, 65–68. *See also* Gangs, in prison
Inquisition, 34–35
Inspections, cell, 153
Institutional review boards, 143–45
Interstate Corrections Compact Agreement, 145
Investigation, police, 11
Ireland, corrections in, 40
Irwin, J., 67–69

Jackson v. Bishop (1968), 119
Jails, 17
Janitorial products, 158–59
Jay, John, 46
Jensen, G. F., 72–73
John Howard Society, 38
Johnson, Robert, 112
Johnson v. Glick (1973), 120
Jones, D., 72–73
Joseph II of Austria, 35

Judge shopping, 15
Jury trials, 13
Justice: beginnings of, 25–26; restorative, 57; states as locus of, 6
Juveniles, Roman legal treatment of, 32

Kassebaum, G. G., 95
Kennedy, D. B., 64
Kentucky, lashing in, 119
Kentucky State Reformatory, 118
Kerber, A., 64
Klotter, J. C., 5
Kruttschnitt, C., 97

La Rochefoucauld-Liancourt, Francois Alexandre Frederic, 45
Latin Kings, 81
Lauen, R., 104
Laundry, 158
Law: civil, 3–4; common, 4–5; criminal, 3–4; first examples of, 26–27
Lawsuits, 118–22
Lawyers: confidential visits from, 170; private versus public, 16, 134; relationship to judges of, 15
Leger, R. G., 95–96
Library, prison, 160
Lockdown, 152
Lownes, Caleb, 45, 46

MacKenzie, D. L., 104
Maconochie, Alexander, 39–40
Mail, 167–70
Mala in se crimes, 5
Mala prohibita crimes, 5
Manslaughter, 5
Martin, M., 98–99
Masturbation, 152
Mawby, R. I., 97
McCabe, M., 71
McCain, G., 82
McLaren, J., 119, 121
Meal times, 166
Media coverage, and sentencing decisions, 15
Medical facilities, 162–63

Menstruation, 96
Mexican Mafia, 81
Miller v. French (2000), 122
Minnesota Correctional Facility, Shakopee, 98–99
Miranda warning, 11
Misconduct, prisoner, 174–76
Misdemeanors, 5
Morality, prison life and, 185–86
Morris, P., 72
Morris, T., 72
Moses, and law. *See* Hebrew Law of Moses
Mothers, in prison, 98–100
Mount Pleasant Female Prison, New York, 90
Multipurpose areas, 160–61
Murder, 5, 8–9

Narcotics Anonymous, 183
National Crime Victimization Survey (NCVS), 8
National Prison Project (NPP), 122
Nazis, 113, 123
New Gate Prison, East Granby, Connecticut, 43
Newgate Prison, New York, New York, 46–47
New York (city): corrections in, 46–47; murder rates in, 9
New York (state), corrections in, 46–47
Noddings, Nel, 93
Norfolk Island penal colony, 39
Nuestra Familia, 81
Nuremberg Code (1947), 123
Nuttall, C. P., 81–82

Office for Protection from Research Risks (Department of Health and Human Services), 124
Ohlin, L. E., 66
Orders to Report (OTRs), 154
Osborne, Thomas, 63

Panopticon, 112–13
Parole: origins of, 40, 50–54; prison-ization's effect on outcome of, 75

Paulus, P. B., 82
Peet, B. J., 75
Penal colonies, 36–37, 39
Penitentiary Act (England, 1779), 38
Penitentiary system, 44–46
Penn, William, 44
Pennsylvania: corrections in, 43–46;
    sentencing decision factors in, 14–
    15
Pennsylvania system, 45–48
Penology, 55
Petersen, D. M., 67, 73
Philadelphia, Pennsylvania, corrections
    in, 43–46
Philadelphia Society for Alleviating
    the Miseries of Public Prisons,
    44–47
Philadelphia system, 45
Physical fitness. See Exercise
Platt, A. M., 90
Plea bargains, 13, 133–35
Police, 11–12
Pollock, J., 54, 78
Pornography, 160, 168
Possessions, prisoners'. See Property,
    prisoners'
Pregnancy, among inmates, 99–100
Preliminary hearing, 13
Pretrial detention, 132–33
Prison, 140
Prison Discipline Society of Boston,
    47–48
Prisoners: assignment of, 142–45;
    classification of, 137–40; dependency
    of, 76–78; deprivations faced by, 67;
    emotional hardships on, 172; first
    days of, 171–72; humane treatment
    of, 113–18; increase in, 18; indi-
    vidual- versus group-oriented, 179–
    80; interactions with offices of,
    176–77; labor of (see Prison labor);
    lawsuits filed by, 118–22; negative
    personal change in, 65, 74–75;
    reception and evaluation of, 135–42;
    as research subjects, 123–24; rights
    of, 111–26; survival mechanisms of,
    177–83; types of, 18. See also
    Convict code

Prisonization, 65, 68–76; antecedents
    of, 70–74; effects of, 74–76;
    institutional goals and, 73–74
Prison labor: for institutional mainte-
    nance, 184–85; in penal colonies,
    36–37; in Pennsylvania penitentia-
    ries, 45–46; Southern leasing system
    of, 50–51. See also Prison work
    programs
Prison Litigation Reform Act (1995),
    122
Prisons: crowding in, 81–82; custodial,
    74; custody levels of, 149–50;
    modern context in, 78–82;
    privatization of, 19–20; as societies,
    63–65; treatment-oriented, 73–74;
    types of, 17
Prison violence, 76, 173
Prison work programs, 145. See also
    Prison labor
Privatization, of corrections, 19–20
Probation, origin of, 48–50
Programs, religious, 161–62
Progressive movement, 90
Property, prisoners', 117, 135–36, 151
Prostitution, 5
Psychological approach to corrections
    problems, 54–55
Public defenders, 16, 134
Punishment: in ancient times, 112;
    matched to crime, 27, 57; rights
    violations concerning, 119; UN
    Rules on, 116

Quakers, 38, 43–48

Race, sentencing affected by, 14
Rand, K. R. L., 102
Rangers, 81
Rape, 5
Reasonable doubt, 4
Recreation, 154–57, 182. See also
    Exercise
Reformation, corrections policy of, 43–
    47, 50–54, 90–91
Reformatories, 51–54
Rehabilitation, 54–55, 64–65
Reintegration, corrections policy of, 57

Relationships, external, 181–82
Religion: prisoners' rights concerning, 121; and reformation as corrections goal, 43–44; UN *Rules* on, 117; varieties of, in prison, 161. *See also* Calvinism; Christianity; Quakers
Research, prisoners as subjects of, 123–24
Resocialization, 64–65
Restorative justice, corrections policy of, 57
Retribution, corrections policy of, 56
Richards, S. C., 100
Rights, of prisoners, 111–26
Robbery, 5
"The rock," 151
Rome, justice and corrections in, 31–32
Rosenfeld, R., 8–9
Ross, J. I., 100
Ruffin v. Commonwealth (1871), 113
Rules. See Standard Minimum Rules for the Treatment of Prisoners
Ryan, George, 6

Sanborn, Franklin, 50
Schuyler, Philip, 46
Schwartz, B., 72
Section 1983 (U.S. Code), 118
Selective incapacitation, 18–19
Self-control, 182
Self-incrimination, 11
Sentencing: components of, 13; decision factors in, 13–16; length of, 18; private versus public lawyers and effect on, 16
Sentencing guidelines: effects on sentencing of, 15–16; in Pennsylvania, 14; purpose of, 16
Sexual assault, 101
Simpson, Nicole Brown, 4
Simpson, O. J., 4
Sixth Amendment, 16
Smith, D. A., 12
Solitary confinement, 44, 45
Solon's Code, 30–31
Standard Minimum Rules for the Treatment of Prisoners, 114–16

State of Prisons in England and Wales, The (Howard), 38
States, legal autonomy of, 6
Stereotypes: death sentences affected by, 105; sentencing affected by, 16
Stevens, D. J., 81
Straus, R., 78
Stress management, 183
Subculture. *See* Inmate subculture
Sumerian Code, 27
Super-max confinement, 19
Supreme Court, U.S., 11–12. *See also specific cases*
Sykes, G. M., 66–67

Talion principle of punishment, 27
Teacher's aides, 146, 183
Telephone use, 166–67, 169
Television, 156–57, 182
Ten Commandments, 27
Tennessee v. Garner (1985), 12
Thomas, C. W., 67, 73
Thompson v. Commonwealth of Kentucky (1979), 118
Thornburgh v. Abbot (1989), 121
"Three strikes" laws, 56, 103–4
Title 45, Part 46 (Code of Federal Regulations), 124
Tittle, C. R., 71–72
Tittle, R. P., 71–72
Tocqueville, Alexis de, 45, 48
Total institutions, 63–64
Transfers, from prison, 117, 146–47
Treatment-oriented prisons, 73–74
Trust, among inmates, 181
Twelve Tables, 31–32

UCR. *See* Uniform Crime Reports
Ulmer, J. T., 14–16
Uniform Crime Reports (UCRs), 7, 8
United Nations Congress on the Prevention of Crime and the Treatment of Offenders, 111, 114–16
United States, correctional history in, 43–58
U.S. Code, 118

Vandalism, 5

Vice Lords, 81
Violations, 5
Violence. *See* Prison violence
Visitation, prison: UN *Rules* on, 117; for women inmates, 94

Walnut Street Jail, Philadelphia, Pennsylvania, 44–45, 46
Ward, D. A., 95
War on Drugs, 92
Washington v. Harper (1990), 120
Weapons: janitorial supplies as, 159; for self-protection, 183; shanks, 164
Wellford, C. F., 71
Western Penitentiary, Pennsylvania, 45–46

Wheeler, S., 71, 78
Wines, Enoch, 50
Winfree, L. T., 75
Women inmates, 89–107; African-American, 96–97; characteristics of, 92–93; current issues for, 103–5; history of, 48, 90–91; and homosexuality, 95–96; increased numbers of, 91–92; management of, 100–103; mothers, 98–100; prisonization among, 72–73; relationships of, 93–97; separate facilities for, 52, 90
Wooldredge, J., 83
Wormer, K. W., 95

Zingraff, M. T., 75

About the Authors

STEPHEN STANKO provides three chapters with a first-person account as an inmate of the MacDougall Correctional Institute in Ridgeville, South Carolina.

WAYNE GILLESPIE teaches in the Dept. of Criminal Justice and Criminology at East Tennessee State University.

GORDON A. CREWS is the Associate Dean of the School of Justice Studies, Roger Williams University.